SILENT
FOOTSTEPS

SILENT
FOOTSTEPS

SALLY HENDERSON

MACMILLAN
Pan Macmillan Australia

FOR JEREMY,
and to my children, Lou and Lachy

Some of the people in this book have had their names changed and their stories merged or separated to protect their identities.

First published 2007 in Macmillan by Pan Macmillan Australia Pty Limited
1 Market Street, Sydney

National Library of Australia
Cataloguing-in-Publication data:

Henderson, Sally.
Silent footsteps : A woman's awakening among the elephants of Africa.

ISBN 978 1 4050 3788 4.

1. Henderson, Sally. 2. Elefriends Australia (Organization)
– History. 3. Wildlife conservationists – Australia –
Biography. 4. Women conservationists – Australia –
Biography. 5. Elephants – Zimbabwe – Hwange National Park.
6. Hwange National Park (Zimbabwe) – Biography. I.
Elefriends Australia (Organization). II. Title.

333.72092

Typeset in 12/16 pt FairfieldLH Light by Midland Typesetters, Australia
Printed in Australia by McPherson's Printing Group

Papers used by Pan Macmillan Australia Pty Limited are natural, recyclable products made from wood grown in sustainable forests. The manufacturing processes conform to the environmental regulations of the country of origin.

CONTENTS

Glossary		vii
Prologue		xi
Chapter 1	Epiphany	1
Chapter 2	Jewel of the Kalahari	20
Chapter 3	Resurrection	32
Chapter 4	Into Africa	43
Chapter 5	Skew Tusk	54
Chapter 6	Return of the elephants	76
Chapter 7	Life in camp	91
Chapter 8	Horace the Horrible	110
Chapter 9	The spirit of Africa	126
Chapter 10	Elephant song	141
Chapter 11	King of the elephants	159
Chapter 12	The song of my son	180
Chapter 13	Spartacus and other lions	199
Chapter 14	Standing on shadows	215
Chapter 15	The good, the bad and the chocolate thief	244
Chapter 16	Jer's health scares	264
Chapter 17	From desperation to elation	281
Chapter 18	Would they remember us?	311
Epilogue	The kettle is smiling – July 2006	345
Acknowledgements		383

GLOSSARY

Askari Swahili word meaning 'soldier'

Bakkie *(pronounced 'bucky')* commonly used reference to a small pick-up truck

Barbeque Australian word for an outdoor cooker

Big Five refers to five of Africa's greatest wild animals – lion, leopard, elephant, buffalo and rhino, and is synonymous with the African bush

Boerwurst *(pronounced 'boo-ruh-vorss')* a spicy farm-style sausage or 'wors' (literally 'farmer's sausage')

Boma enclosure made of branches and sticks

Braai *(pronounced 'br-eye')* the extremely popular South African version of a barbeque, where meats such as steak, chicken and boerwurst are cooked on a grill over a fire

Fisi Swahili word for 'hyaena'

Flehmen a behavioural response of many male animals, consisting of lip curling after sniffing a female's urine

Gap it slang for 'leave the scene'/ 'get out of here'

Howzit a traditional South African greeting that translates roughly as 'How are you?' or 'how are things?'

Is it (*pronounced as one word, 'izit'*) an expression frequently used in conversation and equivalent to 'is that so?'

Jalapalapa one of a number of African pidgin languages that developed during the colonial period to promote ease of communication between European settlers and Bantu-speaking people

Juju originated in West Africa and means 'fetish' or 'charm'. Commonly used elsewhere in Africa to mean 'magic' or 'the supernatural'

Kadaitcha Man an Australian–Aboriginal 'sorcerer'/'spirit doctor'

Kaross traditionally, an animal-skin cloak – more commonly now, 'cloth' or 'blanket'

Keti 'sling shot'

Kopje Afrikaans word meaning 'small hill'

Lekker Afrikaans word meaning 'very nice', 'special', 'wonderful'

Lichunanjani Shona word for 'hello'

Madala (*pronounced 'muh-dah-la'*) Afrikaaner slang – an informal local term of respect for an 'older man' or 'wise man'

Makoro a small, rough-hewn native canoe

Mama Ndlovu another version of 'Mother Elephant', combining English and Ndebele

Mandlovu Ndebele word meaning 'Mother Elephant'

Mazungu white man

Memsahib east African term of respect for a European woman, taken from colonial India

Meru Maasai word, 'Mieru' or 'Mweru', which is a Swahili word meaning 'island'

Mshungu black magic

Munt used among whites in South Africa, Zimbabwe and Zambia, meaning a black person, from *muntu*, the singular

Mushi Shona word meaning 'very nice', 'super', 'excellent'

Muti Ndebele word for 'medicine'

Ndlovu Ndebele word for 'elephant'

Nyanga witchdoctor

Pan waterhole

Rondavel southern African dome-shaped, single-room hut

Sadza stiff porridge made from mealie-meal (maize)

Sahib an east African term of respect for a European man, adopted in Africa from colonial India

Shame unlike elsewhere in the world, this is an expression that broadly denotes sympathetic feeling – even praise. For example, when admiring a pretty woman, the expression 'Ag, shame' may be used

Shumba Shona word for 'lion'

Simba Swahili word for 'lion'

Spoor footprints

Stoep (*also pronounced to rhyme with 'book'*) Afrikaans word for 'verandah' or 'porch'

Veldt Afrikaans word for an open grazing area

Vlei seasonally flooded area

Yebo (*pronounced 'yeah-boh'*) 'yes' in local African vernacular

PROLOGUE

I met Horace on a crisp, golden morning in June 1990 a few seconds before he decided to kill me.

It was a typical winter's day. Sunlight streamed through the window, warming my body after a freezing night spent huddled in an inadequate sleeping bag. I was sorting photographs and assembling files of newly identified elephants at our research base, located beside the grounds of a safari lodge near Hwange National Park. The small room was an obsolete bunker; a relic of the civil war.

A frantic call interrupted my concentration. The wife of a safari guide appeared in the doorway. Angela's face was contorted with concern. She waved me to the entrance impatiently, then pointed towards a group of people standing a hundred metres away on the edge of the grassed area of the camp, very close to a bull elephant.

'Look at those crazy fools, will you? I can't get them to

move away from that big guy. Can *you* do something?'

I raised my binoculars and focused on the solitary bull. I saw at once this wasn't a member of the resident herd. He was standing alarmingly still. I was appalled to hear the noise of excited chatter as the tourists clicked their cameras.

Angela's alarm was warranted. The bull was a wild animal going about his business, and these people were threatening his space. I had met them earlier during a talk on the herd project. Eyes sparkling, the women had described their fear – the rush of adrenalin – whenever elephants approached their safari vehicles. Yet they seemed oblivious to the danger of being down on the ground with this bull. I could only think that the manicured lawns and trappings of human habitation gave them a sense of security – as if the bull were standing behind an invisible wall at a zoo.

I grabbed my own camera with the intention of adding his profile to our files at the same time as I warned the women to move off. I knew that bulls were less likely to react to human stupidity than cows, who might charge to protect their young. The exception to this is during the period known as musth, when male hormones are running rampant. Throughout that cycle of about three months, which occurs once a year when a bull becomes fully mature, he is not to be messed with by any living thing.

I ran towards the women. One look at the bull was enough to fill me with horror. The temporal glands on either side of his wide forehead were swollen and streaming a thick fluid that was quite different from the moisture sometimes released when elephants are under stress. His penis dribbled urine and sagged from a sheath that was frothy and green. The bull was in full musth! *God help us all . . .*

'Move *now*!' I ordered quietly. 'You're in extreme danger. Run fast to the craft *kraal*.'

Conversation ceased, skirts flapped and they ran.

The bull remained motionless for a moment, glowering at me before he dropped his head with deadly intent. I made the split-second decision to run to the research room, rather than follow the fleeing women. It was a big mistake.

I wheeled around and bolted. By the time I realised the distance was too great, I was committed to that path. The craft *kraal* was now further away than the bunker. I heard nothing from behind, but I felt him coming. The bunker looked very far away. Angela stood framed in the doorway, gesturing frantically with her arms.

'He's charging!' she screamed. 'Run faster. Hurry! Hurry!'

I felt as if I were running in slow motion. The rancid smell of musth bull assaulted my nostrils. The long distance to safety never seemed to lessen. Angela's horrified shouts escalated and I knew he was closing on me. He was silent. But I heard his rage inside my head.

Then a figure emerged from some bushes ahead. In the moment when I saw the man, I had the sensation of leaving my body. From above I watched my knees and arms moving agonisingly slowly. I looked down on the huge bull. He was surrounded by a dust haze – tinted red with his fury. He and I seemed to be characters in a play I was observing from a safe place. I heard my father's voice telling my child self not to look back when I was running in the state championships. 'You will lose some impetus and give your opposition a chance to pass you.'

At the same time I was able to take in everything about the frail figure intercepting my path. Dressed in tatty trousers and a red shirt that flapped over his skinny chest, he looked ancient. The old man tottered on, apparently unaware of the unfolding drama. His appearance drew a noisy response from the bull, who was distracted for a split second. But I didn't know this then – or that the old man was visible only to the elephant and me.

An ear-splitting blast washed a cloud of stinking hot air over me. I came back to my body. The bull was very close. *I hear you, Dad. I won't look back*. A fresh surge of adrenalin lifted me higher.

CHAPTER 1

Epiphany

The wheels of the Cessna bounced on to the Kalahari sands. A man and a Land Rover waited beside the cracked beige runway of the Savuti airstrip. Squat, leafless shrubs crouched in a wasteland circled by quivering mirages where the earth met the sky. The intense heat seared my lungs when I took my first breath of the desert. I gulped, but it wasn't from the dryness of the air or from the sand motes that bleached the blue from the sky. I was simply overwhelmed with joy to be on the ground in Botswana; in Africa.

The bearded man approached, tussled for supremacy in a long, wrestling handshake with my husband and swallowed mine more gently. 'Howzit?' he said, 'I'm Nigel. Welcome to hell!'

I knew it was his standard greeting when I saw his dense

1

eyebrows were leaping above amused dark eyes. I looked towards the shimmering horizon. 'How far is the camp?'

'Into the sun that way,' he said, pointing ahead. He then turned to the pilot. 'Let's get the plane inside the hangar.'

There wasn't a hangar. Instead, the men circled the tyres of the light plane with thorn-encrusted acacia branches to protect them from the jaws of curious hyaenas. His words only added to my sense of exhilaration.

We climbed into the back of the Land Rover. Nigel sprang over the half door and into his seat, fired the engine and we roared off at speed across a trackless plain; across stillness. We saw no living thing, but I knew there must be animals somewhere taking refuge from the midday sun.

'Bushmen paintings in that *kopje*,' he pointed as we tore past a lone rocky hill jutting hard above the otherwise featureless landscape. Fifteen minutes later the sand dropped into a dry river course. On the opposite bank, a group of tents huddled beneath the shelter of a stand of stunted trees beside the waterless Savuti Channel.

Nigel introduced us to the other guests, Ira and Miriam from New York, to three staff members wearing khaki uniforms and to the camp chef, Shylock, who boomed a greeting.

Our luggage was stowed inside one of two large tents set close together beside a pit of dying coals. A dining table and chairs stood nearby. Further back, an awning stretched across an open-sided kitchen next to a gathering of pup tents, where I presumed the staff lived. The camp was perfect; it catered to the needs of its guests while minimising their intrusion on the wilderness.

Locals call October 'suicide month' in Botswana – with good reason. Temperatures hover around 40°C during the day, and stay well over 35°C into the night. After lunch I checked the thermometer. The reading was 45°C. It made sense to follow Nigel's suggestion and lie on our camp beds, which the staff had moved from our tents into the shade of scrubby trees. One of the staff handed us wet towels, and placed jugs of water and ladles beside the beds. I changed into a sarong, stretched out and placed the towel over my body. Within seconds it was black, bristling with thousands of mopane flies. The flies and the dry, static atmosphere sucked away the moisture within minutes. Each time the towel dried I dribbled water across it. And the flies descended again.

'This sure *is* hell. The heat's a bitch,' Ira moaned.

No-one replied. Except for the occasional clink of ladles against enamel, sound ceased. I didn't care about the flies or the heat on that first afternoon on safari in Africa. I found the dry heat more bearable than the humid heat in the steaming tropics of my Australian home. The others snoozed while I waited impatiently to leave for the afternoon game drive.

When we finally set off, I greedily sucked in the smells and physical substance of a place that I thought was perfect. I had never been to Africa, yet I felt as if I had come home. It had taken many years, but now I was here. My husband had reluctantly agreed to our stopping over in Africa on our way to attend rugby Tests in Europe. I couldn't quite believe it, or the sight of a small herd of impala that watched us briefly before their golden bodies leapt away to a safe distance. The dust-cloaked zebras refused to flee. They tossed their large heads with annoyance and glared at us, disturbed by the excited shouts of the couple from Brooklyn. I glared as well when Miriam pointed at a kudu and yelped to her husband, 'Look, Ira. That sure is a sweet giraffe.' The kudu bolted in alarm.

I thought I heard Nigel whisper to himself, 'Lord grant me patience', before he swivelled in his seat to set her right. My irritation with the couple was replaced by embarrassment when I was caught out incorrectly identifying a steenbok as a duiker. My husband's smirk was warranted.

The sun was hammering the horizon when we topped a small rise overlooking a muddy seep that was the only source of water in the area. My breath caught in my throat. A mighty bull elephant straddled the tiny water outlet, looming over a host of smaller creatures. I had seen Asian elephants in zoos, but this was my first sighting of an African elephant. I was astonished at his immense size. I smiled at the sounds of sloshing water coming from his distended stomach. Yet he continued to swing his trunk with angry blasts at any animal that defied his supremacy and tried to take a drink. I loved his attitude and that of the bloody-minded wart-hogs who dared to challenge his authority by making mad dashes into the water. Shy antelope watched in longing.

Nigel chuckled. 'That old bugger isn't going to let those guys drink until he's good and ready.'

Darkness descended rapidly, and the breeze of speed cooled my face. Just before we arrived back in camp a leopard peeled its rosettes swiftly through our headlights. For a moment I felt I was once again a tiny child, sitting astride my rocking horse with my father leading me through the long grass of the savannah on a quest for elephants and antelope. Sometimes we were in the Borneo of his war memories, searching the heights of the mosquito net for orang-utans. But for me the place I mainly imagined myself to be was Africa. The names my father spoke sounded magical to my ears: Bech-uana-land, Maf-e-king, Limpo-po, Zambe-e-zi. When I could read he gave me a picture book of African animals, a biography of Dr Livingstone and an atlas. I was hooked. I decided to become a missionary, because girls couldn't dare to dream of being park wardens. Dad filled our houses with native creatures and birds. I loved them, but they lacked the mystery of Africa's creatures. Through my mother I learned to appreciate different aspects of nature. She was an artist who saw subtle shades of colour in patches of dry bark where others saw only a flat grey. She would lie with me on the grass, where we listened with straining ears for the sounds of nature spirits. My parents were always of more interest to me than my peers. They encouraged me to dream, and I never doubted that I would one day visit Africa.

Back in camp I crouched down to wash my hands in a basin filled with water that shimmered in the soft blue glow of a hissing pressure lantern. My skin prickled with sunburn. I peered into the impenetrable darkness before returning to the noisy group sitting behind me around the campfire. I supposed the fire was lit to create atmosphere, because even after dark the hot air seared my lungs. I flopped into a safari chair as Nigel handed me a glass of tepid white wine and a bottle of water. The ice that was brought in with the supplies twice a week was only for keeping meat and other perishables fresh, he explained. He then told us of an incident that had occurred just a fortnight earlier.

A youth group from Germany had pitched their tents three kilometres from our base in the public camping site. Too many people were packed into too few tents, he said. Worn down by the relentless heat, one girl chose to sleep across the open entrance to a tent crammed full with her friends. The combination of body odour and sweat was a potent lure. In the early hours of the morning, a lion dragged the girl away from the tent. She was devoured in sight of her terrified companions. They had no weapons. When they shouted at the lion he left his prey and charged towards them. After that they remained silent. One could not imagine the horror and helplessness they must have felt, huddled inside their fragile hides, while the predator ate their friend. Then the hyaenas took the bones. Only the braces the young victim wore on her teeth were recovered. She never stood a chance. The lion escaped.

I think we must have looked concerned for our own safety, as Nigel exclaimed, 'Hey, guys! Don't look so worried, eh? That lion was aberrant and he's a long time gone – *far* away. There's no question.' He then lolled back in his chair wearing an expression of cool confidence on what could be seen of his bearded face.

I opened my mouth to ask Nigel if the predators were starving because the waterholes and seeps had almost dried up, forcing the game to leave in search of distant water sources. Had the lion been an opportunist, I wanted to ask. I got no further. A deep snarl came from directly behind me. I turned and froze. I was looking into the unblinking, malevolent gaze of a lioness. She was just a body length away, crouched down beside the basin where I had washed my hands minutes earlier. Other shadowy forms were moving in behind her. The lioness grimaced soundlessly, giving an awful display of yellow fangs as she drew in air. My lungs stopped working as her bunched flanks heaved into an explosive roar.

Seconds later, Nigel countered her threat with a primeval bellow. Shylock dropped the loaded dinner tray. The sound of crashing crockery increased the bedlam. We had no firearms. Nigel was on his feet, drawing up terrible, primitive sounds from deep in his belly. His face was contorted in a grotesque grimace – a parody of her own. He grabbed the spotlight from where it lay on the sand and aimed the harsh light at the lioness's pupils. She squinted. My breath returned in pants. My legs began to tremble, and my heart beat so hard and fast I felt the blood pulsing loudly in my ears. I feared that my throbbing head would explode and spray surges of blood everywhere. *Good. I'd be dead without having to know those fangs were crushing my carotid artery.*

But Nigel's aggressive bluff succeeded. Blinded by the strong light the lioness squeezed her eyes shut, sank down, and raised a huge paw to swat at the air; to repel the glare. She couldn't see me and I didn't want to see her. We all stood up and began to shuffle slowly backwards. There had never been a time of greater clarity in my life. Nothing existed except the lioness. Her musky odour filled my senses. Her powerful muscles rippled beneath loose skin. She spat in disgust, wheeled, and loped away into the shadows. The others disappeared with her.

They were out of sight, but how far away? We scanned the perimeter of light. I was drawing short gasps that made me light-headed. Stars blazed in the inky blackness of the night sky; close and friendly without the light of the moon to diminish their brilliance. The Southern Cross was there. A mosquito stung. Nigel added a large log to the fire. *Ah. Now I see why.* Suddenly the flames became welcome and protective. I moved close enough to singe my skin. The others jockeyed for similar positions.

Now here *we* were – where the girl had been taken by the lion – facing possibilities too awful to contemplate. I looked into the darkness and wondered if Ira, Miriam and my husband were having the same thought. There were no solid buildings to offer protection. We were without weapons, dependent upon our own intelligence and an experienced safari guide for our survival in a wild desert place that was home to predators with superior physical strength and a formidable array of stings, bone-crushing jaws, fangs, talons and venom.

By day the surrounding featureless plain had appeared innocuous and safe. Now I peered into a black, mysterious space filled with alien sounds and cruel possibilities. Beyond the false security of our tiny circle of light, I sensed predatory cunning appraising my frailty; calculating my potential as food. Being on the dinner menu for another species had no parallel for me or for the other three travellers, whose faces mirrored my own apprehension. We all came from domesticated cities where humans were at the head of the food chain. But in this place we had only our aptitude to elevate us marginally above prey animals. I couldn't see the lions, yet I knew they were watching us – strong and confident in their nocturnal element.

Like frightened children, we looked to Nigel for direction. He was propped lazily against the ice chest (which I was eyeing as a possible hiding place) with a seemingly nonchalant air. Years later, when I met him in different circumstances, he admitted to his own trepidation that night at Savuti. I told him then that he had been wise to hide this from eyes that were calculating the level of his concern to establish our own.

I began to relax a little when Nigel drew languidly on a hand-rolled cigarette, casually blew smoke rings and spat a stray strand of tobacco off his lip. Could a man be feeling anxious and yet appear so cool? I thought not.

Ira asked anxiously, 'It ain't the one that ate the dame, is it?'

It was a question we all wanted answered.

'No, man, it *ain't*,' stressed Nigel. 'For one, she's a female!'

My shoulders relaxed further when Nigel pointed out that our shelters were strong, four-man tents sleeping only two; that the 'girl-eater' was an aberrant lion; and that this pride was definitely after a kill from the small herd of impala we could hear alarm-barking nearby. He led us into the open-sided kitchen tent. Our tightly bunched group of four bumped into his back when he stopped walking, which should have been embarrassing but wasn't. He turned amused eyes upon our fearful faces.

'Don't worry, guys. *Ay-ay-ay-ay-ay*! I'm not going to throw you to the lions. It's water they want, not us.'

For a moment I felt safe. This was until he betrayed my fragile faith in his certitude by stroking his feral beard thoughtfully, peering into the surrounding dark and adding, 'Still, they're cheeky buggers, eh? Just a bit too willing to come into a busy camp. Let's eat and call it a day.'

We ate our meal in quick gobbles. The food caught in my gullet. Nigel continued to appear confident and self-assured, but I sensed he was on high alert. His spiky black eyebrows lifted and twitched like alarmed caterpillars, giving him away. Shylock was huddled with the rest of the black staff beside the wood stove. Their voices were hushed. Fortunately, I didn't know then that this behaviour was unusual. In time I would learn that it is considered impolite for Africans to speak quietly, in case others think bad things are being said of them.

Nigel escorted us to our tents. 'Goodnight. *Lekker slaap mevrou.* [Sleep well, madam.] Shylock will come with a wake-up call at 5.30.'

The next eight hours remain unchallenged as the longest of

my life; but I suppose that eight hours is really a very short time span for an intensive workshop on the evolution of the soul . . .

The *meru* canvas tent was lit by a flickering lamp placed upon a small table between two camp beds. My husband fell on to one and into immediate sleep. I felt very alone. It wasn't a new feeling, but just then I needed reassurance and support. I drew comfort from the Bronx-accented voices of the couple next door as they prepared for bed. Perspiration dripped from my face on to the groundsheet where I crouched, struggling to close the wayward zip of the entrance flap to our tent.

'Damn. Damn!' I cursed.

Ira and Miriam's conversation was loud, but it was reassuring to hear voices. Should they take sleeping pills? Could they sleep in such cruel heat with all the flaps down? The flaps down? I had forgotten to cover the windows and there were no inner blinds. I looked through the nylon mosquito screening of the unusually large windows that extended down almost to the groundsheet and wished I could leave them open to allow air flow. Ira was outside his tent tying the fasteners over the screens. He was complaining about the sweat box inside the tent. As he moved to the next opening, his wife reminded him of the unfortunate girl.

'What ya doin', Ira? Ya wanna die out there?'

I didn't want to go the same way, but there was no other option. I would cook in the night, but we would be safe. I returned to the doorway. I had managed to close the zip, but now it was jammed shut. 'Bugger,' I muttered. Perhaps Ira would help . . . I returned to the window and opened my mouth to ask for assistance. No sound emerged.

A lioness crouched outside, watching Ira intently. Her sphinx-like form was outlined against the halo of light from the glowing coals nearby, her ears pricked to attention. Ira continued to grumble as he tied down the last cover, unaware of his deadly audience. I willed myself to be silent. Alerting him to the lioness's presence might cause him to panic and run – a move that would act as a prey signal to the female. He was almost finished. I mentally urged him to hurry. Concern for his vulnerability pushed aside my own fears. I didn't even think about the four uncovered windows of my tent; which was just as well. The opportunity to close them had passed.

All secured, Ira muttered his satisfaction and strolled a little distance from the entrance to have a pee. It was a long, loud pee. *Would it ever end?* I wondered. Evidently, Miriam wondered as well. 'Ya wanna wash the tent away?'

Ignorance was bliss. Ira countered Miriam's irritable comments by launching into a Yiddish lullaby which he crooned to the bitter end before returning to the tent. The zip rippled shut in one movement. *Lucky Ira . . .*

I had doused the lantern in our tent when I first sighted the lioness. Within seconds, my neighbours' tent was also dark. Nigel and his staff were in their tents fifty metres away. It was eerily quiet. I wanted to yell out to them that the lions had returned. I picked out two more feline shapes crouched beside the basin, making loud lapping sounds. I wished the water had been emptied. And yet I was glad for the relief of their thirst – however minimal.

Seeking solace I went to my husband's bed, placed my mouth against his ear and whispered, 'Please wake up. There are lions outside.' He didn't stir, even when I shook his shoulder – he had drunk too much wine. At least he was there. I settled cross-legged on the narrow cot, feeling both scared and excited by the close proximity of the predators. The eerie red light from the rising moon dispelled the shadows. If Nigel was right, the lions should soon head off to make a meal of impala.

I was exhausted, and undoubtedly sleep would have come quickly – despite the lethal company – if I hadn't heard the story of the recent tragedy and if my window flaps were tied securely over the gauzed openings. *If this and if that. So many ifs. Stop it, girl. You're here. Breathe, breathe . . .* I soon began to quiver. The internal hum of adrenalin was even worse than the physical tremors. I envied my neighbours their drugged, blissfully ignorant sleep and the deep slumber of my husband.

Outside, a tremendous earth-pounding noise broke the silence, accompanied by thick grunts. *Are the lions playing? If they frolic right into the guy ropes of the tent will it collapse?* Or even worse – if in their rough play they connected with the canvas, would they realise how fragile it was, swat a tear with their powerful paws and have me for dinner? *Oh, God!* Why weren't they leaving to hunt the impala? I got beneath the bedclothes and held the sheet up high so that only my eyes were exposed. The cover was armour of sorts.

A second later my fears became more than fantasy. The bed rocked from the impact against the tent of a bounding form. A silent scream heaved about my throat. The stench of decay filled the air. I peered through slit eyes at the window gauze near my face and wished I hadn't. A huge furry face, mouth open and panting, filled the window, encasing me in a cloud of halitosis.

It was a male lion! But there had been three females earlier. Were there four lions out there? *Oh, God! Is it* him? I thought he must smell me. I knew that cats have night vision; if I could see him, he could certainly see me. I closed my eyes. Returning his gaze would be a definite challenge; a threat. I'd read this

12

somewhere. His breath was hot and fetid on my face. I was still; waiting, waiting for I knew not what. Finally, the rank smell receded. He had moved away.

Very slowly, I slipped over the side of the cot on to the groundsheet in the middle of the tent, where I struggled desperately to control my racking shudders. Animal instincts replaced dignity with soul-crackling dread. I knew there was no point in trying to rouse the man who lay slumped on the bed beside mine. His incoherent mumbles might attract even more interest from the creatures waiting outside. Powerless, I curled into a lonely ball and longed for my mother.

One of the four lions flopped down across the entrance to the tent. Thank God that flap was secured. I could hear pouncing movements and soft snarls. Two shafts of pale moonlight fell on to the floor through the windows. I looked for a weapon. The only things of substance were the lantern, the metal wash basin, a chamber pot and an enamel jug of water. Water . . . I had to empty it somewhere. There was nowhere. A groundsheet covered the sand. I dribbled some of it across my body, then drank, and drank, until I felt sick from the volume and with guilt for the thirst of this part of Africa.

I placed the 'potty' on my chest when I lay down. It was my chosen weapon. Humour prevailed briefly as I pictured the headlines: *Woman repels marauding lions with a potty!* The vision of this absurd scenario settled me a little. I almost giggled. Surely they would have attacked by now if they were aware the prey was easy? The playing ceased. Through the opposite window I could see a lioness collapsed on her side beside Ira's tent. Loud snoring sounds grumbled from the rear. The predators slipped into sleep as my nightmare expanded.

Time stretched slowly over the next hours. The ground

13

between the beds became the refuge where I lay huddled, wrapped firmly in the rough sheet. My stomach swished water. My body had become a furnace, stoked by the heavy heat of the relentless Kalahari night. But my soul was chilled. Each time sleep crept near, a grunt, or a change of position from one of the lions, shook me into a state of wild-eyed alert. I tried to meditate, but my efforts to find refuge in a still mind failed miserably.

At 3 am the male rose and padded to the window beside my bed. He yawned and then gave some tiny grunts before shattering the night with three roars followed immediately by seven descending coughs. He then repeated the sequence, all just a stretched arm's length from me. Once again I screamed soundlessly. Undoubtedly the lions could smell my fear.

The first experience of those awe-inspiring bellows almost destroyed my sanity. For a moment, gripped by an overwhelming feeling of claustrophobia, I considered tearing open the tent and running from my prison. Yet, I knew I needed to stay and watch over my husband, and this knowledge came as a surprise. Since our marriage when I was just seventeen, I had always seen him as *my* protector.

The male began to circle our tent. He stopped occasionally to look in the windows. Three more forms joined him. The mood had changed. I had no doubt they were hunting and were focused on their target. It was *me* . . .

Then, suddenly, they disappeared. My ears strained to hear the slightest sound. A hyaena whooped in the distance. Cicadas chirped. Somewhere, the poignant call of an unknown night bird wavered. Where were the lions, just when I had expected them to shred the canvas? Without any warning sounds, a great shadow fell across the moonlight against the fabric of the tent. I crawled to the window and peered out. A sturdy black presence stood solidly in attendance. Soundlessly, an elephant had arrived in camp. It seemed the predators had bowed to the might of the huge creature.

For two hours the bull stayed with me. He smelled of cattle, manure, earth and sweating vegetation. *Such sweet perfume.* He snored gently. There were turgid stomach rumblings, but for the most part he was silent. I thought how easy it would be for him to rampage through the camp, destroying everything. Yet I knew his intentions were peaceful – even protective of me in a way no person had been. I rejoiced in his company and whispered my gratitude to him. I made a pledge to help his kind. He left as quietly as he had come.

The moon went with him. The false dawn promised an end to the longest night of my life. The heat continued to oppress the silence. Creature sounds had ceased altogether. This was the time of the lowest ebb, when the dying drop the last threads of life; when predators stalk their prey.

And then a pungent stench hit my nostrils like a punch. There was a furtive movement outside, and again my body seized with tension. Every part of me trembled. I clenched my teeth to try to stop the chattering. My tongue bled. *Down to the floor . . .* They were back, looking straight at me.

This time, their intentions were clear from their stealthy tread. I sobbed out loud. Silence didn't matter anymore. They knew me. This was it. *Can't someone please help me? Where's Nigel?* The lions began to roar. I heard it as the sound of triumph. They loped around – and again around – the tent, exuding power. I prayed and sobbed and dribbled and surrendered.

Just then the Land Rover's engine engaged, revved wildly

and came towards us at speed, its horn blasting. I saw the lions wheel around and run, pursued by the wildly bucketing vehicle with Nigel at the wheel. I slumped. My body felt like lead. My eyelids blinked grit. I staggered to the entrance flap. The vehicle returned, skidding to a halt outside. Nigel was at the entrance, but I thought he was really God in disguise . . .

'The zipper's stuck,' I blubbered.

He struggled from his side, cursed and shouted that he would be right back. I wrapped a sarong around my exhausted, trembling body as I watched him run back to his tent backlit by a glorious red dawn. He returned carrying a knife. The blade appeared through the flap and slashed down the canvas. He pushed his way inside, knelt down and pulled me to him. I was weeping with relief. Nigel's caterpillar eyebrows rose in query as he took in my still-sleeping, oblivious husband. His gaze returned to mine. My throat ached harder when I saw the sympathy in his eyes.

He patted my head clumsily, saying: '*Ay-ay-ay-ay-ay*. Steady on. They won't come back now. Shhh. Shhh.'

Between my hiccups and sobs, I told him of my night of the lions. I thought my body must stink with the sweat of fear. I was sliming his shoulder with nasal tears, which was disgusting. But I was beyond caring about my dignity. Finally, recovering a vestige of my sense of humour, I asked: 'Do you always use these tactics to get into a woman's tent? You promised you wouldn't throw me to the lions!'

He threw back his head and chortled, '*Sis*, man, I've been sprung. But, seriously, I didn't get too much sleep. I heard the cats come back into camp.'

He paused, looking puzzled. 'I didn't think they'd hang around once they'd drunk. Christ, I must've slept for a few hours until they roared just now. Man, when I looked out I could see them circling your tent. They looked serious, eh?'

He dragged me close to his chest. 'Sorry, girl, I didn't know your flaps weren't secured. I would've made a run to the vehicle early in the night if I'd known.'

Stroking my back with clumsy comfort, he produced a leather flask from his pocket. I took two burning gulps of whisky and lurched outside. The elephant was standing on the edge of the camp. He was facing us, swinging one leg backwards and forwards as if uncertain about whether to advance or retreat. Did the bull return when he heard the lions roar? I thought he had. Now the dusty giant turned and plodded away into the desert. In time I would know that this elephant had been more than he seemed. When the rhythmic rumbles shivered the fabric of my tent, it wasn't just the sound of an elephant. The spirit of Africa had come to my rescue; as it would again and again in the years ahead.

Excusing myself I tottered on floppy legs to the canvas-walled thunder-box. Three impala were nibbling the sparse grass stubble in front. *Why didn't they want you?* I wondered. It was a peaceful scene. A yellow-billed hornbill watched me from a branch, clicking and tutting his displeasure. 'Hello, beautiful bird.' I threw him a kiss and revelled in the glory of being alive.

Nigel was talking with Ira and Miriam when I returned. The Americans were expressing their annoyance at having slept through the drama. Ira was still wearing a nightshirt. His thin, hairy shanks quivered and his basset hound eyes rolled when I told him of his deadly spectators at bedtime.

Miriam stood rigid in shock and then murmured an un-accustomedly soft, '*Oh my God*'. They clutched at each other and pulled me into the embrace. Their kindness was endearing and I wept again. My husband appeared looking groggy. Nigel didn't spare him when he told him of my terror in the night. I knew my husband was angry when he crossed his arms across his chest and asked for a coffee. That was it for me. In this place where he had no power, I knew I could escape. I think he saw it in my eyes as we drank steaming coffee laced with brandy sitting by Shylock's fire.

I stayed behind when the others left for a game drive. I needed to be alone. I felt overwhelmed by bizarre and wonderful feelings. Colours, sounds and smells swamped my senses with intense clarity. For a while, I felt adrenalin bursts, like sizzling mustard seeds. And then I felt elation. I had never experienced such strange and wonderful emotions as I experienced that day. I felt I was having an epiphany! I wanted to consult a dictionary to understand the extent of an 'epiphany'. And then I *didn't* want to attempt to define it in case logic destroyed simple knowing. I knew that the marriage was over; that I had the strength to let go and move on. This would free us both. How could a twenty-seven-year-old man have known how a seventeen-year-old child would evolve? On that day when the child bride came of age I knew I would be judged and vilified. I also knew that in time my husband would be grateful for my decision. I had a sense of having been reborn. I was only in my early thirties, yet I felt as if I had been married forever – to a man who had become a stranger. I had no doubt it would be a hard road for all of us. Nevertheless, I felt joyfully alive, emotionally awake, present and free in a way I hadn't known since childhood. I savoured having survived actual blood-and-bone predators, but also I felt free of the fears I had been living with for many years: the fear of being hurt, of losing my self, of loneliness, of being punished, of not being able to provide for my darling children. And this glorious epiphany had come about because I had experienced a tangible and understandable fear – the fear of dying in the jaws of a lion. The experience stripped me naked and transformed me. When I surrendered to the lions, I surrendered control. It seemed that a higher force said, 'Ah, she's got it at last', and granted me freedom in the guise of an elephant that brought with him the possibilities of a new and better life.

In the African desert I emerged from a spiritual desert to begin the long journey from unhappiness to fulfilment. It would also be a journey towards the elephants.

CHAPTER 2

Jewel of the Kalahari

When we flew away from the Savuti Channel I held tight to the knowledge that an elephant and I had an agreement. I would be coming back. The aircraft droned deep into the miraculous Okavango Delta. This time the plane landed on a grassed strip flanked by the dense forest of the Moremi wildlife reserve. Nothing had prepared me for the astonishing beauty of the giant jewelled oasis of the Okavango.

I felt safe there, sitting on the verandah of a thatched *rondavel* that overlooked a cool, clear stream of the Khwai tributary. The lush waterways soothed my soul after the intense experiences of Savuti. It was hard to believe that this place existed in the midst of a great desert. I watched sleepy hippos lolling in the water beside the reeds. Their peaceful sleep was broken by occasional yawned warnings to each other before they gave vent to their increasing indignation with loud, pig-like snorts. Crocodiles basked on the banks in the company of cheeky blacksmith and crowned plovers, a family of Egyptian geese, long-toed jacanas and a pair of stunning saddlebill storks. Majestic fish eagles surveyed their realm from the branches of tall trees. Pleased and proud, they threw back their fine heads and throbbed their ode to joy. For me, their song is the sound of the African day. I know I am home now when I hear their haunting call.

Each morning before dawn, I joined my fellow wanderers for tea and hard rusks around the fire. Armed with cameras and binoculars, we set off in the open Land Rovers for never-long-enough game drives. I wanted to whistle the tune from the movie when we crossed the rickety pole bridge over the River Kwai. The soft light of dawn cast a mellow golden glow upon the waving grasses. Above, the dust coating the exotic trees gave the leaves an aura of rose pink. The air was cool and fresh, cloaking the aroma of Africa that would come with the heat: it held the smell of animals, wood smoke, earth and sweating vegetation, sometimes tinged with decay. It is a smell I have grown to love.

My purpose in visiting Botswana had been to meet with the indigenous San people (known more commonly by the term 'Bushmen'); hunter–gatherers I was studying in anthropology. These remarkable, gentle souls, who had lived for millennia in harmony with their harsh environment, have been taken to the brink of annihilation by both white and black settlers. But after surviving Savuti, I let go of that wish. It was enough just to be in the land of my longings; to sight greater kudu, glossy black scimitar-horned sable, rare roan antelope, and the dainty if ubiquitous impala. Semi-aquatic lechwe fed on the water plants of the river meadows. I even caught a glimpse of the shy sitatunga disappearing into the water and papyrus jungle. It was as if I had always known these creatures, and yet everything was a revelation. I was astounded that protected wild Africa shelters, camouflages and feeds a perfectly balanced diversity of species in what appears to be disproportionately large numbers for the carrying capacity of the land. It is God's perfect plan. Browsers, grazers and predators utilise divergent foodstuffs – nothing is wasted. But the wilderness has been reduced alarmingly since Europeans shattered the perfection of the vast savannahs and forests with bullets, and invaded the natural habitats with domestic stock.

By my second day at Kwai I had become determined to be fully present in the now, and not to worry about the future. Africa does that. It focuses one on the present moment. That evening the safari guide drove the Land Rover on to an open plain where he found a cheetah on a kill. The panting cat still had her muzzle clamped over the windpipe of her prey, a lechwe calf. She lifted her small, dainty head, painted with two elongated black teardrops beneath the eyes, and growled a high warning. Her long, elegant legs straddled the carcass as she swung her face from side to side like a metronome. She was beautiful, perfect. Without taking her golden eyes off us, she quickly tore an opening in the calf's stomach, working rapidly and nervously until the gaping hole was large enough to pull out the steaming bag of stomach contents. This she discarded with obvious disgust. She began to eat quickly, stuffing herself with a haste that seemed indecent for such an elegant creature. *Fangs-in-tear-chew-gobble-swallow*. Soon I understood the reason for her haste.

Three spotted hyaenas, trailed by two jackals, were closing

fast across the plain. The exquisite cheetah twittered and snarled at the approaching threat. She ripped off another chunk of meat. Loping faster, the hyaenas shrieked and whooped. Saliva dripped in gruesome, slimy strings from their huge jaws as their heads dipped and swayed. Their horrible giggles and shrieks of excitement made my skin crawl. Hyaenas move with a craven creep, but their topsy-turvy (to my eyes) conformation produces the action. Their hindquarters slope away from high, strong withers. Contrary to popular belief, they are not cowards. They are excellent predators, but when the occasion presents they are even better opportunists. And this was the case here. The black-backed jackals hovered behind, exacerbating the cacophony with their eerie, wailing howls.

They were almost upon her when the cheetah bowed to the pressure and slipped away, grasping a last desperate mouthful from the carcass. Her streamlined, slender form looked defeated and unsatisfied. She had almost stayed too long. Her small teeth were no match for the mega-jaws of the hyaenas.

When we returned to the place in the morning, nothing remained: the death of one gave life to others. Scavengers had licked away the stain of death. Now a distracted impala buck herded his ewes with bossy thrusts from his lyre-shaped horns as they ducked their pretty heads to feed on the trampled, bloodstained grass.

Later, I showered in the company of strange flat spiders who cared even less for my presence than I did for theirs. Glittering, holographic eyes caught the light and sparkled red, while I cringed into the centre of the flow of water, never presuming they wouldn't suddenly leap at me. *Shame and embarrass-ment . . .* I had locked eyes with a lion at a distance of a metre, so what was this to compare? But these were early days in my getting of courage with arachnids. Even now, I would rather face a venomous snake at five paces than a spider of any species.

An hour later the spiders were forgotten. I sat with my fellow travellers in the open bamboo and thatch-roofed bar drinking a sundowner. Fabulous wooden masks acted as light-shades. Rays streamed from their eyes and mouths: they looked like gargoyles and demons. Intricately designed woven baskets were scattered around the floor between the bleached skulls of hippos, baboons and an elephant. Heads of mighty horned antelope watched us from the massive posts with dead eyes. *Shame . . .*

The camp manager, Raphael, was a long, lean, handsome Zimbabwean who had fled to Botswana to escape post-civil war Zimbabwe. He exuded sexual energy in every movement of his graceful form. We held glances a little too long and I was astonished at my daring. 'Rhodies' are an angry, exiled people who still refer longingly to their homeland as 'Rhodesia'. But that place no longer exists – not since independence was declared in 1975 when a dictator displaced democracy.

Raphael poured Castle, Lion and Leopard beers into enormous glass jars beside the cheerful Tswana barman named Hello, who was making shandies of ginger ale, lemonade, orange cordial and bitters mixed in differing proportions for either the sweet Malawi brew or the drier Zimbabwean variety. The shandies were served in long iced glasses dusted with sugar. They were decorated with fluorescent miniature parasols, preserved Amarillo cherries and slivers of orange. The drinks were glacier cold, unlike those at Savuti. At Kwai River Lodge there was a refrigerator drawing power from a generator that throbbed during the hours clients were away on game drives. It was almost *too* civilised. But after Savuti I needed safety.

Suddenly, Hello clapped his hands to attract everyone's attention. Silence descended. He came from behind the bar and stood before his captive audience, looking at each of us in turn. With the air of a great orator, he began to speak.

'My friends,' he said gravely. 'There is a great thing I am wanting to tell you. My people made this Okavango a wildlife reserve in the year 1960 plus three.' His face shone with pride as he held his hands together before his chest in thought.

'Ah, yes,' he continued. 'It was a very great happening, you see. This decision that my wise fathers were making has been described as a shining light in the tribal history of my people. And that is what I had to tell you. Thank you too much for listening to this small man.'

We burst into spontaneous applause as he bowed before returning to his post.

Just then a vehicle rumbled to a stop outside. The actor George Clooney's clone sauntered in and straddled a stool. Except for a collective female gasp, silence fell. The man leaned his elbow on the bar, rested one foot upon the rail and cast a slow gaze over the assembled guests. Hello beheaded a Castle beer and handed the man the brown bottle. He tossed the contents down without pause. I was mesmerised by his bobbing Adam's apple. He was dressed in stained, crumpled khakis and wore a wide-brimmed, battered felt hat tipped back from his deeply tanned face. His presence was powerful, even dangerous. Not a word had been spoken since his arrival. The hush deepened as he put the bottle down and walked slowly towards me. Placing his hands on either side of my chair, he thrust his face close to mine and growled, 'You have ten minutes to decide if you want to come for a two-week trip by *makoro* into the Delta.'

Startled, I looked into his haunted brown eyes and opened my mouth to speak. Before I could utter a word he placed his forefinger against my lips, caressed them gently and repeated, 'Ten minutes!'

He turned and swaggered outside. My husband snorted, lifted his glass to his lips and turned to address the woman sitting beside him. It was another scar on the backdrop of closure.

An American woman sighed, 'Did you hear that?'

Another said, 'What a hunk.'

Suddenly, everyone was talking at once.

Raphael beckoned me away from the group. His face was dark when he said, 'Howzat? Are you going to pack your bag?'

I retorted, 'I'm here to see four-legged animals, not the two-legged variety in trousers!' However, I was feeling light-headed and more than a little intrigued.

Raphael's frown disappeared. He laughed. 'Buck will be disappointed. He's just wound up a stinker of a hunting trip with difficult clients. He's a wild guy. But this is a first.'

I realised the stains on the hunter's clothes must be dried blood. I excused myself and slipped through the back entrance into the dark. The floorshow was over for the others. I heard the vehicle depart soon after I sank into a canvas deckchair in the gloom by the fire. Was I so transparent that the highly tuned intuition of the hunter sensed what he thought was a wounded creature and came in for the kill? I hoped not, for, if so, he was wrong: I had already started to heal. Or was he simply a lonely man who made an impulsive, random choice of female company? It remains the strangest compliment I have received – if a compliment it was!

A woman approached and crouched down beside me. She touched my hand. 'Life can be a bummer, can't it?'

I smiled at the pretty blonde Canadian who had arrived in Botswana for a two-week safari three years before and had never returned home. Susan managed the kitchen and domestic staff at the lodge. She sighed, 'Be careful. You could lose your heart to this country.'

My heart swelled. 'I lost my heart to Africa long before I came here. There has never been a time I haven't yearned to visit since I knew it existed.'

'You, too?' she replied. She took my hand between hers and continued, 'I think you're very sad.'

Tears filled my eyes. A warm embrace of air encircled us both and I felt safe in sharing with her revelations about my changing circumstances. The need to draw comfort from such a kind woman overcame any loyalty to my husband. Besides, I knew I would never see her again. It was as if she had been sent to me when I most needed guidance, for she had a similar tale to share with me. We were kindred souls, and in those few moments we were able to be honest with each other in the way that very old friends can be.

We moved beyond her past and the possibility of my future course. She spoke of the present and told me of her difficult relationship with a research scientist working on the tsetse fly problem. They were at loggerheads over an ideological question. He was working to eradicate the fly for the benefit of cattle producers. Domestic animals have no immunity against

27

the toxin. Susan pointed out that, conversely, wild animals are unaffected and this has been a godsend for them. But destruction of the tsetse fly tolls the death knell for the game, because human greed is demanding more and more of the marginal country that is the last stand of Africa's animal heritage. I thought of my elephant friend and sympathised with Susan's fervent hope that common sense would prevail. We stayed talking until the dinner drums invited us to eat.

Three heavy ironwood tables formed a semicircle beneath the stars, bounded on two sides by a reed *boma*. Lions wouldn't be joining us for dinner here in this paradise of bounteous food and water. Our meal was equally sumptuous: fresh bass doused in peri-peri sauce, thick marbled beef with gem squash and native spinach, and tangy citrus tart washed down with excellent South African wines. Conversation and laughter levels rose to a raucous pitch as Dionysus weaved his magic and our defences dropped.

My heart was at peace. I felt replete. I left the party early and fell into bed. I could hear the hippos grazing nearby. In the distance, lions roared. They didn't bother me. In this safe place I snuggled into the soft bed beneath a whirling fan and listened as the stars murmured to me of their dreams. I stirred when my husband returned. An elephant arrived soon after. I lay in my bed listening to gentle murmurs as he rested outside. Like my champion at Savuti, this elephant was very fine company.

I was woken before dawn by ground hornbills booming their percussion. Dressed in beige shorts and shirt, I stepped outside to look for them. The game vehicles were ready to leave. My husband was still sleeping when Raphael asked if I would like to go with him in search of a breeding herd of elephants. So far my experience had been with bulls, so I leapt at the chance to see cows and calves. He said he was very cautious with the local breeding herds, which had a reputation for aggressive behaviour towards humans since several had been shot when they strayed into a neighbouring hunting concession. Raphael had reason to avoid any close encounters with the understandably wary herds. The previous year he had been hospitalised for two months with a serious back injury after surviving a charge from an angry matriarch that left his vehicle the shape of a sardine can. Like the squashed Land Rover, his present vehicle had a diesel engine. This meant there was a delay between turning the key and starting the engine while the fuel line filled: a delay that had proved costly for Raphael and that would bring us close to the brink again on this final day of my visit.

In the heavy mist of a humid morning we drove through the dense bush bordering the floodplains. Within an hour we came upon a ninety-strong herd of elephant cows and calves browsing across our route. Raphael cut the engine quickly. We were upwind, and they seemed to be oblivious to our presence. We settled with poised binoculars to watch them feed. I was incredibly excited to see my first breeding herd. A huge bull trailed behind.

Several calves played around their mothers' legs. *Ring-a-ring-a-Rosy* appeared to be a favourite game. They ran in circles, chasing each other's tails until one fell down. Then the rest clambered gleefully over the prone calf until it was obscured by a waving mass of trunks and stolid little legs. Eventually they all tottered to their feet and repeated the performance.

Without warning, a huge cow with sunken temples and long, worn tusks broke from the bushes a hundred metres away and headed for the bull, which turned and ran with his tail held aloft. The cow wheeled around, screamed once with her trunk lifted high and then dropped her head, curled her trunk beneath her chest and charged at us. Raphael turned the ignition key without taking his eyes off the fast-approaching female. Her family had disappeared in a cloud of dust, signalling their departure with blaring blasts as their great bodies beat against the bushes, breaking thick branches as if they were twigs.

The engine remained quiet, despite the clicking fuel line. *Oh God!* The matriarch bore down on us, filling the sky with her bulk. My sphincter muscles threatened to relax. There was nowhere to hide. Cursing quietly, Raphael switched the ignition off, and then on again. *Tic-toc-tic-toc-bloc.*

The charge was silent, which made the throbbing sound as the throttle engaged all the more shocking. She was almost upon us when we finally shot forward. The acceleration threw me down. Recovering my balance, I crawled on to my knees and looked behind.

I shouted, 'She's still coming! Hurry, hurry!'

Raphael had the accelerator flat and we were beginning to pull away, but the cow's pace was unchanged. Wild elation replaced my cringing fear. The brave cow thundered on, disregarding her own safety in order to protect her family. I was filled with awe at her single-minded courage. Raphael purposely maintained a speed that kept us just ahead of her, to judge the degree of her intent. After five magnificent minutes she stopped, smacked her ears against her shoulders in a defiant head-shake and unleashed a mighty trumpet. Her trunk was pointing high and was stiff with rage. We left her to return to the herd that would be waiting patiently for their matriarch.

Raphael's face was glowing with excitement as he took my hand. 'Howzat?' he asked.

In the evening I watched a strategic drift of salmon-pink cloud float over the horizon and reflect the glow of light from the sunken sun. It was the end of my first week in Africa. My body swayed with the throbbing of the drums that were inviting us to dine, but which also spoke of death, of sexual tension, and of jealousy.

CHAPTER 3

Resurrection

I did a secret thing when I returned to my home in Australia. The first tree I had identified in Africa was a sausage tree blooming with deep-throated, carmine-coloured, velvety flowers that would turn into heavy, sausage-shaped fruit. I watched elephants straddling the decaying pods while they stretched their trunks high to browse on the leaves. The giant fruit is inedible and the flowers are said to be eaten only by the delicate nyala antelope, but the tree is sacred to many African tribal people – perhaps because the bark has healing properties. Within days of my return I found a nursery selling tiny seedling sausage trees and bought the one that liked my touch. I planted it in a sheltered position near a spring-fed dam on our ten-acre property where it would be safe from the hooves and teeth of the horses. Only my silky terrier and I knew. Each day

I took a watering can, filled it from the waterhole and sprinkled the tender plant. It responded magnificently to my care and to the summer heat, while the indigenous giant Moreton Bay fig beside the house began to die. I saw a parallel in my own life, as my marriage slid inexorably towards divorce. I was shattered when my husband and I separated, but I hoped to find peace where chaos had reigned.

The tiny, thriving sausage tree became for me an icon of freedom. It gave me comfort on what would be a long and convoluted journey before I returned to Africa and the Kalahari. I never doubted that I would fulfil the promise I had made to the elephant and to myself, although I knew it would be a difficult process. But the loneliness that had filled my life prior to visiting Africa was now replaced by relief and a gradual gaining of confidence, and even though I stumbled many times I was never again afraid of the future. My spirit felt light.

The economic and emotional struggles of being a single mother were mitigated by an overwhelming sense of relief. I was intoxicated by choice and the freedom from expectations. I wreaked vengeance on my wardrobe. Out went the designer clothes prescribed for the wife of an upwardly mobile man and in came the faded jeans, Indian blouses, Jesus sandals and untamed hairdo of the university student. I was in my final year of studying archeology and anthropology, but I hadn't felt like a student until then. I had been catapulted straight from school into marriage at seventeen without knowing the irresponsible freedom of youth.

My girlfriends brought to the house flagons of wine that tasted better than the fine vintages of my previous existence. We danced and sang with the children and their friends. Even my classical piano training went out the window. Beethoven's

Ninth evolved into Billy Joel's 'Piano Man', and my children were delighted. I declared to my friends that men were off the menu. But the Cosmic Comic had other plans.

I met a man named Jeremy at a bus-stop. His ten-year-old daughter, Kate, was a friend of my children and of mine. Jeremy had been involved in cattle business with my husband years before, but I had never met him. I was running late on the morning Kate was due to return from a school skiing trip, having offered to meet the bus and take her home for the weekend. When the doors parted, the pretty blonde child was waiting with a beaming smile and outspread arms. I remember feeling surprise, as Kate was not usually so demonstrative. Delighted, I stepped forward to take her in my arms. Instead, she ran past me into the crushing embrace of her father. Jeremy hadn't told her he was returning to Australia after a period of time living in the Pacific Island state of Vanuatu. He wanted to surprise Kate and his older daughters. We shook hands, locked eyes and fell in love.

At first I was attracted by Jeremy's stillness, far-seeing blue eyes and strong cattleman's body. But it was his kindness, beguiling charm and wry, often self-deprecatory sense of humour that captivated me. From the beginning he made me laugh. He was an intriguing mixture of dignified pride and quiet humility. He took me from the city on walkabout into the vast spaces of the dry western country of Queensland that we both loved, where kangaroos vied with cattle for feed. We swam in mysterious billabongs, hiked through barren gorges, boiled the billy over tiny fires, and he sang to the stars and to me with a voice that could melt the hearts of angels. We shared the pain and sorrow of our failed relationships, and we wept for our children who were also suffering. Jeremy had been divorced for many years and he told me that my grieving had just begun; that it would be a long time before I would heal. I didn't believe him then, but he was right.

I took Jer to see the sausage tree. I told him of my promise to the elephant at Savuti. Other friends had mocked me when I spoke of it, and I wondered sometimes if I truly was the crazy person I saw reflected in their eyes. But Jer heard me and said he understood. Incredibly, he agreed to join me on my quest. I doubt that he anticipated quite how much his life was to change.

We were married in the beautiful garden of his youngest sister, Joanne, with the blessing of our five children. Jeremy lost his heart to Africa during our belated honeymoon. He told me so when we sat beneath a mighty baobab, dipping our tongues into the sharp, tangy fruit we plucked from a low branch. I took him to the Kalahari. The haunting beauty of the desert wove a spell of remote, unspoiled magic. I felt utterly at peace sitting beside my soulmate. It was a very fine thing to feel understood – to understand each other. I had always felt like an outsider looking in at a world I couldn't understand, as if I didn't belong. My values were different from those of the people who inhabited that world. For the most part I had judged myself harshly, believing that I was a very strange person indeed, wanting desperately to know why I was unhappy in the midst of a plenty that seemed to me to lack substance. I tried very hard to be what others wanted me to be.

But it was nature, wild nature and its creatures, that gave me joy. It put me in touch with the sacred. I had tried to see what others saw in the blobs of colour in modern paintings, but they were meaningless to me. I could admire the form of a building or a piece of sculpture, but I was never struck with awe in the way that I often was by nature. Nature is the perfect work of art. I wasn't judging what art forms gave others pleasure. I could only know my own experience – and the natural world was my sanctuary.

Jer told me how he also had bound himself into a conventional life. He'd experienced similar feelings of alienation, but had lacked the motivation to go his own way. As a youngster his dreams were of becoming a patrol officer in Papua New Guinea, which wasn't so different from my own dreams. Both of us had rejected those longings and taken our responsibilities to others very seriously. I had always told my children, 'Anything is possible', but I hadn't believed it for myself. Visionaries don't always know they have choices, or the means to fulfil their dreams. When two such souls come together, anything *is* possible. And so Jeremy and I made a plan.

If we established an African art gallery in Australia, we decided, we could fulfil two ambitions: helping to support struggling African sculptors and artisans, while also raising funds for conservation projects.

We moved to the beautiful hinterland behind the Sunshine Coast, bought and began renovations on a derelict pink house (sheltered within a run-down orchard), and restored another place in the quaint mountain village of Montville which we turned into The African Gallery. Here we sold images of Africa's wild animals, and other works. Our plan was taking shape, but I disliked being under public scrutiny in the gallery. I was always happiest working in the orchard.

For two years we poured our energies into regenerating the old trees and planting young striplings. We grew organic avocados, macadamias and vegetables, which I sold at a roadside stall, at the same time as we operated the gallery. We worked seven days a week between the two operations, only stopping to sleep. Jer also worked part-time as a cattle consultant. My children often helped out, seeming to enjoy the change of circumstances despite the economic hardships. Life was exhausting, but we were content. Personal happiness is a great source of energy. Even so, I wonder that we survived.

We visited Africa frequently to purchase artworks from remote rural areas and that was fun. The hard part was returning to the cities to complete the paperwork required to export the works. The cities seemed far more dangerous places to me than the rural areas. For a few precious days at the end of each buying trip we would escape to the ever-diminishing wilderness to draw strength from wild nature and to seek a way to answer the call of my elephant. With each visit we became increasingly alarmed at the escalating violation of the animal kingdom. The human parade pressed hard into these struggling sanctuaries. Along the way we established firm friendships with remarkable people who were devoting their lives to the preservation of wildlife habitats and threatened species. We met saints who do the same for impoverished Africans.

I longed to be in the close company of elephants, yet I began to think that my promise to help African wildlife would have to be carried out from a distance. I hatched a plan with Jer and some friends to establish the non-profit organisation Elefriends Australia. Elefriends was soon set up as an autonomous conservation group that continues to raise funds to assist struggling researchers working with endangered species and habitats. By osmosis, poor Africans benefit from the wildlife through tourism.

During our brief sojourns in Africa, elephants continued to steal my heart. Establishing Elefriends wasn't enough. Elephants thundered through my dreams at night and filled my thoughts by day. It was a longing I found impossible to resist and I understood the call to religion. However, I was unable to see a way to make my promise to the elephant reality.

Until, that is, while visiting Zimbabwe on a buying trip for the gallery, we met a man we knew as Mandebele, who leased a vast concession of land that lies adjacent to Hwange National Park. Mandebele operated safari camps there; however, he saw his main role as being custodian of a special herd of elephants that ranged across his leased holdings. He was in the process of establishing a research program that would also have the effect of protecting his charges.

Wildlife management bodies were calling for yearly culls to diminish the number of elephants in Hwange. Ecologists were justifiably concerned that the burgeoning elephant population was unsustainable, and causing increasing rates of tree loss within a confined game reserve. The issue was highly controversial. Culls require the slaughter of complete families. No one was happy about the extinction of entire gene pools and Mandebele wasn't convinced that major culls were the only answer. He was determined to examine the possibility that natural attrition, through the cycles of drought and plenty, would keep population levels steady; that elephants are natural conservationists – selective browsers. He had already found an ecologist who was prepared to work with his herd to investigate their browse habits and impact on vegetation. She had recently volunteered her time outside of her official job in Hwange and was already struggling to cope with the massive task.

Butterflies of excitement fluttered in my stomach. I told Mandebele about my experience and epiphany at Savuti. There was nothing to lose, and I sensed he would understand. His narrowed eyes settled on mine and I held his gaze for a long, silent moment. Then his stern features softened; he nodded and gave a small grunt.

'You're mad. You know that, don't you?'

'Oh, yes,' I agreed brightly. 'But it's a madness that won't let me go.'

Once again he withdrew into silence. I stuck out my jaw and maintained eye contact with him until he spoke. 'I see you,' he said. 'It takes a mad person to recognise another.'

Jeremy hadn't spoken. I think in that moment we both knew our prayers were about to be answered.

Mandebele leaned forward. 'You'll need the kind of obsession I'm hearing here to stay the course, girlie. Would you like to come join my project?'

I was out of my chair and hugging him in true demented-woman fashion before he could retract his words.

Mandebele turned his attention to Jer. 'How do you feel about being the guy who looks after these women? I figure that your knowledge of cattle and living hard in the Australian outback will take the worry off my shoulders. I haven't got the time to watch over them.'

A slow smile spread across Jer's face. 'I thought for a moment you were going to forget me. You're asking if I'm prepared to be Man Friday. No worries there, mate. I'm in.'

We spent hours discussing the project. It didn't matter to Mandebele that neither of us was an animal biologist, although my anthropological background would equip me with the tools to investigate social behaviour in the herd. The project would be a dedicated scientific study, but Mandebele also wanted to investigate the possibilities of mysterious interactions between species that defied scientific evaluation. He needed a bona fide scientist to give the project respectability and clout, but he had been searching as well for committed naturalists who would work within, and without, the mechanisms of science. Jeremy and I fitted the bill.

Mandebele made it clear that apart from having a place to sleep and fuel for the vehicle we would need to purchase, our work would be voluntary. I told him I would have paid to do the work, so everything else was a bonus. Momentum grows when we are on course. I didn't sleep that night.

We returned to Australia. Jer and I were adamant that no funds should be donated by Elefriends Australia. I think Mandebele wondered at our staunch refusal to accept a cent from the organisation we had established. But doing so would have raised doubts about our integrity and that of Elefriends, which already had to refuse many worthy conservation projects.

A week after our return I drove for three hours to the acreage outside Brisbane where I had planted the sausage tree. From the road I saw the fig tree had died. Away in the distance, to the right of the dam where I'd nurtured the tiny seedling, I spied a young tree bursting with green life. And deep in the leaves I thought I saw a crimson flower.

The next day I began the process of liberating us from the things that bound us. We had to sell everything quickly. *Let me go. Let me go*, I sang to the pink house within the avocado grove. A friend had told me the spirits of the house would hear me and understand if I really meant what I said. Old houses probably all have spirits, but if you don't believe you won't see them. Dancing through the evening light that bathed the rooms I felt like a whirling dervish. I wanted to believe my friend.

Perhaps it was just wishful thinking, but my peripheral vision glimpsed shimmering, silvery green sprites whispering in the corners. I addressed them earnestly. 'The elephants are waiting for me. Someone who wants to make you their own for a long, long time is waiting to buy you.'

Were my imprecations earnest enough? I stopped to listen. The floorboards groaned. The iron roof creaked. Otherwise, the house was silent. I thought of the tiny set of rosary beads we had found two years earlier, beneath the five layers of wallpaper that overlay the fretwork above a door. Perhaps they had been placed there by the people who built the house, to protect it and create harmony within its walls. It was certain they had loved it well. I had, too, when we came there to begin our married life. But now it was time to move on; to go walkabout along my essential Songlines. In my mind and in the room I felt a shift of energy. My focus was so intense that I knew now it would sell quickly.

Outside, a high country currawong carolled. I ran to a window and saw it perched deep within the closest macadamia tree of those we had harvested for their organic nuts during our two-year tenure. Underneath the great tree sat the 'boy's toy' quad bike I drove at dawn each day, carting the mobile water tank to the young avocados we had planted in disorderly rows – because avocado growers we were not meant to be. The Kalahari Desert and the elephants were calling us far away from these beautiful mountain meadows. We would replace rainforests and a sweeping view across green valleys to the Pacific Ocean with a flat, parched tawny land where my unicorns wore jutting tusks.

Within a week we sold our business, and our home and orchard. We were assured that the large, sagging shed would be preserved – where the mighty diamond python lived now; where the Italian internees had lived and served their time during the Second World War. I would miss the company of the curious, glitter-eyed snake, which would watch from the rafters above as we pushed macadamias through an ancient nut crusher and classed and packed the hand-picked avocados. I wouldn't miss the rats. One had bitten my ankle as I sat on a stool balanced precariously on cracked and sinking floorboards sorting nuts and dreaming of Africa. The wound had become infected. Living in the misty coastal mountains seemed now to have been an interlude of grace, a time when Jeremy and I came to know each other before we launched into an existence that would be even stranger than our wildest imaginings.

When the children heard that our initial stint in Africa would be for only six months, they happily encouraged our commitment. They were teenagers, all busy with their own lives. We purchased expensive photographic equipment, took a crash course in film-making, updated our inoculations, submitted our bodies to a physical fitness regimen, and assembled vital supplies that would ease the rigours of life in the wild. Every part of my life was transformed. The journey into the world of elephants had begun . . .

CHAPTER 4

Into Africa

All night the aircraft flew over Africa into a dawn hazy with smoke and dust. My spirit was already there, but my brain wasn't so certain that body, soul and spirit would be reunited. The cabin tilted steeply downwards. Our bodies pressed hard against our seatbelts. The engines of the shuddering jet whined as we made our final descent into Gabarone's international airport.

'Wonderful. Bloody wonderful.' I muttered between clenched teeth. 'We've got a fighter pilot.'

Practice is supposed to make perfect but several similar approaches during visits to Africa in the preceding three years hadn't decreased my fear that the nose cone would plough into the Tarmac. I figured that the odds were stacking up against us.

With a wolfish grin, Jeremy joked, 'Remember what they say? The best pilots in the world fly in Africa. They have to be.'

I recalled the theory a fellow passenger had expressed after my first experience of almost vertical descent to Lilongwe airport in Malawi. On overhearing my gasps and whimpers, the eyes of the English missionary twinkled as he told me that he believed the Zimbabwe pilots (who were trained to fly during the civil war) habitually evaded heat-seeking missiles. Considering that armed conflict was wracking neighbouring Mozambique, I had wondered whether a stray projectile might have crossed the border and locked onto our aircraft; perhaps even lured there by my searing fear. Yet our landing was as faultless as our gentle touchdown at Gabarone.

Weighed down with camera equipment, we stepped on to the Tarmac. We had arrived in Botswana. Excitement, fuelled by nervous energy, replaced bone weariness after the long flight. Jer's wide, straight shoulders bounded back to being square, and I stretched with relief and gratitude. Jer tried hard to provide me with more space on long flights, but his strong physique could only shrink so much.

Smiling African officials, clothed sensibly and crisply in shorts, long socks and short-sleeved white shirts, processed our disembarkation with brisk courtesy. The usual colourful band of noisy sightseers jammed the neat, modern arrival hall.

If I needed convincing that we were on the right path, then our first day in Gabarone provided proof. Equilibrium returned quickly, bringing body and soul together. Feathers left my head and everything else fell into place. Customs opened their doors after closing time and rapidly cleared the unaccompanied baggage we had sent ahead from Australia. The only problems were a pair of binoculars in a camouflage case and similarly cloaked khaki water bottles purchased from an army disposal store. Within weeks we had tossed away the bottles, but the essential and irreplaceable binoculars were an ongoing hurdle during our travels. At border posts and military check-points they would be examined with deep suspicion by frowning interrogators. We believe our Australian citizenship and relaxed smiles often saved us from internment as potential spies. On this first day the officials' doubts were quickly laid to rest.

Reliable second-hand four-wheel-drive utilities were as scarce as hen's teeth in most African countries except South Africa and Botswana. In Zimbabwe (if by some miracle, a vehicle were available), when the time came to sell, the money must remain in the country. South Africa's policy of apartheid meant that South African numberplates spelt trouble in other African countries, which was why the expedition was beginning in Botswana. The next day we found a vehicle: a baby-blue Toyota HiLux. Our hopes of finding an off-white vehicle were crushed when we realised how fortunate we would be to find *any* four-wheel-drive that was roadworthy. Our inappropriately coloured vehicle was soon known as Bluey. She would become an identity, our greatest tool and sometimes our refuge.

We shopped for water, petrol containers and pharmaceutical supplies. I was astonished at the range of goods available in the shops – everything from caviar to vintage French champagne. Gabarone was reputedly the fastest-growing city in the world, buzzing with excitement and expectation. Botswana has vast diamond mines and mineral resources – and thus a huge input of precious foreign exchange. Millionaires were being made overnight; developers were unable to keep up with the demand for housing, and satellite suburbs were springing up seemingly without any town planning.

The indigenous Motswana people looked prosperous and confident, in sharp contrast to people in Zimbabwe, Malawi and Zambia. I was saddened and humbled often by their frequently obsequious manner, especially that of the elderly, who were a product of the servant mentality of the colonial era. In an awful encounter in Malawi, an old man fell to his knees at Jer's feet. 'When are you coming back to take care of me, my father?' he pleaded. 'This is not a good place since you left.' The dictators who replaced the ruling white governments in many African countries have not proved to be the saviours of their people.

Botswana is a different story. In 1966, Sir Seretse Khama led the country into independence and a democratic system of government quite unlike any other in southern Africa. In Gabarone, I was delighted to see the people walking tall and proud. I found it easy to understand and forgive the occasional surly reactions to our presence.

I was impatient as all hell to get to Zimbabwe, but we were forced to detour to Pretoria, in South Africa, to purchase a fibreglass canopy and other essential goods that were unavailable in Zimbabwe: a groundsheet, mattress and pillows, an extra tyre, spotlights, a tool kit, engine oil, brake and clutch fluid, a tyre pump and spare fan belts, radiator hoses, points, spark plugs, condensers and fuses.

Two days later we were ready to leave Pretoria. As Jer pulled into a petrol station, a vehicle driven by an obese white man with a florid face stopped near us. The driver stomped to the rear of his car and opened the boot. An old black man in dusty, torn clothes crawled out coughing. I couldn't help myself. 'What have you done?' I shouted.

The doughy face of the white man split into a crocodile grin. 'Ach, man,' he chortled. 'We must keep the bloody kaffirs in the trunk, hey?'

I wanted to hit him. 'Get in the car and be quiet,' Jer said. Then he said to the man: 'You want to wake up to yourself, mate. That "bloody kaffir" is a human being just like you.'

The attendants looked astonished. So did the gross man. He balled his fists, but before he could move we roared away on course for the border post at Martins Drift.

My spirits lifted as we passed between vast fields of sorghum, sunflowers and barley that were flourishing after good summer rains. Tall, purple-hazed mountain ranges rimmed the valleys. Our guidebook assured us there was simple lodge accommodation eight kilometres off the main dirt road just over the border in the Tuli block. As evening fell, we crossed back into Botswana and re-entered a desert landscape.

We located the lodge, but the owners were away. There was nothing for it but to push on to Francistown. Driving through the African bush is hazardous at any time, requiring complete concentration to avoid hitting cattle, donkeys, goats or wild animals. By night it is an ordeal. Two hundred and forty kilometres, several close shaves with kudu and three hours later, our strained bloodshot eyes moistened at the sight of the welcome lights of the Marang Hotel. The thatched-roof buildings sprawled along the banks of the dry Tati river bed on the outskirts of Francistown.

I was hungry, and roaring sounds were booming from Jer's stomach. We dumped our luggage in our room, paid a security man to watch our vehicle and found the restaurant. A waitress loomed beside us. Her jiggling, massive breasts were balanced by a jutting derrière of imposing proportions. She recited the menu in a booming voice that rose above the din. Her impressive body quivered like jelly as she bellowed our order to a petite waitress who piped the message further down the line.

My eyes were riveted on the woman, who returned my stare with a smile. I wondered how much of the Bushmen she carried in her genes.

As far as we could see, the role of the statuesque woman was to move as little as possible and to use her vocal cords often. Eventually, the tiny, apricot-hued waitress arrived with our food stacked on a tray balanced upon her delicate head. Beneath the soaring, frond-lined ceiling we dined on a casserole of game meat, which was the only meal available at that hour, and watched the passing parade. Choking on bitter coffee laced with chicory, I took in the scene through dust-shot, jaded eyes. Informally dressed, faded white women and their red-faced men sported colourful African print clothing, while well-groomed blacks wore understated, smart European attire. They couldn't have known how strange they looked to the two weary travellers in their midst. Our ears were battered by the dated music that blasted from crackling speakers, and my sense of humour deserted me.

We were confronted by a drunken, red-necked, ageing expatriate who had urinated in his shorts. *Phewwwww!* He launched into a garbled story about 'the ferkin' good old days', before reeling away to find a more appreciative audience. The blacks watched the spectacle impassively; the whites appeared to ignore him. I felt shame at my response to the man. Who was I to sit in judgment of such people? We were guests in their country. *I'm tired, that's it.*

The music stopped at 2 am. The party folded and the guests staggered away. *Thank God*, I thought. We had stayed rather than become increasingly frustrated in sheet-tossing efforts to get to sleep. We returned to our room and dropped into an exhausted sleep. Six hours later I bolted upright into the mosquito net. I had left my handbag containing our passports, credit cards, and all our money and valuables, under the table in the dining room. I made a frantic call to reception. A bag had been found and was locked in the hotel safe, I was told. But it couldn't be opened until the manager arrived.

We hurried to the office where we waited for half an hour in a feverish state of worry. I was overwhelmed with guilt – and fully expected to find the wallet empty. Eventually, the manager arrived. He unlocked the safe and gave me my handbag. 'I don't fancy your luck,' he said gravely. 'These guys collect only twenty pula [US$10] a week.'

I hardly dared look inside. Then, joy, oh joy – nothing had been taken. We would be able to keep our appointment with the elephants. The security guard, Anson, was still on duty and accepted our heartfelt thanks and reward with puzzled dignity. 'Ahhh, *Rra* [father],' he said to Jer, for this was the way of things. 'The mother and I will remember you to God in our prayers.' He gave each of us the African handshake of palm-thumb-palm with his eyes downcast.

I have continued to remember Anson and his family in my prayers as well. His honesty was a wonderful advertisement for a country where '*pula*' not only describes a unit of money but is also a courteous greeting and the word for rain. Anson's faith in God was reflected in his tranquil expression, which filled me with a sense of peace. I wanted to know what he knew.

Clutching my handbag closely, I returned to our room to pack. Snorting sounds rumbled from the bushes near the door. I investigated, expecting to find a wart-hog. Instead, the sad expat drunk of the previous night was lying comatose on his back, clutching a half-filled pot of stale beer upon his sunken chest. The pot rose and fell with his breathing, somehow managing to stay aloft. Distressed by his state, and saddened by the intractability of many such old colonials who refuse to accept the new order I located the manager, who summoned Anson. 'The cavalry,' the manager groaned, 'to mount the colonel's usual Sunday morning rescue operation.'

I knew that Anson would treat the colonel with dignity.

We loaded the Toyota with water, fuel and stores for our journey across the eastern corridor of Botswana's Kalahari to the northern border town of Kasangula, and on into Zimbabwe. We anticipated a very late arrival at Victoria Falls.

The lonely highway stretched straight between horizons, across a vast thirst-land of scant vegetation. Scrubby thorn trees fingered towards the purple-black sky, cast into surrealistic spectres against the gloom. Intermittent showers blessed us with cool relief in a place of harsh silhouettes and arid spaces. The smell of wet earth is like perfume in a dry and barren land. I inhaled with pleasure. We passed isolated small settlements of thatched-roofed mud huts, where small, sinewy native cattle somehow found nutrition from the sparse spiky grasses. Bantam-sized boy herders watched our passing, propped against their strong crooks with one foot resting against the knee of the other leg.

One hundred and ninety kilometres later, we reached the outpost town of Nata, which lies close to the mystical Makgadikgadi salt pans. I stared longingly into the distance where the white sand shimmered. We pulled into a solitary fuel pump standing before a shabby corrugated-iron building. Saliva-inducing cooking smells filled our nostrils.

Munching the best beer-battered fish and chips I have ever

tasted, we wandered around the Sua Pan Bottle-store. It boasted a fine selection of excellent wines and spirits, as well as exotic liqueurs. The prices were equally exciting. I purchased a vintage bottle of Chivas Regal Scotch for ten US dollars.

A long-eared Boer goat, with twin kids, shared the verandah with us. She gobbled the greasy paper after we polished off the contents, although I tried to wrest it from her. Liquid-brown-eyed tots peeped shyly from beneath unblinking lids as we consumed orange ices. We bought more for them, which they gravely accepted as their due. Few European children have such quiet dignity that erupts suddenly into a spontaneous dance and unselfconscious laughter. Our ignorance of their jokes was probably for the best. We laughed along with them and they forgave us for being different. Somehow it didn't matter whether they were laughing at us or with us.

The Toyota's oil pressure gauge was dropping and the engine began to wheeze and cough as we limped into the tiny, but busy, border town of Kasangula. On the Chobe River floodplains below, distant herds of elephants reflected the silver light of late afternoon from their wet, slate-grey skin. Reluctantly we turned away from the inviting scene to join the queue waiting patiently to pass into Zimbabwe for the last seventy-kilometre stretch to Victoria Falls. The gates would close at 6 pm and we were eager to reach our final destination the next day.

Except for potential attacks from humans and mosquitoes the greatest threat to my peace of mind in Africa is the sound of a mechanical problem in a vehicle. It never fails to elevate my blood pressure to dangerous levels. By the time we laboured into our favourite budget lodge on the banks of the Zambezi River, smoke was pouring from the bonnet and threatening to expel from my ears! Both sources of potential fire abated quickly. We had arrived and help was close at hand.

The usual family of wart-hogs was down on its knees grubbing in the lawns and the usual irate staff intermittently chased them away. Cradling long, frosty drinks, we collapsed into wicker chairs to enjoy the colours of the sunset bouncing off the clouds and casting rainbows through the distant rising spume of the falls, *Mosai oa Tunya* – 'The Smoke that Thunders'. I was in an African heaven. My exhaustion was tempered with excitement as tiny moths of anxiety fluttered beside butterflies of joy in my stomach at the prospect of reaching the end of my long journey to be with the elephants.

That night I dreamed of spirit things. I returned to Australia and felt a deep connection with the land. I saw the earth blending into the shimmering timelessness of never-ending plains dotted with silver-grey gidyea trees and mulga scrub: the never-never of my childhood. Once again I ran with my Aboriginal friend Lily across a dry creek bed into the shade of a great white river gum – but never as fast, or as quietly, as she ran. Beneath our sandy toes, the Australian landscape began to dissolve into this Africa, where mopane woodlands throbbed with animal life. I was aware of an equally intense connection with the elephants and the buck that watched us pass by. I knew the silence and dreamtime of my birthplace. But I also knew the heartbeat of eternal humming life in Africa, where even the stillness of an empty place hints of hidden creatures.

When I awoke from the place of dreaming I felt a great sense of peace. I knew then that there could be several homes where my soul would sing. I understood what my father had meant when he spoke to my brother and me of his love for Borneo, Sumatra, and orang-utans and elephants as we fished together for yellow-belly in a creek. His personal battles fought in the jungles of Indonesia against the invading Japanese during the Second World War had been mitigated by his enjoyment of the wildlife and the local tribal people. Dad carried his happy memories of a strangely treasured killing place always, and spoke of them with me when we were at peace in our own land. His heart wasn't divided. It was content with being in two places at once – even if one of them was physically distant. When the dawn came, I knew that I could do the same. I was filled with excitement at the prospect of reaching our destination, near the village of Dete and close to Hwange National Park. It would be home for the next six months.

CHAPTER 5

Skew Tusk

Those anticipatory butterflies and moths fluttered harder in my stomach during the final 320-kilometre leg to camp. Alongside the road, artisans sold wood and stone carvings and small sets of marimba drums made from gourds; their wives and children offered melons, baobab fruit and vegetables.

Near villages, the road swarmed with walking, cycling humanity. Slick, modern African youths, wearing mirrored sunglasses and vividly coloured shirts and caps, swaggered with unconscious grace and rhythm. *Cool, man . . .*

Their heads draped in brightly coloured scarves, barefoot women swung their *karosses* to the front and breastfed their woolly-headed babies as they swayed along the roadside with languid grace. Others strolled slowly, knitting luminous pink and green garments. Donkeys – three and four abreast – and lumbering oxen doggedly hauled wooden-wheeled wagons piled high with firewood.

The mud walls of many huts were decorated with brightly coloured painted pictures and slogans. One read, 'Jealousy is not acceptable.' I wondered if this were a command and warning from a husband to one of his several wives. Perhaps she was a rebel railing against a lower-ranking position in the household. *Go, girl* . . .

Progressive thinking was evidently needed in other aspects of these people's lives. Even at this time of nature's benedictions the environmental damage wreaked by man was obvious. Over-grazing of domestic stock (particularly goats, which destroy the root systems) had laid bare the soil around the villages. Trees were stripped of their branches to keep the cooking fires burning. But what else could the people do? They needed cattle, goats and wood to survive. Spindly, fast-growing eucalyptus trees were planted in groves that could never keep up with the demand. But at least there was thought for the future.

It became apparent that the rains were long overdue in the Hwange area. Away from the settlements the country was thirsty, but despite this, the stunted mopane trees sprouted green foliage. Even the great baobab trees wore leafy hats. During the dry season, the baobabs seem to rise from the grey, powdery pans, their root-like branches stretching above over-sized bloated trunks as if they are growing upside-down. Perhaps Titans had thrown the vegetable giants skywards to land hard, burying their canopies below the soil? Their eerie forms obscure the riches they offer, of hidden water, nutritious fruit, and shelter for myriad birds, small animals and insects. When I hug a baobab, its body feels warm like no other tree. Each giant is a Lord of the Plains.

Outcrops of boulder-strewn *kopjes* marked a shift in the ecotone of the Kalahari sands environment. Tall teak forests and stands of elegant, wide-canopied acacia trees replaced the baobabs. We left the main road at the 254.5-kilometre marker between Victoria Falls and Bulawayo to push deeper into game country for the last stage of our journey. Bluey rattled along the rough bush track that skirted a parched *vlei*. I peered into the tree line searching for signs of the safari camp. After an hour, I saw a few pole-and-thatch tree-houses and *rondavels* well camouflaged among the trees above a diminishing waterhole edged by well-trodden, cracked dried mud.

Accumulated memories crowded my mind; of my daughter Mary-Lou's entranced face as she watched my son, Lachy, play his latest composition at the Christmas table; of his unique voice singing the beautiful melody for our pleasure; of my mother's graceful movements while she danced with an unseen partner to the rhythm of Lachy's guitar. Distance is an illusion. Even the distance of death. Dad was there, too, telling his enchanted daughter stories of his hero, Dr Livingstone. Magical woven words. The living and the dead were with me as certainly as the man who sat behind the wheel. Jeremy's cool blue eyes looked far away. I thought he must be seeing something similar.

We returned to the waterhole and each other. I leaned over and kissed his ear. 'Let's go and make some foundations for our dream.'

A man strode across the sand and thrust out a huge hand. 'Howzit? I'm Des Delange. We've been expecting you for days.'

My hand was engulfed by the paw of this man who would become one of our closest allies. His small head rested easily on slightly hunched shoulders crouched above a long-legged, sinewy body. He towered over me. He reminded me of someone, but then I thought it was an animal. *Aaah, yes!* Des has the form and grace of a cheetah.

A slender redhead hurried towards us, giggling. 'It's so good to see you here safely. We've been worried about you. I'm Jenny, Des's wife.' Her huge blue eyes dripped with concern that was tipped with laughter. 'You must be so tired. Come, we'll have some tea and you must meet Aubrey Packenham before he leaves.'

I followed Jenny to the main building. It was stunning. Tall, thick gnarled poles soared upwards to an intricately shaped thatched roof. In the centre of the room, a circular wooden stairway led to a platform overlooking the pan. The floor looked like marble, but was highly polished concrete. Huge woven baskets and carved wooden statues of animals and tribal people perched at the base of each pole. There were no exterior walls. Dense mown buffel grass stretched away to the trees that defined the line between human territory and the preserve of the wild creatures.

A small, wiry man with twinkling grey eyes rose from the depths of a fat chintz-patterned sofa. I put out my hand. 'Is it woman?' he mocked, brushing it aside. 'Hows about giving an old man a *mushi* cuddle?'

I squinted over his shoulder at Jer as Aubrey crushed me to his chest after planting a sloppy kiss right on my lips. I wasn't sure about this. 'You'll have to get used to Aubrey's cuddles,' Jenny laughed. 'He fancies himself as a ladies man.'

He let me go to grab Jer's hand with a vice-like grip. 'Howzit, Jeremy? Come, sit. Tell me all about it.'

We dropped into armchairs arranged around coffee tables made from wide slabs of local timber and topped with silver canteens, elegant china vases, and lamps with animal-skin shades. Rugs of zebra and impala hides were scattered on the floor.

A waiter emerged from behind a bar topped by a long bench made from a wide slab of glossy timber. He was dressed in a crackling starched white uniform that didn't begin to rival the blinding flash of his welcoming smile. Offering his hand (with the forearm clasped carefully by the other hand in the traditional African manner) he rumbled, '*Mhoroi, mhoroi. Titambire*! Welcome, madam and madala. I am known as Elton. Your coming has been awaited for very long.'

'*Ndatenda*, Elton,' I replied, pleased I knew how to thank him for his kind welcome in the Shona language. Tears tickled my eyelids. I couldn't think how we had deserved such warm greetings. Jer's glance caught my eye. His expression was questioning, but he looked happy.

Jenny took my hand. 'Come, we'll make tea.'

I followed her to the outside kitchen. 'I'm betting Mandebele didn't tell you about Aubrey?'

I shook my head. 'Is he for real?'

'Oh, yes. He's harmless, you know. He's a great guy, Mandebele's right-hand man. You won't see much of Mandebele. He set up the project, but Aubrey's the face of things.'

She spoke of the great friendship between the men and of their association with the elephant herd stretching back half a century. Mandebele leased the land they roamed, but Aubrey would direct operations. His knowledge of the elephants' history would be invaluable to the project as he devoted enormous energy to coordinating official business with the establishment of the fieldwork. Jenny explained that this would allow us to concentrate on our subjects, while Aubrey struggled with the bureaucratic minefield in the city. When we returned with the tea tray it was a relief to see the three men sitting forward with their heads close together chatting like old friends.

Elton rushed to take the tray from Jenny. 'I will do that, Madam.'

'It's all right, Elton,' she replied in a breathy voice. 'You have enough to do. The clients will be back from their game drive now-now.'

Jenny would become a great friend. I soon fell in love with her compassion for others. She seemed to tune in immediately to their needs, and this concern for their wellbeing extended to all living things. We would discover that even when Des had moments of cheetah ire, she maintained her equilibrium and soothed his cat irritability with her gentle manner – and always with giggles.

The men were so busy bonding that our presence seemed superfluous.

Jenny's eyes sparkled. 'Do you play Scrabble – or chess?'

My eager nod produced a jump of joy and a tiny squeal of pleasure.

'*Lekker* [fantastic]. We'll play, huh? But first I must settle you in before the troops return.' Concern rippled across her face. 'I'm afraid the digs are very basic. Ours are, too, but we can always come here to relax and play Scrabble when it's quiet.'

I reassured her. 'Goodness me, this is just wonderful, Jenny. I thought we would be camping rough from the first day.' We had known that our initial base would be adjacent to this safari camp while we familiarised ourselves with the territory and learned to find our way around the uncharted bush tracks.

Jenny led me along a path that wound past the luxury guest

rondavels to a small, rough-hewn slab hut squatting solidly at the edge of the staff quarters. Our few possessions were soon arranged inside. Loved faces watched me from lightweight, cloth photo frames which I perched precariously on the beams of the unlined walls. We spread our sleeping bags on the lumpy horse-hair mattresses of two single iron beds. Other than a rickety dining chair, our only furniture was three wooden crates we turned on their sides to serve the dual purpose of storage and benchtops. There was one window with a cracked pane that looked out on to the dense bush. I thought it must hide a thousand secrets.

Aubrey gave me another rib-cracking squeeze before he departed reluctantly for Bulawayo. I was puzzled when he farewelled us with 'See you just now', as I knew it would be several weeks before he returned. But I would soon learn the idiosyncrasies of the local lingo. What he had said was: 'See you in a while'; 'See you now-now' meant: 'See you very soon.'

That night the elephants came to drink at the pan. The camp cook, Shadrick, had just brought cold gazpacho soup to our table beside the fire when the sound of mighty splashing rose from the waterhole below the central building. The head guide, Brian, leapt to his feet. '*Lekker*! Into the Land Rover now-now before the ellys gap it.'

Once again I was bemused, though the general stampede to the vehicle left no doubt as to his meaning. In essence, he had said: 'Marvellous! Into the vehicle this very minute before the elephants leave.' The enchanting mixture of Ndebele, Afrikaans and English idiom that makes up the appealing Jalapalapa vernacular would eventually become familiar. But then I was in the dark, literally and figuratively. The night was as black as the inside of a cow's belly. I fell up the running board and into the front seat beside Brian.

'Haven't seen the ellys for over a week,' he chortled. 'They must've come to welcome you. Hold tight. I'm going to drive without headlights.'

Trumpeting sounds could be heard above the drone of the engine as we bucketed wildly down the rough track to the waterhole. The Land Rover rolled the final few metres without power or lights. 'Be absolutely silent and still,' Brian hissed, before he shone the spotlight over the giant forms that loomed above us. I needed no warning. My body was stiff with excitement and tension, and we all gasped.

The first elephant I saw held her head and trunk high, with ears stretched wide away from a long, narrow face. One of her tusks was strangely deformed, sloping in an arc beneath her chin. We would come to know each other well. She was known as Skew Tusk and was the matriarch of her herd.

For a moment the elephants stood stock still – then all hell broke loose. Mud thunked into my face as the giants wheeled away in panic to circle their bewildered calves. Then they ran; jostling and pushing along a narrow game trail that led into the tree line. Babies toppled and fell in the turmoil. Frantic mothers butted them back to their feet. Their squealing and screaming were both thrilling and disturbing. My eyes filled with tears as I witnessed the fear our intrusion had incited.

Within a minute they were gone. Stunned and saddened, I listened to the diminishing sounds of crashing vegetation and strident blasts of alarm. I became angry. But these were early days, and I knew I must keep my silence. Still, I didn't accept Brian's theory that their terrified behaviour could be attributed wholly to a previous close encounter with hunters or poachers. We had overstepped their line, invaded their space and insulted their trust.

From that time on, Jer and I would leave at once if we happened upon elephants at night. Even unintended brief encounters convinced me of their aversion to artificial light. We planned our observations of their nocturnal behaviour around the full moon. It would take time, but when we began to know something of their movement patterns we could often antici-pate the herd's presence at an optimal viewing site. Armed with cameras, recording equipment, fruit and drinks, we could arrive early, conceal Bluey and retreat to a tree hide. If our calculations were wrong, we would enjoy time out watching the other creatures of the night.

That rude encounter was to be our only sighting of the elephants of the study for many weeks. Our arrival coincided with the coming of good rains to the Hwange area very late in the wet season. We were christened 'the rainmakers', which was a good name to receive as newcomers in a parched land. Everyone had been worried that the overdue 'long' rains wouldn't come at all that year. Suddenly there was water in abundance, and the elephants and other woodland creatures were able to survive in the peace of the deep forest without needing to emerge to drink at permanent water sources. I was glad we had met the elephants, however briefly and traumatically; otherwise I might have doubted they really existed in this place. They simply disappeared.

Almost every night a storm illuminated the clouds with a spectacular sound and light show. Cascading rain pelted the thirsty earth until it could drink no more and became a place of glorious mud. Late wildflowers burst into rainbow colours, luring massed legions of buttercup-yellow butterflies to their pollen. Birds swooped from the soggy trees into the clouds of yellow, hardly disturbing the purpose of the pretty things.

When there were no clients, Jen and I played Scrabble and chess until bedtime. *Stop cheating. That is not how you spell 'alliteration'* . . . Sometimes we sat either side of the board with our feet soaking in basins of hot, soapy water. Then we painted each other's toenails, although not for public viewing as our feet were mostly hidden by our sensible boots.

I liked to think about my elegant pink twinkies and secret sexy undies tucked away beneath the ubiquitous khakis. Jen and I giggled about these things and shared other secret women's business while our men sat by the fire arguing the finer points of rugby and cricket.

When I went to bed I snuggled into my sleeping bag on the hard mattress, lulled to sleep by the gentle cadence of rain pattering on the tin roof. Sometimes the tempo lifted to a frenzied cadenza when the thunder clapped at the moment the lightning flashed overhead. In those moments I felt deeply content – just grateful to be there. Nonetheless, as the days passed, my frustration and impatience began to escalate at the absence of the herd. Yet, there was also a sense of relief, for the delay gave us time to become familiar with the habitat and the people who lived there, and with the research methods we would be using.

Shadrick (Shaddy) created miraculous dishes out of the simplest of ingredients, using only worn-down wooden spoons and sharp knives as his tools. His enormous hands gently kneaded dough that metamorphosed into the lightest of bread and delicious pastries. He taught me to fillet precious, hard-won, freshwater fish with a few elegant swipes of a boning knife. Well-blooded bass caught by the boys on their days off was as delicious as caviar.

Each day I asked what was for pudding. I wanted to find out if meringue would be on the menu. I never tired of watching Shaddy beat egg whites with his huge bare hands into towering mounds to make delicate soufflés and pie toppings. 'You see,' he would thunder. 'It is the hotness from Shaddy's hand that is making life in this kitchen.'

Shaddy wore his pristine white chef's hat proudly and insisted that anyone who entered his work space must tie a fresh bandana around their hair. He was fastidiously clean in the open-air kitchen, where cast-iron pots and pans were strung in a very specific order on the surrounding ropes. Flies and other insects were pursued with murderous rushes and shouts, until sections of mosquito netting were secured protectively over prepared foodstuffs waiting to be served.

A large copper boiler like the one my grandmother had used to wash clothes was filled with fresh water each morning and kept simmering on the coals for use in cooking, and for washing hands and forearms with the precision of a surgeon between each foray into different food types.

A particularly lethal-looking *panga* (machete) was used to kill any hapless snake that dared to invade Shadrick's kitchen during the day. At night, he hurled buckets of hot water at hyaenas, occasionally even at wild dogs and once at a leopard that had followed its nose to the alluring smell of meat. When it came to protecting his cuisine, nothing got in Chef's way. He was a tyrant, and his minions were the head waiter Elton and Jabulani, who woke the guests for early-morning game drives, set the fire and brewed tea. Jabulani had aspirations to become a chef despite Shaddy's declaration that, 'This boy is very foolish. He is full of it, Sally. Full of it!' I understood Shadrick's gentlemanly reference. The man who owned the lodge, and called 'The Big Boss', used the expression 'He's full of shit' as often as possible.

But Jabulani would not be denied. One morning I saw him sneak out of the kitchen carrying a bowl of egg whites in one hand and a cup of sugar in the other. I followed and asked him what he was doing. With a dark look he muttered, 'I am wanting to beat the "feathers to be" to prove to Chef how this boy can cook.'

With narrowed eyes, and determination firming his facial muscles, he sat near me and went to work on the mixture using his fingers. I knew it would be useless when I spied some yolk amid the opaque whites, but I said nothing, for this was a lesson he had been taught over and over. Perhaps Shaddy was right after all.

And so it was that Jabulani began to beat the egg whites. His method was excellent; his energy was immense. He began to drip sweat after fifteen minutes. The concoction was softly white, but that was as stiff as it would get. It was time to say something. 'You know, Jabulani,' I said. 'When you broke the eggs you let some yolk into the mixture. It will never become meringue if the whites are not pure.'

He stopped beating. For a time he sat staring into the bowl with his hand still immersed in the froth. Suddenly he jumped up, threw the contents away, tossed his handsome head back and laughed. 'I am a man. Men do not cook. This is what I know. I will become a carpenter like Stevie Mpofu,' he declared, making an instantaneous decision about a career change.

The next day I saw him following Stevie about. A week later he was hanging around the mechanic. And so it went. This was Jabulani. He never quite finished things. When he failed in his aspirations, as he inevitably did, his personal logic always saved his pride. In the end he became a good jack of many trades, which is, I think, a very useful thing to be.

Bheki was the cleaner who also lit the lanterns at night. Just sixteen, he had the gravity of a man in middle age. I understood Bheki's stance and empathised with his dilemma. Marriage to a lawyer at seventeen had weighed me down with responsibilities way beyond my years. I wanted to see Bheki laughing and fooling about, but he had the added misfortune of having the build of a young Lobengula. There was no doubt that his powerful presence, dignified demeanour and dedication to his work commanded respect. Despite my wish to see him behaving like a wild young man I had an insane desire to curtsy whenever he passed by. He would nod his large moon-shaped face gravely, as if he sensed my respect.

Very early in my acquaintance with Africans I heard their unspoken words. It wasn't that their body language expressed emotions – quite the reverse, as they have learned to hide their feelings from white people. The anthropologist in me thought also that their DNA was more pure than mine, for they sprang straight from the womb where humankind evolved. Perhaps they sensed my empathy, for they sometimes let me into their space.

Lovemore (who did our laundry when we set up our own camp) was the 'stand-in' for everyone. Dingindawo took care of the general camp maintenance and made us laugh with his jokes. He had an incredibly mobile face which told a tale better than his words ever could – except when he didn't want us to know what he was feeling and his face became mask-like. But

I still read many of his feelings, and sometimes they were resentful of us white fellas. On his days off he wore a T-shirt emblazoned with the face of Fidel Castro and I wondered.

When I first met Stock, he was drunk. He was always drunk, yet it didn't affect his ability to maintain and drive the ancient tractor that kept the bush tracks clear and roadworthy. His job was for life. During the civil war he argued for the life of his white employer. Stock's courage saved the man, but he was tortured for his efforts.

His brother, Pious, fired the boilers and tended the garden. He spent more time chasing baboons, and grumbling about his hard lot, than actually working. He was far from pious, smuggling in a series of voluptuous girls with promises of marriage and fame.

Steve Mpofu became a dear friend. He was an innovative and inventive carpenter who built many of the safari camps in the area. Steve was unaware that his devastatingly handsome 'Marlon Brando' face mesmerised both men and women. He made our life easier, and I loved him for his generous spirit and gentle heart. We soon knew him as Stevie Wonder.

Brian, Rob and Ross were white guides who took the visitors on game drives and entertained them in-between. Their sighting skills were often eclipsed by the extraordinary dedication and aptitude of the black guides, Ekaim, Raphael and Dickson. No one envied the guides their work. It was constant, and often thankless.

For the next few weeks we would live closely with these people. I believe our personal differences were minimised because of the need to cling together for support in a dangerous world. Since we were unpaid researchers, Jer and I were removed from workplace politics. Unfortunately, this resulted in another unsolicited and unwelcome role. We became the designated peacemakers once they realised they could safely vent their frustrations on us whenever tempers became frayed – as they do where personal space is limited. If Dingi came to complain about Ross, we could be sure that Ross would appear soon after, full of testosterone and self-righteous indignation. In Brian's case I found it difficult to listen to his moans with equanimity. He wasn't called 'The Hairy Rat' for nothing! Mostly grievances were settled quickly. However, I think it was a blessing that the woman who would be our workmate and closest companion lived in another camp.

Kathy Martin had already begun work on the project as a volunteer. She worked for National Parks as an ecologist in Hwange. Her black-haired, sloe-eyed looks attracted attention whenever she slipped into unknown company. She wasn't beautiful in a conventional sense, but her unusual features were striking and she emanated a serene grace. We shared a deep affinity for nature. I learned much from her through verbal instruction, and even more from our silent interactions. We reacted similarly to the spirits of the wild when they whispered their songs. Sometimes savage instincts emerge in humans where the wild dictates the rules. But we were women; nurturers who understood a different way might be possible where men were not always able to cool their reactions. When Kathy and I sat together in silence, we occasionally touched a source of understanding beyond words.

Kathy introduced us to the methods of elephant identification. These seemed to be remarkably basic, and simple, from the distance of the research room. But our belief that herd identities could be charted quickly would be dissolved by the elephants themselves. When they did return, the laughter of irony replaced our presumptuous assumptions. The elephants would humble me as they tipped their trunks at my confident assumption that I would quickly identify individual animals. At the vital moment the selected elephant often merged back into the grey block, refusing to cooperate with our efforts to photograph and imprint its features on a card bearing an image of an elephant head, with ears outstretched. The length, shape and angles of tusks and the nicks and holes in ears were drawn on to individual images during encounters.

Kathy explained that we would also need to add the images of venations (vein patterns) on the ears of the elephants to the images on the cards after our photographs were developed. This would be the most important feature of identification, as venations don't change over the lifetime of an elephant whereas everything else does. When an elephant was firmly identified in this manner the data could then be entered into a prehistoric computer that crashed frequently during power failures and surges. At such times I would shout, 'Africa strikes again!', in the hope that by acknowledging the raw power of the dark continent I might assuage its vagaries. Expecting to find order in a continent of immense complexity was arrogance personified. Africa would always have the last laugh.

Every day, the country threw frustrations at us, but none was more aggravating than the long wait for elephants. Sometimes I heard distant elephant speak which prompted frenzied rushes to Bluey to drive in the direction of the sounds. Either our radar was deficient or the elephants conspired to taunt us. They would not be found.

I filled in time by measuring out hundred-metre lengths of

twine to mark transects which we would place in varying habitats throughout the territory of the elephants. These lines of twine would be staked into the ground. The trees, plants and grass growing there were classified every two metres. This would help the team to chart the pattern of movement and browse habits of the herd. I sat for days tying each two-metre section with a piece of string. It was tedious work, although I enjoyed the peace and solitude from my position beneath a graceful camel thorn tree overlooking a pan visited by numerous species of game.

Dingindawo ragged me constantly. 'Madam, this is a VERY important thing you are doing. Your fingers are marching across this string. Is it a cloth you are weaving to catch the elephants?' he teased.

The diversion always went the same way. Feigning disgust, I would throw a stick at him as he vaulted high on to the lowest branch of a tree in one great leap. The resulting belly-rolling laughter infused the tedium with glee. Africans know how to play. They taught me that life is a game, so why not play it?

Each morning we left early, armed with mud maps and a compass to acquaint ourselves with the area. I was even more surprised than Jer to discover I had an innate skill at navigation. Especially so, considering my ineptitude as a scholar of maths. After the first few arguments about the direction we should take, and one memorable 200-kilometre diversion when Jer doggedly disagreed with my directions, it was accepted that I had an ability to figure out maps and astronomical movements. My talents were seen as an aberration by the white men. Women weren't supposed to be gifted with such skills.

Like me, Jer had spent much of his life living in remote Australia, 'west of the Black Stump'. He is a man of the bush, able to negotiate treacherous tracks of slippery mud or deep sand without fuss. He rarely lost his cool, even when the vehicle was up to its axle in sand or bogged deep in sludge. Jer isn't a man to be rushed. He would stand, pondering, with his hand holding the stem of the pipe that he clenched firmly between his teeth in comfort mode. He strode off the road often with his treasured tree book to identify an unknown specimen and enjoy the moment, as if the issue with the vehicle had been God-sent, rather than the devil's curse.

Sometimes he would return and say, 'This is as good a place as any to have smoko [a snack], squirt,' and we would sit on the ground beside the bogged vehicle to eat boiled eggs sprinkled with salt from a tiny twist of grease-proof paper – *just like Mum's school lunches*. Jer scoffed great slabs of Shaddy's legendary rich fruit cake and I knew it wouldn't affect his perfectly toned, powerful physique. *Not fair at all*.

There wasn't an ounce of surplus fat on his body; not even after he consumed entire containers of ice cream in one hit (*otherwise it will melt away*) when we went to Hwange town. He would lift his bushy dark eyebrows and twinkle his 'Paul Newman' eyes over the top of the laden spoon at astonished local passers-by, while he stood outside the store polishing off the contents of the container. I hid my laughter at their reactions to his exaggerated, greedy guzzling and at his charm and jokes when he bought sweeties or sticky buns for the children and for the blind women who sat propped against the wall knitting. Their warm reactions to him were genuine. They liked him a lot. He was a man for all people, which made my life a lot easier.

Our unplanned picnics beside our bogged vehicle in remote locations always ended calmly, although sometimes I had to become a little proactive when Jer was happily tree spotting as the light failed. Once, a spectacularly intoxicated Stock appeared as if by magic when we were about to set off home on foot.

'Ahhh,' he slurred. 'I have come.'

His cap fell into the mud from his swaying tortoise head and he joined it with the formless grace of the inebriated. Eventually he rose as if a puppeteer were pulling the strings on his loose limbs. Jer attached the rope to the vehicle, while Stock crawled with strange dignity back into his seat.

'Modom, the hat,' he gestured, making a concerted effort to focus on my face. It was extraordinary that a man who couldn't find his own head to replace his cap could efficiently pull us out of the quagmire and then proceed along the track on a straight course. It is the only time I have been glad to welcome a drunk.

We learned invaluable things during those first weeks when the elephants were absent. But even Kathy began to wonder if our first night's encounter had been an illusion. Later I would be grateful for this time spent learning, and there were the resident animals that were always fun, even when they caused havoc. No workplace politics there. They were busy being animals and we could react honestly to their challenges.

Visits to the toilet were always fraught with tension because of Roy the wart-hog. He had a habit of sleeping on the cool floor in front of the long drop. Roy and I had a run-in the morning after a midnight encounter with a hyaena that had sprung me using the bush loo (the ground) outside our hut. I had been forced to stand up mid-stream to make myself taller than the ugly creature as he bore down on my crouching form.

This resulted in my having to take a sponge bath by candlelight while Jer crowed with laughter. So I wasn't in a good mood when I forgot to check first, threw open the half door of the toilet in the morning and fell upon a startled aggressive hog. The Hairy Rat was showering next door. The wart-hog knocked me off my feet as he fled, but far worse was the sight of the heavily matted legs of an otherwise palely naked man who appeared on a dubious rescue mission. Equally hirsute arms took every opportunity to lunge and grope as he purported to save me. My screams of disgust sent both creatures running for cover. Each was a stubborn opportunist, but I would become very fond of Roy.

Even the local wart-hogs seemed to bow to his might whenever he decided to leave camp for a foray of strutting dominance. After witnessing his prowess in fights and the resultant victorious couplings, I felt sure that most of the off-spring were fathered by the wily boar. However, he absolved himself of any responsibility for the ensuing progeny. He lolled in the shade of the hut watching the family trot by with the losing male in charge. Not for Roy the burden of finding a secure home for the wife and kids, or the bother of leading them to food or protecting them from predation. His wasn't an ordinary wart-hog life.

Ricky was a sweet, banded mongoose infant who followed me about and cheeped constantly for food. Rob rescued him from a predator. During a game drive, the gentle giant saw an eagle steal the youngster from his family. But the bird of prey had taken on more than he could chew. Clutching the squirm-ing infant in its talons the eagle managed to flap heavily just a short distance, about a metre above the ground, before it dropped the unwieldy cargo.

Ricky sustained a terrible neck injury that swarmed with maggots despite daily flushes with antiseptic. We had to pick the disgusting grubs out of his neck, one by one, until the wound began to heal. We even fed him his own maggots, which was a strange justice! Ricky was always hungry. Everyone in camp swooped upon grasshoppers and insects to cater for the dietary needs of the fast-growing ball of fluff. Despite his pleadings I refused to let him sleep in our hut, knowing his instincts would have him spray and mark urine to declare the territory as his own. It was enough that a family of night apes (bush babies) skittered and cried through the rafters at night. The hut already reeked of their acrid urine. One even managed to pee straight into my eye.

Sadly, little Ricky wasn't meant to have a long life. Early one morning he rushed into the cookhouse to beg for breakfast. He hopped on to a step just as Bheki's large boot descended. Rob and I heard Ricky's terrible scream and ran to find a distraught Bheki crooning over the tiny mongoose. When Rob attempted to check the extent of his injuries, the terrible pain caused Ricky to bite his friend. The mongoose died a few minutes later.

We buried him beside the termite mound where he had loved to stretch out on his back for a sunbake. Rob left for Bulawayo immediately to be inoculated against rabies, which wasn't a pleasant experience. He told us the doctor inserted a massive needle into his stomach. Rob had faced perils in the wild with calm good sense. But he returned from Bulawayo whimpering like a baby. I thought of my daughter Lou's abhorrence of injections after a phlebotomist broke not one, but three needles during a blood test, and shuddered.

The least welcome of all the resident animals was a local troop of baboons, who persistently crept into the compound intent on mischief. They would peel back their lips over their mighty canines and laugh as people rushed to close doors and windows in often useless attempts to foil their plans of destruction. The fearsome dominant male startled me many times by creeping up silently as I sat working beneath my tree, facing the waterhole. He would settle nearby in a position that aped mine. When I turned my head slowly to look at him, he would mirror my movement, so that our eyes locked for a moment before we both hurriedly looked again to the front. It was an understanding we arrived at after some unpleasant initial encounters.

The first time we met, the large male terrified me with a rush that filled my vision with his dog-jaw face drawn back in a rictus above frightful fangs. His beady brown eyes darted when he ripped a sandwich from my hand and fled in barking triumph, leaving me fully aware of his capacity to tear me to shreds. I never took food with me again unless a man was present, for he respected the presence of men.

After the second unpleasant encounter, when he grabbed some papers from my lap, I kept a hefty stick and *keti* (shanghai) with me. The baboon seemed to understand that I meant business. Eventually I allowed him to come closer without raising my stick. We would sit together in a certain harmony. One day the old fellow barked a warning, looked beyond me with a frightened expression, and then bounded away to his screeching troop. A large shadow fell across the grass in front of me. I looked to the right and into the legs of an elephant. He had arrived in silence and stood peacefully beside the closest *rondavel*. *Woo hoo! They're back!*

CHAPTER 6

Return of the elephants

Unlike the fleeing baboon, I was overjoyed to see the elephants had returned – too much so to be frightened. Within seconds, Des appeared with Jen. She had been alerted by Elton, who was now looking for Jer. We ran to the main building and climbed up to the viewing platform. From tree line to tree line a mass of great grey bodies covered the *vlei*. It looked like every elephant on the planet was out there.

An engine started below. I looked down to see Jer gesturing for us to come. He was in Bluey's driver's seat and a mass of bodies was already in the back, with Bheki forgetting his dignity and scrambling to get on board. Jer revved the engine while the three of us slid down the stairs. I jumped into the front and squeezed Jer's cheeks with pleasure as Jen settled on to Des's knees beside me. Bluey was loaded. I looked behind me into five excited faces.

Jer drove to the top of the ridge, turned off the engine and rolled Bluey quietly on to the edge of the *vlei*. And there before us was Skew Tusk, puffed up with importance and indignation. She dropped her head, whipped her ears against her mighty shoulders and came towards us. Emboldened by Kathy's advice, Jer stayed put.

'Shit, man. Let's gap it!' Des shouted, completely forgetting the rule about being silent in the company of wildlife.

'Absolutely!' I agreed.

'Oh, dear me. Oh dear,' whispered Jen, who remembered to keep her voice down.

Meanwhile, fists were beating out a similar message on the divide behind our heads. I looked back into several pairs of scared eyes.

'She's stopped,' Jer said calmly. 'Let's wait and see.'

Five metres away Skew Tusk towered, watching us. All was silent. My heart was hammering and I could feel Des trembling, but my fear receded. A tiny infant wandered out from beneath Skew Tusk's legs. She ran towards a group of calves further away who were playing happily. Our presence wasn't affecting their game. Skew Tusk looked at them as if to assess their mood. Other cows peered at Skew Tusk to assess hers. She visibly relaxed, as did we.

Des was still very nervous, though, which surprised me. This was 'Cheetah Man', wasn't it? Later he spoke of his fear of elephants. We thought that with habituation to the herd he would overcome his anxiety, but he never did. After this close encounter he made it his business to keep a long distance between him and elephants. We all respected his decision, as he respected our particular foibles. Each of us experienced fear of at least one wild creature. Spiders gave me the wild willies. Leopards sent shivers up Jer's spine, Jen loathed snakes, and the locals were united in their abhorrence of hyaenas and snakes.

Poor Des was ignored and forced to deal with his phobia as we spent a glorious couple of hours watching the herd from a reasonable distance. It wasn't feeding time; they were having fun. The newly watered pan copped a beating from the pounding of giant bodies as they wallowed in the mud. Skew Tusk kept us well in her sights, standing guard between us and them. I wished she could join her rollicking peers, but she took her role as matriarch seriously.

We returned to camp well before the light faded and before the guides arrived back from game drives in Hwange. Determined not to confuse the elephants in the darkness, we waited until they left before we drove to Main Camp to tell Kathy the good news. We celebrated too well. Kathy and I held our sore heads the next day after drinking the dodgy local wine that was infamous for causing hangovers. But we were determined that not another day should be wasted. We forced down some greasy food, guzzled litres of water, swallowed paracetamol, ignored Jer's rude cracks and embarked on our study.

In the beginning, we tested the ground gently to habituate the herd to the constant presence of humans. And this human to the close company of elephants! At first they watched us closely, often blasting warnings with awesome shows of strength. Once again my heart responded with galloping attacks of tachycardia. My body didn't simply tremble; it betrayed me with monumental quakes and embarrassing sweats. But these symptoms of fear were soon replaced by sensible caution as I forgot myself in order to enjoy the elephants.

None fascinated me more than Skew Tusk. There were still heart-stopping moments when she vented her displeasure through mock charges. But more often she relaxed and so did her extended family once they recognised us. I felt privileged and humbled by their trust, by just about everything that life was offering me. Within a couple of weeks the herd accepted us and each day became bright with expectation. What would we see around the next corner? Every moment was filled with excitement rather than fear. Kathy knew the elephants' moods well. She never panicked, even when there was a minor crisis. She was alert and careful, quietly suggesting that we move off when the herd displayed signs of being agitated. It was important that we respect the moods of the moment, to retain the special privilege of being accepted and trusted by these marvellous creatures.

I was now grateful for the time we had been given to learn the ropes. I think Jer was as staggered as I was by the physical and mental effort required in photographing the animals and recording their distinguishing features on identification cards when confronted with a large group of unidentified animals. Even counting the numbers of a herd was difficult. When the entire herd gathered together the figure was around 180. However, they were more often separated into distinct family units. Keeping track of one elephant as it slipped in and out of the mass of bodies was difficult. There wasn't much point in sketching the shape and size of tusks, or the nicks and tears in ears, without a photo of the individual. But most important was getting close-ups of the patterns of the ear venations. Without these images our efforts were for nothing, for these maps defined who an elephant was more certainly than anything else. If I managed to take a clear photograph, it had to be numbered to match the card one of us was filling out. Each elephant received a number beginning with 'E'. Kathy followed the system that had been established with the Amboseli elephants by Cynthia Moss. Since 1968, when she joined the father of elephant researchers, Dr Iain Douglas-Hamilton, Cynthia Moss has worked in Kenya studying the elephant herds in Amboseli National Park. My admiration for the patient efforts of both women increased in line with my levels of frustration. At the vital moment, the chosen individual often eluded the final stroke of the pen on the ear chart or the defining photograph. My neck and shoulders seized with the tension of juggling cameras, clipboard and pencils while trying to follow the movements of a specific elephant. I needed to do both at once, while Jer gauged the mood of the herd; ready to fire the engine and flee if an elephant protested at our presence. So much for our carefully planned strategies.

Although we strove to avoid attributing anthropomorphic significance to social behaviour, we found it impossible not to give names as well as numbers to certain individuals who, due to their distinctive features, were easily recognised in the crowd when we came upon a large gathering of elephants. In this way we saved valuable time while working frantically to chart new individuals before the animals moved away in an amorphous mass of bodies. Back in the research room we could clarify the presence of these individuals easily, knowing there was no need to pore over our identification sheets searching for particular vein patterns.

The first group of elephants we identified was a group of eleven bulls that became known as the Gang of Eleven, for they were always together. Ripley (E3) was immediately recognised by the great tear dividing one ear that flopped askew. Kathy had already named another bull Rembrandt (E5), because of his large head and palette-shaped ear. He was often with a male who was missing half an ear – Van Gogh (E1).

It seemed logical to name some of the others after artists. A bull with a small trunk that he dipped about with delicate movements was christened Renoir (E2). Toulouse-Lautrec (Tou-Lou, E4) was the smallest bull in the Gang of Eleven. Shotgun (E8) was the oldest, and Sabre (E6) the youngest. We named him for one enormous thick tusk that pointed straight down and narrowed to a sharp tip.

Shy Henry (E7) was named after a great Shona sculptor, Henry Munyaradzi. There was a sad-faced comedian we named Popov (E11). He was the joker in the pack. Fat, round Stan (E9) and long-faced Laurel (E10) were inseparable. Other elephants were given monikers based on their distinctive personality traits or physical characteristics that reminded us of acquaintances.

In only one case we named a cow after a contemporary Hollywood actress. Bette Midler was a matriarch of note. She kept her small family apart from the herd, rarely joining their communal meetings. I suspected that her ego wouldn't permit her to sublimate herself to other matriarchs, especially the supremely powerful Skew Tusk, even for a brief interaction. Bette's head size matched her ego. It was quite out of proportion to her body. She had only one tusk and her legs were short. She always greeted us with a loud, trumpeting, feisty charge. She vocalised more than any other elephant we knew. She bossed and bullied her family in a loving manner, shamelessly hogging the limelight. It was wise to respect her space by keeping a good distance between us. She was unpredictable – once making contact with the vehicle after a prolonged chase.

We didn't make a habit of inflicting foreign names on the few designated elephants that made our lives easier by presenting very specific attributes and features – especially in the case of the cows whose gatherings were always larger than those of the bulls. Generally we kept the faith with the local Matabele people by also giving the elephants Ndebele names, translated from English by Kathy. In the final analysis the Zimbabwean people were the custodians of the herd. And once shown particular characteristics, the local guides were also more able to recognise those with names than the others with less distinctive features, which added value to their accounts of sightings. If Dilingane (Beauty) was described as having been in an area, behaving in a particular manner, we could be sure that her family was there as well.

I think the local people must laugh out loud at the didactic sensibilities of scientists (or naturalists, in Jer's and my case) who have set themselves rules to do with anthropomorphism that are incredibly elitist, if one thinks about it. They probably consider this dogmatism silly. *I do too*.

Africans give animal names to people as well, but in that case they *are* imposing animal characteristics, or commonality, upon the recipient. In no time I became Mandlovu (Mama Elephant), which is endearing there, where it would be insulting back home! An old European rancher of dubious morals was always referred to as 'The Old Rhino'. Another burly cattle farmer was known as 'The Great Bull'. One elephant was named after a safari operator by a black guide. His boss was arrogant, pigheaded and vain. His namesake was all of those things. After a time, it seemed to me that the elephant even looked like this man.

Likewise, they bestowed upon other species the names of

humans with whom they shared certain characteristics. The dominant male rhino of the incredibly precious 'Kennedy Family' was referred to as 'Joseph' by us and 'Lobengula' (the great Matabele/Zulu King) by them. Oh yes, the Europeans named the female rhinos 'Rose' and 'Jackie'.

I will always remember our first meeting with Dilingane. The day was bright in the smoke- and dust-hazed African way, which is quite different from the clear, glaring brilliance of the Australian bush. We were idling beside a well-trodden pan watered by a series of reed-fringed, wide lagoons. A pair of saddle-billed storks fossicked after insects in the grass. Nearby, a small herd of fat zebras shared their space with a group of impalas, a pair of wart-hogs, and a troop of baboons whose tiny black babies played a game of tag and wrestle close to their feeding family. When the going got too rough, squealing balls of indignation scrambled back to their mothers for reassuring hugs and suckles. Clutching elongated nipples in their mouths they swivelled their little 'old man' faces for curious peeps at their waiting playmates before starting a new game. It was quite easy to lose several hours watching the antics of baboon youngsters.

Further away, three alert kudu ewes and their tawny calves dipped their delicate kangaroo-shaped heads to drink in the manner of their kind. They never seemed to relax – both blessed and cursed by their exquisite sense of hearing. A group of disembodied giraffes lifted their towering necks above the surrounding bush like giant flower stems, slowly swaying their tiger-lily faces back and forth as they browsed. They created surrealistic images of weird beauty.

Myriad species of small birds crossed the airways, creating a blazing mosaic of colour and a melodic symphony. Even the abrasive *'go awa-a-ay'* call of the grey lourie had its place in the percussion section of the orchestra. We were hard pressed to know which way to aim the lens and recording equipment amid such a feast of colour and sound. Not for the first time I understood the concept of a Garden of Eden. I wondered how many city people, accustomed and attuned to strident sounds and high stress levels, would really enjoy this open-eyed meditation of harmonious nature. But nature likes to trick us. She reminds us that everything is in flux. Over and over again, when I was revelling in the sweetness of a gentle sighting, chaos would erupt – as it did that day.

Suddenly all sounds ceased. Every head turned in the same direction – towards the tree line. The nervous kudu cantered the other way. But not in panicked leaps, which would have indicated the presence of a predator. Our gaze followed theirs. Silently the bushes parted as six red-dust-coated elephants emerged, quickening their pace as they closed upon the water. More and more appeared, until a solid block of bodies stretched along one side of the lagoon. There were cows of every shape and size and their adolescent youngsters, toddlers and tiny babies. Everything else gave way to the presence of the monarchs of Africa.

By now our company was acceptable to the herd: the more so if we were in position when the elephants arrived. All trunks were seriously busy drawing up water and depositing copious quantities into thirsty throats. Each swallow sounded like a flushing toilet. Even the toddlers subdued their wilful trunks to test the water. The smallest simply had no idea how to cope, aimlessly splashing the surface like babies in a bath before turning in frustration to place their trunks in the mouths of their elders to investigate the contents.

I watched one frustrated calf try endless times to siphon water into her straw-like trunk. If elephant cheeks could flush pink with exertion, hers would have been scarlet. Eventually she achieved dodgy success, falling back with horror as the liquid shot straight up her nose and into her sinuses. Her tiny eyes ran with tears as she blew and coughed away the irritation. Observed by her mother, who I swear was enjoying a silent chuckle, the distressed calf stood in a hunched, forlorn posture, rubbing one eye with the tip of her offending digit. The cow stretched her massive trunk along the relatively diminutive back of her child with a comforting caress, before pushing the reluctant toddler back to the water's edge. Thirsty and tired, the little one sank to her front knees, lifted her bottom high and curled her tiny trunk out of mischief on to her shoulders in order to drink straight from her mouth.

Counting such a closely bunched herd of elephants is almost impossible. We eventually agreed on eighty-four. There were several known individuals. Files were opened on unidentified members of their families. I was drawing the ragged ear marks of a young tusk-less female I had often sighted with the matriarch Skew Tusk, when a new group of seven elephants broke from the trees, rumbling and blaring with excitement.

Raising puffs of dust with each stride, the lead cow approached Skew Tusk in an amiable floppy run. The ears of both cows were spread wide and held far forward as they met. They entwined trunks and gently placed them in each other's mouths, all the while squealing with the intensity of their affectionate greeting. At the same time, their families were sharing similar salutations while reinforcing familial bonds. For several minutes they consolidated their relationship with touching and rumbling before they settled down and moved together to the water.

The new matriarch was flawless. Her ears were unmarked and in perfect proportion to her beautiful face. Two ideally matched long white tusks curved gently upwards in a graceful sweep. She was tall with a fine conformation: even her straight long tail was tipped with thick, flowing black hair. Kathy suggested we give her the Ndebele name for beauty – Dilingane. Her sweet male infant was still able to walk beneath her body. He stood knee-deep in the water to suckle from her heavy human-like breasts as she drank her fill.

We watched the two matriarchs standing contentedly together and wondered if they were closely related. Despite her deformed tusk, Skew Tusk is a handsome cow. I saw a facial resemblance between them. Skew Tusk's matronly back sagged lower; testament to the fact that she had borne several calves. Certainly the depth of feeling displayed in the greetings indicated a close bond between the families. Dilingane's group of seven had arrived well after the rest of the herd, and from a different direction, so perhaps they had been separated for some time. After that first sighting of Dilingane the two families were mostly observed in close association. Dilingane's vivid personality always guaranteed glorious encounters. She never objected to our presence. That task was left to our beloved Skew Tusk, or to her ally Inkosikasi, a large tusk-less cow, and Bette!

The best of times were the carefree days at the end of the wet season when nature's benevolence allowed the fat adults the energy and time to express their contentment in joyful games. One memorable morning in May the herd allowed us to be among them during an unparalleled display of elephantine joy.

Well rugged up against the early-morning chill of autumn we had been driving since dawn. We found, and followed, the spoor of a pride of lions along a sandy track until they veered off deep into my favourite teak forest. Where the tracks left the road we called a halt to eat speckled, shrivelled apples and to swig from our water bottles. In this season the mopane scrub and teak trees drop a gentle drift of russet-gold leaves that form a crackling carpet on the sand. I leaned against the bonnet, lifting my face to the fingers of soft warm sunlight piercing through the rapidly thinning canopy.

The crispness of the air constricted my throat into an involuntary cough. At the sound, unseen creatures crunched the leaf layer beneath their stride as they bolted away from us. I hoped we hadn't frightened them straight into the jaws of death. Somewhere nearby the lions would be resting in a sunlit glade, recovering from the exertions of the cold night. Perhaps they had already killed and were enjoying the feast. Undoubtedly they would retire later to a patch of shade to escape the heat of the day and do what lions do best – sleep. I soon discovered that small insects such as dung beetles and termites offer more excitement in five minutes than an entire pride of indolent lions does in eight hours of daylight.

We set off again, towards a well-watered pan that was a favourite place of the elephants. Often we stopped, turned off the engine and listened to nature's messages. Even before we came to the pan we could hear the strident sounds of excited elephant speak. Arriving after the elephants wasn't an ideal situation. Still, we decided to risk disturbing their equilibrium for a quick glimpse of the behaviour associated with such an unusually long session of bellowing and trumpeting. Jeremy eased Bluey between the bushes bordering the large clearing and switched off the ignition. A frenzied spectacle of sight and sound was well under way. Had we been accompanied by a hard-rock band, I believe our arrival would have been disregarded.

Dignified, placid cows forgot themselves and thundered about in circles; chasing each other, or adolescents, with tails and trunks held high. I was astonished, and delighted, to see the usually haughty Skew Tusk looking absurdly amusing as she stumped backwards into one after another of her companions. With each great, grey ram from her baggy bottom she assumed a brief stance of pretend anger; froze, puffed herself up, flared her ears and expelled a throaty blast before once again hunching into the comical reverse shuffle.

The cows she bumped displayed equally aberrant behaviour by ignoring the highly respected matriarch, or responding to her blasts with daring bellows of their own. But the funniest part of the whole show was the bewildered band of calves bunched together at one side watching with obvious shock the excesses of their elders. Tiny trunks urgently touched each other, feeling for reassurance and comfort in the face of such irresponsible goings-on. One sweet baby sucked her trunk and peeped from behind the slightly larger body of a toddler who swayed one of his front legs back and forth with obvious dismay. I wondered whether their mothers had parked them there out of harm's way to ensure their safety, for they would surely have been trampled if they joined the party.

Suddenly the mood changed. In an instant the entire breeding herd came to a standstill and looked in one direction.

We heard a tremendous crashing of bushes before a wild-eyed young cow ran from the trees. Her trunk stabbed the air with a series of short, sharp blasts as she fled past the breeding herd.

A huge bull broke from the scrub and lumbered across the pan between the motionless cows and on towards the opposite tree line where the female had disappeared. The cows' heads followed his course until he disappeared from view. Then they swung back to watch the bush where he had entered the clearing. Somewhat hamstrung by their swinging, partially erect penises, three amorous young bulls followed in hot pursuit. Once again all eyes followed the passing parade; like spectators watching the passage of a tennis ball at Wimbledon. For a few seconds after the band of five vanished into the forest the cows remained still, then they quit being observers and threw themselves back into their own wild game.

I wondered whether the presence of the obviously oestrous cow within their ranks had induced the excited interactions in the breeding herd. Our brief glimpse of her fleeing form suggested the bewildered confusion of a young female experiencing her first season upon reaching sexual maturity. Cynthia Moss describes similar reactions to courting males from inexperienced cows within the Amboseli herds. I thought such a rampant display of hormonal activity and nervous energy was bound to affect the equilibrium of these sensitive animals.

To my mind it seemed the bout of elephantine madness came more as a result of great good humour during nature's bountiful harvest. Or perhaps our herd was responding to a combination of both: the result of cause and effect. The rains produce the food and water, which brings the elephants to peak condition. This prompts the reproductive organs of unencumbered cows to ovulate, which attracts the bulls. Stomachs are filled much faster with vast quantities of plentiful sweet herbage, so there is time and energy for fun.

Certainly, as the good times passed and the food and water sources diminished, so did the fat, along with the feisty energies of the elephants. But on that day tears of pleasure smudged the camera lens as I revelled in the expressions of rapture radiating from those beautiful, intelligent creatures. It was Elephantasia.

CHAPTER 7

Life in camp

The elephants' return to the valley changed the dynamics of our days. Even though I would never relinquish feelings of unreality and gratitude at my great good fortune, I was by now at ease with the terrain and with the people who lived there. I knew the time we had been given to settle into an alien world had been a period of grace. The comfort of living in the staff quarters of the safari camp, though temporary, had given us the opportunity to connect with the people. This was crucial for our future wellbeing.

Now it was time to leave a certain amount of luxury and move from the safari camp to a rudimentary hut Mandebele had commissioned Stevie and Jabulani to build for us deep inside the elephants' territory. Our new home was called Farm 41. Singing along with every stroke of his hammer, Stevie

erected the shack atop the concrete foundations of a homestead that had been razed during the civil war. The farmer was
long gone after losing his own battle with animals that ate the
crops, and lions that ate his cattle.

Finally, the house was re-tenanted by a National Park
ranger and his wife, who lovingly refurbished the building and
restored the charming garden. They kept horses and pigs
there, continuing to cling to their tenuous existence amid the
escalating hostilities well beyond the limits of safety. They
were determined to retain a semblance of normality. But the
nights were long and fearful. Rifles and handguns carried by
day were placed by the bed at night, when they barricaded
themselves into one bedroom with the dogs. The ranger was
conscripted as a police reservist. He disappeared into the bush
periodically, and when he did, his wife relocated to a heavily
guarded lodge.

Late one night he joined her there after a two-week stretch
away on duty. The next morning he refused to return to the
farm. Distracted and depressed, he was unable to explain to
his wife his feelings of foreboding. All day she worried about
their hungry livestock and pets. That night, rebels from the
Zimbabwe African National Liberation Army (ZANLA) fired
the house with petrol. They shot the horses and butchered the
pigs, leaving some of the horribly maimed creatures alive in
their agony. The spear used on the pigs was the only item
the family recovered from the smoking ruins of the house. The
dogs escaped.

The drums of civil war had ceased long before we arrived,
yet there was ongoing disharmony between old enemies. Each
side continued to suffer. Many *mazungus* (white people) were
negative and many *muntus* (black people) were angry. However,

in the wild places where we lived we saw little of this and the animals knew nothing of it. It was only when we visited cities and towns that I became aware of the dark feelings of discontent. It saddened me, though it wasn't my business. Elephants *were*.

By the time we set up camp at Farm 41, nature had obliterated the horror. Only once did I sense darkness, but not from the ghosts of sad human history. We settled in quickly to our new life – grateful for the isolation and at last able to establish a routine revolving around the movements of the elephants.

Our little camp was a haven after long days spent following the herd. Sometimes the elephants joined us there and we didn't have to travel far to observe their movements. Often they tore up the pipe running from the small waterhole to our basic roofless shower enclosed by a *boma* of bound reeds.

One evening, a young male searching for water dropped his trunk over the two-metre-high poles that encircled the shower while I was inside. Naked and vulnerable, I turned off the flow on the canvas bucket and cowered hard against the poles while his wrinkled, hairy trunk weaved and flopped all around me. He shuffled firmly against the fragile structure, grumbling his frustration. I closed my eyes and focused on sending loving thoughts his way.

It wasn't my day. When he gave up in disgust and wandered away I faced a new and infinitely worse terror. I turned to see an immense bird-eating spider just a few inches away. I was more fearful of this awful creature than of the elephant whose companions were all around camp, and nothing was going to stop my escape from the giant monster that leered at me from the post. The towel was out of reach behind the spider. Jer was away. With my hair full of suds, I ran. At that moment, Rob careened into camp. He was met by the startling sight of a naked woman sprinting towards the hut, obviously undeterred by the close proximity of a number of wild elephants.

If I had to be sprung by a man during an act of naked cowardice, then 'Gentleman Rob' would have been my choice. He was truly a gentle giant with a degree of discretion missing from many of the other guides.

'Is it?' he muttered, looking serious, when I emerged wrapped in a sarong. But his twinkling eyes betrayed his amusement.

Africans say 'Is it?' instead of 'Is that so?', 'Did you?', or 'What happened?'. When I asked Rob to get rid of the spider so that I could finish my shower, he said it again. He didn't laugh at my frailty, nor did he tell anyone else. If he had, my arachnophobia would soon have become common knowledge and I would have found spiders at every turn.

Each night before bed, Jer checked the hut or tent for spiders, but many times hairy legs would scuttle across my face, waking me into a conscious nightmare. It was a losing battle. A night without incident was a good one.

Whether housed in our simple shack or camped under canvas, the mechanics of waking took the same course. Following a domestic routine gave me a sense of order. It became a means of maintaining personal discipline in a world gloriously untamed by humans – where nothing else was predictable.

Winter had arrived and the air was cold; sometimes below freezing. On those mornings I snuggled deeper into my sleeping bag for extra warm moments until Jeremy lit the fire and heated the water for our sponge baths. I relished the heart-stopping vigour of washing hurriedly and rushing to dress, hopping from leg to leg while pulling on my stiff cotton trousers. My numb fingers would battle to tie the laces of my eminently suitable, but horribly rigid, hiking boots.

I grew to love the grainy maize meal porridge I cooked in reconstituted milk over the flames. Jer never did. Until we discovered we could buy delicious canned guavas and grapefruit, we endured pretend orange juice – a powdered, over-sugared, orange compound. Stale bread made excellent toast when speared by a long fork or straight stick and seared over the fire, especially when topped with a poached egg or the finest black marmalade I have ever tasted. Because our days were long and exhausting, and lunch was often a meagre meal of dried fruit, long-life cheese, peanuts and crackers, a hearty breakfast became an important ritual.

The local bird life and the resident troop of vervet monkeys made it their business to visit our camp at mealtimes. Determined not to encourage wild things to become dependent on our presence, we never consciously fed them – though enough crumbs of food escaped our plates to tempt the shy creatures into the company of humans.

Vervet monkeys, apparently wearing hobnailed boots, greeted the dawn by galloping across the tin roof of our shed or swinging about the guy ropes of the tent and chattering excitedly. The noise they made prodded us out of sleep. Even now I wake, bright-eyed and foxy-tailed, at around 5.30 am.

With the grey light of the false dawn, the plaintive calls of owls and nightjars and the cries of bush babies sounded harsh, before the liquid melodies of the diurnal bird song gathered force signalling a welcome to the sun. I slipped into yoga poses in my own salute to the sun and listened to hyaenas whooping contact and farewell calls to each other as they plodded home to their dens. Jackals wailed messages of success or failure before settling into their burrows for a long day's sleep. Often we heard lions roaring victory over their kills before the silence of the feast. Sometimes a solitary, slinking leopard sawed its eerie call, setting off hoots and barks of alarm from terrified tree-bound baboons. Dawn and dusk are the noisiest hours in wild Africa.

At exactly six each morning a flock of guinea fowls marched in convoy into camp. I always swung a salute at their leader and Jer always said, 'Use the right hand, not the left, Squirt,' and I would right the wrong. Such rituals were important.

My interest in birds developed daily. I consulted my bird book to identify glossy starlings, delicate waxbills, finches, weaver-birds, yellow-billed hornbills and a pair of stunning crimson-breasted shrikes that grew in confidence until they would even hop under our makeshift table to steal tasty morsels as we scrubbed the dishes. Such familiarity at these times made me froth with impatience as I stalked my photographic prey among the bushes later in the day. The birds always kept just far enough ahead to defy my efforts. Eventually, I took to lurking in a deep hollow beside the hut. No matter how cautiously and slowly I lifted my face and camera above ground level, one bird would spy me and flee; alarming its feathered friends into frantic flight. However, they often gathered close as I wrote when the camera was just out of reach. The moment I picked it up, they were off.

That was until I met Effie. She was a yellow-billed hornbill who became quite a star after I saved her from a jackal. I was writing in the shade of an acacia beside the hut when I saw the jackal sneaking about looking for titbits. Hornbills were mobbing him. One bird in particular swooped closer and closer, taunting his efforts. She fluttered low, screeching her contempt and batting her wings in fury. Within a wink she lost balance and fell to the ground where her desperate flailing caused one leg to lodge beneath a stone. The jackal and I rushed to her together. I won the race and snatched up her struggling body.

Unfortunately, the leg was broken; it dangled down uselessly beneath her fat body. Effie's great orange eyes rolled within comical, wrinkled grey bags as I placed her gently on a branch. She sat for a long time; thinking about her plight, I suppose. Finally she tested flight, but it was a long time before she could steady herself to land on one leg with the other sticking out stiffly beneath her body.

From that moment, Effie trusted us and allowed us to hand-feed special treats into her great curved, garden-clipper beak. The camp became her territory and she tutted and shouted her authority and possession to all her comrades. She seemed to know to pose for photographs with film star postures, and greeted us with obvious pleasure on our returns home. I knew the relationship was based on need. Even so, I loved Effie and was sad when she disappeared.

Within weeks, we could recognise many of the animals living on the *vlei* near our camp. They became relaxed about our presence. When we approached they tensed, ready for flight, until they saw it was us.

This habituation to the close company of humans caused me concern. Trusting us as they did, I worried that they might extend the same honour to poachers and unwittingly offer a quiet, standing target for the bullets. But there was little any of us could do to discourage their relaxed attitude.

Perhaps they knew we were of a different kind from the poachers, in the way they were aware of the differing rhythms between hunger and lack of interest in their natural predators. It was a pleasure to observe their bodies relax at the coming of the light when we crossed the mist-veiled *vlei* at daybreak. It was quite different on the evening return as the perils of the approaching night began to loom. Yet, it was important that we discouraged any efforts by frightened animals to make our camp a refuge from predators after dark. Excepting pesky baboons, they seemed to know to avoid the less-friendly settlements, which blocked their old migratory routes. Sadly, it was to be elephants that stepped over the boundaries into human territory when the crops were ready to harvest, creating conflict between the species.

Our wildebeest seemed content enough with a life well settled. Perhaps the old instincts were sometimes triggered at the time of year when their ancestors had 'gone walkabout' following ancient migratory routes. A zebra family that comprised a testy stallion, three mares and two youngsters shared space with the wildebeest. This symbiotic relationship offered each species certain qualities the other lacked, thus improving the chances of each being forewarned of the presence of predators.

Giraffes emerged from the forest to drink at the waterhole and browse on the fresh green tips and flowers of the bordering scrub. It wasn't possible to recognise individuals among the swaying tiger-lily faces unless they had unique features. In any case, it wasn't necessary. I simply revelled in their grace and beauty whenever I saw them passing by. At one time a herd of females and their similarly aged calves lingered longer than usual near camp. The youngsters gambolled with a carefree abandon that in their aloof and elegant parents would have been undignified. When their impossibly long eyelashes drooped and play was done, the youngsters gathered into a nursery where one of the mothers stood guard over the sleeping bunch.

There was a day when I almost drove the vehicle into such an assemblage of giraffes where they lay resting in the long grass. Although their necks and heads remained erect, they were camouflaged exquisitely among the long stick-like beige and brown weeds. I seemed to be the only concerned party. Five sets of lashes closed again over large, beautiful eyes and the nurse who had been quietly browsing high into a nearby tree returned there to feed.

An ageing male giraffe with a disfiguring growth on his chest seemed to be a permanent resident. He spent as much time chewing bones – in search of some much-needed minerals – as he did actually feeding. For this I named him Predator. He was very patient with my presence when I craned out the window to film the strange sight. Female giraffes were confronted often by the startling vision of the gaunt giant hurrying towards them with ardour on his mind and jaws working furiously over a white bone that hung out of his loose mouth. He performed *flehmen* with that bone still clamped firmly between his grimacing lips.

I became very fond of a lonely old gemsbok, the sole survivor of a group which had been introduced years earlier by a local game farmer and hunter. At home in the most arid of deserts, here the striking antelopes had been systematically hunted for their superb trophy horns, or devoured by nomadic lions that fell upon them as they stumbled through the unaccustomed dense bush.

There were families of black-backed jackals that filled the evenings and dawns with their wailing arias. The calls always made my hair stand on end, reminding me of the spooky sounds my friends and I made as children when we told each other horror stories.

Above all I loved the sable antelopes who had once reigned supreme on the *vlei*, and now fought so bravely to protect their calves from the spotted hyaenas. After dark the night belonged to the nocturnal predators. Theirs was a reign of terror over our community of animals. Because there had been no resident lion pride for a long time the population of hyaenas had exploded out of proportion to the capacity of the land and the prey species available. Here they were hunters, rather than thieves.

I would drift off to sleep to the haunting sounds of communicating whoops, only to be startled awake by shattering shrieks, giggles and growls as the clan squabbled over their kills. It reminded me of lawyers posturing and preening in the courtroom. They were the sounds of hell – guaranteed to send shudders of revulsion through the most heroic of spirits. Some terrified creature had died out there; possibly a youngster I had watched during the safe hours beneath the sun, racing and leaping its celebration of life in wild tag games with others of its age set. Which member of the community would be missing in the morning?

Once I interfered. There was nothing unusual in finding the elephants had pulled up the pipe running from the waterhole to our drum. But the evening of our intervention we returned to a waterless camp too late to try to fix the damage. We decided to make do with water fetched from the waterhole for cooking and bathing. I left to fill the container from the pipe where it flowed clean, fresh from the bore. For a while I watched the herd of sable that had gathered nervously by the waterhole at dusk. Two sable calves had been taken in as many nights by hyaenas. This was both alarming and surprising. Sable cows were excellent mothers, corralling their offspring within a tight circle of adults when danger threatened. I had learned from the African women how to protect my shoulders and back while carrying heavy loads. I was about to heft the container upon my head to leave when I saw the first of seventeen hyaenas trotting purposely towards the herd of sable. It was an enormous pack. They came fast, already vocalising obscenely. I knew that such vast numbers couldn't be repelled by any number of sables. My heart was hammering with shock. To see such a large pack swarming towards an already desperately depleted and rare species was tantamount to observing genocide.

I was angry. These antelope had been reintroduced into the area only recently. Human hunters had caused the indigenous sable to be killed out. I wasn't going to watch another new life taken by a species of predator that had grown excessively due to the imbalance of nature created by my own kind. I ran for the vehicle, revved the engine and charged towards the hyaenas. In the dying light I spun the wheel in every direction to chase the pack of cantering, giggling creatures. One disappeared into the bush as another reappeared to pick up the chase. In the end I won the battle, but my chest was sore that night from battling to turn Bluey as if I had been working the reins hard while mustering outback cattle on horseback.

Eventually, the last of the hyaenas vanished into the tree line for good. Strangely, the herd of sable hadn't moved – as if they knew I was coming to their aid. In the morning, Jer reported the problem to the warden. Frank was aware of the situation. He had been watching the ranks of hyaenas escalate as the number of lions in the area decreased from over-hunting of their kind in a nearby concession. This had been stopped a year before our arrival. But by then the lions had retreated deeper into Hwange National Park and were only now beginning to return. Their absence from our area created a population explosion of hyaenas. Frank took action to cull their ranks shortly after the sable incident. It was a problem created by human mismanagement of a wildlife habitat; it required humans to redress the balance.

One of Africa's most striking creatures has been given the ordinary misnomer 'wild dog'. In Australia the term is used for a variably mixed breed of domestic dog and dingo which is infinitely more dangerous than either species. The African wild dog (more aptly called the 'painted wolf') is a unique social carnivore that may have diverged from the European wolf millions of years ago. Perhaps it is more likely that the African species was the first of the canids from which all the others evolved – like the human species.

And like early hominids, wild dogs hunt as a group, covering vast tracts of savannah and woodlands in a flowing stream of strategic force which makes them the most efficient predators on the African plains. Unfortunately, their speed and endurance cause them to breach the territories of livestock farmers who treat them as vermin. When they leave the safety of the wilderness in search of easy prey the painted wolves face both a firing line of bullets and contact with domestic dogs that pass on diseases such as rabies and distemper. Consequently, they are now a highly endangered species.

Our first meeting with Africa's painted wolves was close to camp during a wood-gathering trip. It was late on the afternoon of a golden autumn day. We were driving along the edge of open savannah land in the shadow of the surrounding forest, stopping at intervals to fossick for sticks and tinder among mounds of fallen leaves. Each corner of the trail offered the promise of a new creature sighting. My eyes tracked the curves like the lens of a camera. Anything was possible in the silent anarchy of the African bush – including Stock on his tractor.

We came upon Stock and Inkosikasi's family of seven elephants at the same moment. Without looking to either side, he was chugging doggedly straight through the middle of a twitchy group. Two cows mock charged the tractor but got no response from Stock. He just ploughed ahead as if there were nothing there; most probably, he was too drunk to care. Eventually the elephants gave up and Stock disappeared around a corner.

My laughter changed to astonished excitement when two wild dogs broke from the bush ahead to run along the road. Within seconds, seven others had emerged in a fluid wave of brown, black and white. They streamed along the track with intense urgency. Their large, rounded ears were erect. Whip-thin bodies gathered and stretched above long, loping legs, and their white-tipped tails waved messages of pleasure and excitement.

The elephants saw them, too. They'd had enough. Inkosikasi trumpeted a final insult and led her family into the forest. Our presence was ignored as we hurtled along behind the dogs, certain that they were hunting. Eventually the caravan of painted wolves and us burst on to the familiar *vlei* near our camp. Within seconds the zebras and wildebeest grouped into a stamping, snorting mass of fear. Kudus cleared the grasslands in a few mighty leaps. The sable family circled their young. Chaos ruled. I was amazed at the beautiful dappled markings and distinctive conformation of the carnivores. I had seen photos and documentaries, but nothing prepared me for their strange beauty. They were like no dog I had ever seen.

It was all we could do to keep up with the pack. When they peeled away on to the *vlei*, Jer drove across rough terrain in bucking pursuit while I clawed out the window and on to the bonnet with the video camera hanging from my neck. With one hand I hung on to the strut holding the visor. With the other I filmed. Later I wondered how I did it.

The dogs bypassed terrified groups of game without a glance. They broke the line to spread out in a wide arc. Each head was intently aimed in one direction. Within seconds they closed on a patch of longer grass and disappeared in an instant. We arrived to the sounds of horror. Yipping, yelping dogs were tearing a bleating kudu calf apart. Nothing ever after caused me to lose my lunch. This did. The dogs were a killing machine of invincible might. There was nothing left within minutes. The steaming body was devoured in great gobbling gulps. I didn't film the orgy.

I *did* film what came afterwards. Individuals licked each other clean of blood, displaying deep affection in a gentle manner which made me wonder whether I had imagined the horror of the kill. Now the pack played like domestic pups; twittering their joy. Painted wolves don't bark.

A female came to the vehicle to look at me where I sat – still balanced on the bonnet. Her intense brown eyes weren't gentle. She stared into mine with chilling intensity for a long time. My pet dogs had never held my gaze as this wild beauty did. With them I was the leader of the pack. With her, I didn't know. It felt like she was considering my potential as food. A dingo in Australia had taken baby Azaria Chamberlain from a tent, but I had never heard of Africa's painted wolves preying on humans. I decided her gaze was an assertion of her superiority.

Still shaking from the violence, I pulled my legs close into my body and inched into the centre of the bonnet. She was confident of her dominance – a glorious, wild, knowing thing. This moment was all there was for her. It was all there was for me.

We took our footage and photos to a wild dog researcher who would become a friend. Josh Ginsberg is a warm, hospitable American scientist who was studying and fighting for the cause of his beloved wild dogs. They soon became one of my favourite animals, too. Josh shared sightings of our ellys with us as we did of his dogs with him.

Josh had an experience with elephants in Kenya that calmed my fears of sleeping in a frail tent when the herd was all around us. Our tent was four times the size of the tiny pup tent he was using during a stint in the Masai Mara. Josh told us that he loved lying in his sleeping bag looking at the stars through the open vent a metre above. He woke at dawn one day feeling hot and sweaty. He checked his watch and thought the sky must be overcast because he could see neither a lightening of the darkness nor any stars. Hearing the sounds of elephant rumbles he eased forward, lowered the door flap slightly, looked out and saw a huge leg. He fell back on his sleeping bag. Then he heard the rolling sound of a tummy grumbling above him. Josh said he thought he was a dead man when he realised that an elephant was straddling the tiny tent. He had been looking up at its belly!

The elephant didn't move for long minutes. Josh suffered the torments of the damned; he pleaded with his God and anyone else who might be listening. When the bull did move, he eased his huge bulk very gently over the tent without making contact with the sides or touching the small guide ropes. The careful placement of those huge feet, and those of his companions, meant that nothing was displaced in Josh's camp.

I always think of Josh when I watch other elephants pick their way delicately over saucepans, baskets and camping paraphernalia with amazing precision. Often we have woken to see elephant spoor criss-crossing our campsites, but we never heard their presence in the night. It was as if they didn't want to create any disturbance. I'm not sure that I have always trodden so carefully in their space, although I've tried hard to blend into their world.

Josh lived at Hwange National Park headquarters, near Kathy who had also been allocated digs there in an old colonial concrete house surrounded by a tall wire fence. A few nights after the wild dog kill, Kathy's Jack Russell terrier, Jessie, went into a frenzy of yapping in an effort to wake her mistress. Kathy could sleep through most things and said she was vaguely aware of the barking. But she didn't react until Jessie jumped on to the bed and licked her face. It was a hot night and the windows were open. Then Kathy heard the sounds of a large creature panting and running hard in the garden. The electricity was off as it always was after 10 pm. She turned on her flashlight, picked up Jessie and a machete, and crept to the window.

What she saw sent her running through the house to close the windows. A mature black-maned lion had come over the fence. He was trapped inside the garden. Perhaps he had been lured by the smell of Jessie, or the fussing of free-ranging chickens which Kathy had forgotten to lock into their coop in the evening.

When the lion began to roar, Josh came to investigate. Soon, there were half a dozen men, including the warden, watching the fear-crazed cat clawing up on to the fence between wild rushes at the lights of the vehicles outside. Kathy secured Jessie inside the pantry, but her excited yapping and the lion's enraged roars overwhelmed the calls of the men to her mistress. They were shouting to warn Kathy that the front door of the house was wide open. She watched events from a barred window, quite oblivious to her own peril.

The warden eventually managed to open the gate while the lion was distracted at the rear of the house. But it was hours before he found the way to freedom. And all the while Kathy enjoyed the spectacle, unaware that at any moment the mighty cat could have found her doorway instead.

Sleep was over for that night. When the sun rose, Kathy found the entire flock of hens intact. They cackled their distress from high branches, refusing to alight even when she tempted them with mounds of seed and lettuce leaves. Jessie followed the scent trail of the lion around the garden all day, barking with importance where the pungent odour was especially strong. Kathy responded to Jessie's urgings with serious attention, praising and petting her admiration of the busy little Jack Russell that had probably saved her life.

The wave of unprecedented predator activity settled and peace returned to us all. Jer and I were well settled into Farm 41; almost jealous of our solitary state. Except for browse damage from feeding animals, the only change to the foliage outside our frail habitation was imposed by the passing season that altered the texture of the leaves and the intensity of the green on all but deciduous trees, which only lost their leaves as spring arrived.

Our weapons were the faculties of self-discipline, vigilance and anticipation. Our shield was a vehicle that sometimes refused to start. If one measures order by the power of humankind to ordain life and death over all things, then this would be seen as chaos. I have never subscribed to this belief. Instead, I rejoiced in a simple co-existence with the earth, the flora and the animals. I had chosen to come to a place where humans must submit to the dictates of nature. It would be nonsense to try to bend this austere Eden to my will.

However, self-preservation required heightened sensory perceptions. My being felt charged and filled with light, and my body responded to the vibration. As the bleak veneer of 'civilised' living peeled away, so did restrictions of sight. No longer did my vision sweep casually over the landscape. I started to notice previously neglected details. What had seemed to be almost monotone colourations of beige and silver began to offer myriad hues, until the formerly well-camouflaged body of a motionless antelope, or a lion, presented a slight difference of shade among the tawny grasses. While still quite far away I could pick out the solid grey bulk of an elephant standing at rest within steel-coloured bush. We could strip the perfect disguise of leopards before the exquisite creatures melted away. I would point to the position of the cats for frustrated visitors who remained unable to see despite my desperate directions. Mind you, our developing senses paled beside the acute vision of the safari guides and indigenous people.

As a new world of sound emerged, we found ourselves speaking more softly. Sometimes I felt that my ears were about to leave my head as I strained to hear the minute sounds of unseen creatures in the bush. Always a light sleeper, I entered a new realm of cat-napping, so light that I woke at the tiniest disturbance. Suppressed instincts began to operate independent of my rational self. But instinct wasn't enough. Ever since my salvation at Savuti I had known that another force walked beside me. And then the presence took a physical form.

CHAPTER 8

Horace the Horrible

Jer had taken Bluey for a service to the workshop at Hwange Main Camp. The enforced grounding offered an opportunity for me to attack some overdue paperwork. I settled down to sort photographs and assemble files of newly documented elephants.

The work steamed ahead, except for brief visits from a group of American women interested in the project, and Kathy, accompanied as always by Jessie. The feisty little dog wore a cumbersome cast on a front leg she had broken during an attempt to bring down a duiker. It was no deterrent to her hunting instinct. Their visit was brief, but even so Jessie managed to flush out a guinea fowl, which she dragged inside to show us. Her injured appendage stuck out from her body at a grotesque angle. Between vigorous shakes of the once beautiful bird and winces of pain, she glanced at us with understandable pride. The bird was almost as big as Jessie. No one condemned Jessie for her occasional kills of wildlife – especially after she alerted her mistress to the presence of the lion in her garden. Kathy lived alone in an isolated and dangerous world.

Kathy dispatched the culprit, and the corpse, into the tray of her battered old utility. Jessie straddled the dead bird. Her excited face peered over the side wearing a moustache of soft plumage. Kathy leaned out the driver's window while we made hurried plans to meet that evening for a *braai* (barbecue) on the banks of the Gwaai River at the digs of her fiancé, Neil Rogers. As usual, my friend belied her languorous manner by gunning the engine like Michael Schumacher before screeching away in a cloud of red dust.

I returned to the bunker, flopped down on the bare concrete floor amid the pile of paper and photographs of elephants, and basked in the sun. The rays soaked into my body and melted through my closed eyelids, warming my eyes. The feeling of bliss chased away the memory of a long cold night. I loved the juxtaposition of freezing nights and sunny days. I felt happy and content, until the indolent moment was shattered by the agitated arrival of Angela Brightman. Angela is the wife of a professional safari guide. Her normally rather haughty face was contorted with concern as she urged me to go to the group of women I had met earlier. They were standing dangerously close to a bull elephant. Their noisy chatter and insouciance was remarkable considering they had spoken of their galloping pulses during encounters with the herd on game drives.

A minute later, I met the bull we would name Horace the

Horrible. I sent the women fleeing to safety, and then made a crazy choice about my own escape route. The musth bull's silent charge was terrifying in the most elemental way. I knew his intention was to kill me.

An old man tottered across our path. He appeared to be unaware of the danger. My lungs were empty; I couldn't shout a warning. When I heard my father's voice and leapt the last few metres to safety, my thudding heart had moved into my throat. I sprawled through the doorway of the bunker onto my face. My video camera was on the floor where I had left it. Sucking in desperate gulps of air I grabbed it, rolled on to my back and filmed the bull. I was surprised that my hands were steady. A portion of his enormous grey bulk filled the doorway. The room was filled with dust. I rolled the camera. The sound of an approaching engine merged with short, sharp, agitated trumpets. Slapping extended ears against his body with frustration the bull wheeled about, set his sights on the acacia tree beside the porch and attacked it.

A Land Rover gunned into view driven by Angela's husband David. He was standing behind the wheel with one hand clamped on the horn and the other waving his hat. It was enough. The bull wheeled around, screamed his frustration, then thundered away in the high, proud posture of musth. I noticed that his left tusk had been broken off deep within his jaw, leaving only a jagged, bloody edge exposed. The combination of musth and toothache must have been causing him considerable confusion and pain. His rage was understandable.

We made a bee-line to the bar for a stiff drink. It was only then that I began to tremble.

Despite endless enquiries I never found the old man whose timely appearance had saved my life. The extraordinary thing was that only the bull and I saw him. No one else did; neither Angela nor those who watched from the *kraal*. What they did see was the bull check in his stride momentarily: long enough for me to get to safety. A solution to the mystery would appear within a week; it would blow me away.

The bull hadn't finished for the day. Anticipating a few problems in our search for Neil's isolated plot on the Gwaai River where the *braai* would be held, we made a plan with Jen and Des to sleep at the safari camp in our old hut. The camp was located halfway between Farm 41 and Neil's place. This would make our journey an hour shorter each way. We set out before dusk in a rejuvenated vehicle, hoping to arrive before dark. I clutched a rough mud map which Kathy had sketched hastily that morning, but after an hour of searching we realised we were lost.

The main arterial dirt road wound through dense forest and there were numerous tracks branching off it which Kathy had forgotten to mark. Beginning with the first we investigated each one, only to find that every track soon finished at a wall of vegetation.

Neil's camp was on the river bank and normally one would scan the countryside in search of the tree types that line waterways. We soon grasped that in daylight our search would have been just as difficult within such an impenetrable grove. Even the shapes of the surrounding trees were obscured by the deep dark which had now descended. I peered as if from the inside of a cow's belly at the directions by torchlight.

Baffled, irritable and hungry, we cut the engine to try the sound test. Silence fell. It was suffocating. We strained to hear human noises. What I heard was Jessie's distant barking. Following the drifting sound we eventually stumbled into a warm circle of faces. The group was crouched on logs around a fire that was the open-air kitchen of Neil's home: a three-sided shack beside the stream. A large wok and cast-iron kettle rested on a solid grid straddling the burning wood and coals. His ancient iron bed was pushed against the outside of the rough shanty. Neil and Kathy had recently announced their engagement. I watched him where he squatted over the wok, stir-frying a colourful mound of crisp vegetables that had been picked fresh from his own market garden. The many varieties he grew there thrived on a cleared acre surrounded by a tall fence. A small generator powered an electric wire he had strung along the top. Neil had a brave plan to create a tempting smorgasbord of produce, deep within game country. If he succeeded, the local tourist trade would have a constant source of fresh seasonal vegetables instead of travel-weary, ageing goods, freighted in by road from Bulawayo. But he was battling huge odds in the form of antelopes, baboons, monkeys, birds and insects, all of which had designs on his produce.

Neil is a handsome man with a deep, rich voice. Like Kathy, he is unself-conscious and has a total disregard for the conventions of dress. When he is deep in thought he has a habit of thrusting his lean fingers through his thick brown hair, causing it to form a Rastafarian mop. It shook wildly when he waved an imaginary baton as Olga Borodina's voice soared in 'Softly Awakes My Heart', from *Samson and Delilah*. His one indulgence was a stereo system and a superb collection of eclectic music. No wonder Kathy had fallen for such a man. Her appreciation of fine things, stoic pioneering spirit and lack of guile made it a perfect match.

Neil had turned his back on his career as a professional guide when it became obvious that he must occasionally shoot animals. His respect and love for nature and her creatures even caused him to embrace a vegetable-growing and vegetarian lifestyle, so our repast was stir-fried vegetables and steamed rice. For the protein element we had hummus, which Kathy had made from her precious cache of olive oil and dried peas and seeds.

I was intrigued to meet our fellow guests. We had heard much about the quietly spoken couple who had established a pottery to teach the local, struggling villagers a cottage industry which they hoped would ease their economic plight. When pressed, the pair spoke of their work. They sounded almost hesitant, as if they feared we might think them presumptuous.

Normally, I would have been entranced by the stimulating conversation, but now my woes were exacerbated by a horrible headache and aching joints. I took my bottle of Lion beer and perched at a distance from the others to contemplate the many aches and pains I had no doubt were the result of my encounter with the bull. I sat back in the shadows stroking Jessie, who was my partner in pain. Her broken leg had stiffened, causing her terrible discomfort whenever she needed to move. Desperately delayed toilet squats were accompanied by pitiful squeaks. On the other side of me crouched Neil's large dog, a German shepherd named Rastus. He had problems of his own. He found it difficult to walk, but for an entirely different reason.

That morning the shaggy animal took his usual morning dip. Neil had given up trying to keep him away from the dangers of the river. He figured that a dog who had escaped being dinner for a leopard by slipping under his master's open-air trestle bed

while he slept was sufficiently wily to avoid the jaws of a crocodile. Unfortunately, he was proved wrong.

Neil was working in the garden when he heard a terrible
commotion coming from camp. He downed tools and raced to
the water's edge, arriving in time to see a battle between Rastus
and a submerged enemy. With Neil's help, the dog eventually
dragged himself free of his attacker and out of the water. What
must have been a very small crocodile had recognised a tasty
morsel when he saw it. The croc had latched on to the poor
dog's penis. A quick examination assured Neil that Rastus's
most precious possession would heal and he would live to woo
another Jessie. The dog never again ventured deeper into the
water than knee depth.

I could swear that the poor dog's furry face took on the aura
of canine blushes as we laughed at the sad tale. Casting shame-
faced looks our way, Rastus lifted his head from his paws and
staggered upright to slink into the shadows. When the conversation took a new tack, away from his personage, he returned to
sit with Jessie and me in a sorry state of united misery. Like
theirs, my body was rigid with high-wired tension. My pragmatic
self knew that the danger was over but flashbacks of the bull's
charge kept playing in my monkey mind. I simply was unable to
take a deep breath. I played with the food in the tin plate
feeling disappointed that I couldn't enjoy the good company.
There were very few opportunities for us to have a night out.

My normally taciturn husband carried my end of the conversation, but eventually our fellow guests became aware of my
plight. Moving to stand behind me, they asked if they might be
allowed to help. They explained their belief in the power of
healing by harnessing energy from the universe to transmit
through the hands. Without hesitation I accepted their kind

offer. Soon, I experienced glorious warmth seeping into my back although they didn't touch me. The tension began to dissolve and the electric pinging in my head disappeared. Within minutes I felt better, even elated. When I attempted to thank them, they replied that they were simply tools being used by a greater force.

I had encountered something similar before, but I didn't know it could work on animals. I watched them place their hands just above Jessie's sore little body. They whispered that animals respond well because they have no inhibitions, doubts or learned fears. Jessie became very agitated, but allowed them to finish. When they returned to their seats they were followed closely by a fawning, grateful friend who perked up to the extent that soon she was chasing imaginary guinea fowl about the clearing. It was amazing. I think her instantaneous recovery proved to me that this form of healing has great merit. Hands-on healing might help a person to cure himself through faith. Surely Jessie didn't have the capacity to know faith, let alone to *have* faith.

I returned to the fire for a singalong. Neil stopped the music when Jer began to sing to the stars. It was a night to remember after an unforgettable day. When I couldn't hold my head up any longer we left the circle of light. Still floating on a cloud of wellbeing, I kissed Kathy good night. She was planning a hot soak in an ancient enamel bath. She noticed my longing glances at the antique vessel.

'*Sis*, man. You must come sometime, to use the bath while Neil is working. Just stoke the fire, and fill the kerosene tin and kettle from the stream. They will soon boil.'

After making do for weeks with just a lap bath, until my shower in the safari camp earlier, I could think of no greater luxury. However, bathing receptacles are very private things and I balked.

'Tut-tut-tut,' Neil insisted. 'Too silly. Plan a bathing mission soon, my girl.'

With such pleasures in mind we took our leave. Unseen creatures moved about in the bush on either side of the path we followed to the vehicle. I dozed for most of the return journey. My body had finally relaxed, although my mind continued to go over the remarkable events of the day.

An ancient black angel had saved me, and two caring white healers had cured me. Exhausted and finally relaxed, I slipped into sleep as Jer drove us home.

I woke with a start when the vehicle pulled into camp. We crept out of Bluey, gently pressing the doors closed so as not to wake our friends and their guests. I huddled near Jer as we wearily trod the path lit by the flashlight. Our old hut was a long walk from the car park. We could see the tiny blue glows from the paraffin lanterns that were placed on each porch of the eight guest *rondavels*. Several had gone out and, as we passed, another guttered. Close by, branches crackled as elephants browsed. Otherwise all was quiet.

'Hoy! Is that you Hendersons?' whispered Des. 'There's been a riot here tonight. Come, let's have a snifter.'

I jumped. Des had arrived as quietly as a prowling cat or a charging elephant. Shaking off our tiredness, we backtracked to the bar and perched on stools. Des prowled behind the bar. Soon Jenny arrived wrapped in a towelling robe. Wild-eyed wonder had replaced her usually soft expression. Even so, she was full of endearing giggles.

'Guys, have you missed some wild action. We're too nervous to sleep.'

By now more than a little curious, I took the tiny glass of potent Kenya Gold liqueur from Des. I washed it down with my ritual silent toast. *Here's to you, Dr Livingstone.* Des's hand was trembling. I was intrigued. Jer looked puzzled. What possible threat had given Des and his capable, calm Jenny such a fright?

'I think we might have met your new friend, Horace,' Jenny gasped, rolling her blue eyes heavenwards.

Des threw back his deeply tanned face and tossed down a Scotch. He wiped the back of his hand across his mouth. His soft voice was deceptive. 'We were sitting having dinner. Without that snotty wind that's been giving us grief we got the staff to set up the tables outside by the fire. Very *mushi*.'

Such was the rule on balmy evenings. After the meal, directors' chairs would be set up by the crackling flames for the telling of tall and shaggy yarns.

Des continued: 'The waiters had just finished their "hallelujah chorus".' (He was referring to the majestic Ndebele style of singing hymns by the staff, which was always a huge hit with the guests and a great joy for the enthusiastic performers.) His eyes narrowed. 'Your bloody ellys had been hanging about,' he grumbled. 'You know, they tore up the waterpipes while the clients were on a game drive. No surprise there! I had to take Dingindawo to repair the pipes so the guys could have showers.'

'I nearly bumped into one on my way to organise the kitchen,' Jen said. 'I got such a fright. Good thing it wasn't Horace.' Her already large, sympathetic eyes grew enormous beneath her halo of wild red hair. Even her sandy freckles seemed more prominent against the unnaturally white skin that she protected fiercely from the sun.

I was intrigued at the continual mention of Horace. After all, he had only received his 'Horrible Horace' mantle that day. And here he was – already a legend. What had he done? We learned to be patient in Zimbabwe. Great storytellers abounded in a country where television had yet to destroy the art of conversation.

Des poured himself another Scotch, which told me that he was suffering from shock. He was only an occasional drinker.

'Shadrick had really pulled out his thumb with a *lekker* impala stew.' Des licked his lips at the memory.

Inconsequentially, Jen said: 'It was really delicious, Sal, one of his triumphs. It's so sad – we didn't get to eat much. Anyway, there we all were having a lovely time when we hear this really loud trumpeting and all hell breaks loose!' She paused, frowning into the distance as she remembered the scene.

'Des and Rob jumped up and held their hands out like this to tell the clients they needed to be quiet.'

She was on her feet with her hands thrust forward aggressively in the braking position. Settling back on the stool she continued: 'The strange thing is that no one made a sound. Everyone just sat there as if they were stunned.'

Jen placed one hand across her mouth in a gesture of surprise. 'Then we heard the sound of a humungous body crashing through trees – coming towards us!'

Des interrupted: 'A huge jumbo came hell for leather across the compound. Straight for the teak tree beside the fire. Right next to us. I tell you, it was bloody frightening. Then the bastard dropped his head, tusking the tree trunk over and over. He was really boiling! I didn't need to tell the guests to gap it for the closest *rondavel*.'

Jenny laughed. 'Honestly, if it hadn't been so serious it

120

would've been terribly funny. People jumped over the rail, with inches to spare – even the elderly couple from Plymouth! I've never seen anyone move so fast – and they were falling over each other to get through the doorway.'

Assuming her role of carer she stopped laughing. 'I think I would've been the first inside if I hadn't been supposed to be responsible for their welfare.'

I knew just how seriously my kind-hearted friend took her job as den mother to sometimes fearful tourists, many of whom didn't realise the dangers of the African bush or anticipate their primal reactions to perceived perils.

Des continued urgently. 'I didn't see any of that. I was too busy waving a flaming stick I grabbed out of the fire. But I can tell you I was shit-scared. That jumbo was on a mission to kill somebody! Rob jumped into the Landy and started the engine. He kept his hand on the horn. I grabbed a burning branch from the fire and waved it at the bull. Man, it felt bloody useless.' Des was sweating with the telling.

'Even then I thought the big bastard might have me. He just kept belting the branches. That guy was huge! He was set to have me – until Rob charged him in Chariot. Only then did the bastard stop thrashing the tree. He tossed his head before he ran off to give another tree a real snottie.'

Jen gasped. 'I was terrified for Des. We watched the whole thing from the *rondavel*.' A chuckle replaced her expressions of concern. 'After it was over, we saw Shaddy and Elton hiding beneath the bar. Do you know, when we looked around we saw that each person was still clutching a white serviette. Can you believe it? What a hoot.'

Once again, Jen collapsed with laughter. This time Des joined her. 'I think they were waving flags of surrender,' he grinned.

The mood had changed from fear, to the merriment that would hereafter accompany the telling of the tale. They had visibly relaxed.

'Why do you think it was the same bull who charged me?' I asked. I was amazed that two violent attacks could have occurred on the same day, just fifteen kilometres apart. The herd ellys were such trusting, peaceful creatures. This was decidedly aberrant behaviour.

'Do you remember describing the broken left tusk to Rob? Well, this guy fitted the description. God knows, I had a bloody good look at him,' Des growled. This was our boy. Des was now back in control of the situation.

I shook my head as I touched his arm sympathetically. 'Hang on, Des. I'm not doubting you. I believe you. I was just astonished that his intent was so atrocious. The poor old chap must be really hurting.'

Jer tapped out his pipe on a post. 'Ha! I wonder how Horace will make my acquaintance. I seem to have missed out on all the fun.' He winked at me as he lit two lanterns. 'Anyway, I'm for bed and I think we could all do with a few hours in the cot.'

He handed Des a light and took my hand. I jumped at the far-away sound of an elephant rumble. The distance between our huts and the bar seemed even greater than usual. I wondered if Horace were still there, waiting to vent his spleen yet again. Sanity prevailed. What were the chances of three skirmishes in twenty-four hours? I, for one, yearned for a comfortable bed as a change from a sleeping bag on top of an ancient mattress on a hard floor.

We all took deep breaths. I attempted to disguise the ragged nature of my laboured efforts. Moving in a tight bunch we quickly and silently covered the fifty metres to safety. My back cringed. I felt exposed, intensely aware of the unseen eyes of Africa's night when her predators rule the wild.

Three years later Horace was murdered. His death wasn't in retaliation for threatening humans. He simply persisted in being in the wrong place at the wrong time.

Except for Des, we all became fond of the feisty bull, although on our first few encounters after his initial frenzy we handled him with respect. Whenever we met him, we left our engine running while we gauged his mood. Although he often tossed his head about with irritation and occasionally mock charged, he never again displayed excessive rage. During that extraordinary sequence of events I think his broken tooth must have been infected by an abscess that literally drove him mad with pain. Combined with being in musth, it would have been a potent recipe for fury.

After our return to Australia we continued to follow the progress of the herd, often hearing about the huffing and puffing of Horace. We remembered him with wry pleasure. So, it came as a shock to hear of his death. These are the facts as recounted to us.

Horace often kept company with two younger bulls. The three friends were browsing on trees beside the airstrip at the time when the acacia *erolobia* trees offer their tasty harvest of pods. They were by no means alone in this habit. The herd knew all the stands in their territory. We always knew where to look for the elephants during the harvest season. The bulls were more popular with the females during this time. With their superior strength they could give the trees a hefty shake to dislodge more pods. I was charmed by the egalitarian spirit of the large lads over this prized food source, for they certainly refused to share the precious fresh water as it flowed straight from the pipes at pumped waterholes.

How often I watched dominant bulls like Horace, bloated with their fill, still hog the first position at the trough. Like schoolyard bullies they would dig in, stubbornly blocking the pipe with the tip of their trunk while their companions jostled and jousted for the next turn.

On the day of his death the breeding herds were elsewhere, and Horace and his companions amiably shared their favourite delicacy. They strayed on to the verge of the runway to collect pods that had fallen from the adjacent acacias. As usual, when elephants roamed on to the airstrip, a vehicle was dispatched to drive them away. Horace refused to budge far. He lingered among the acacias. Certainly, the presence of elephants near the strip could manifest as a danger to aircraft. However, the warden's headquarters were close by and it wasn't a large task for him to assemble a unit to move the animals along.

Unfortunately, on this day, the warden was away at a conference in Harare. It was always his decision which decided the fate of elephants that raided the crops of villagers. Habitual elephant thieves were shot because they not only threatened the livelihoods of the people, but often menaced their lives. The death of an elephant was a great cause of celebration for the villagers. To them he appeared as a walking butcher shop! So, the scene was set for a great feast if Horace stood his ground. A few half-hearted efforts were made by the locals to send him packing, but Horace was really enjoying those pods.

Alerted to the unfolding drama by a concerned member of the airport staff, a local safari operator tried hard to intervene.

He was ignored. Horace was shot. He died hard. The amateur marksmen made a misery of the end of a superb, proud bull.

But Horace had the last laugh. What was left of him after the meat had been hacked away created problems for aircraft for many days. Low-flying vultures were a far more serious hazard to landing and departing planes than a recalcitrant bull, and the disgusting odour of putrefaction filled the nostrils of tourists as they arrived for the holiday of a lifetime. Their cameras recorded the obscenity after they heard the sad tale. Conservation groups drew the attention of the media, and footage of Horace's remains appeared on prime-time television around the world.

It has been said that the slaughter of Horace served a worthy purpose. I think the price was too great for the lesson.

CHAPTER 9

The spirit of Africa

A week after I first made the acquaintance of Horace we were visited by Golden Mbvaira, a representative of the Ministry for Tourism in Zimbabwe. He arrived with a coterie of underlings. Among other business, Golden had come to investigate the progress of the elephant work and to ask me to give talks to the women of local villages on subjects ranging from birth control, to cottage industries that could profit from tourism. I was already tempting providence as a student of humankind assisting a scientist with elephant research. And I was neither counsellor nor business adviser. I said so. But Golden was undeterred by either lack of credentials and made it clear that this was a duty I must perform.

The fact is I was much happier working with animals than with people. This may have been the nature of my beast.

Despite having what I am told is a vibrant personality, I have always suffered from extreme shyness (the kind of shyness that sometimes makes one garrulous) which is apparently hidden well behind a mask of confidence. The upside to my dilemma is that I am sensitive to the possibility that others may have similar issues to deal with. Extroverted introverts can suffer torment through their capacity to hide their true natures. I certainly fit that niche and wish it were otherwise.

However, with indigenous people I find it easier to relax. They seem to understand me better than my own kind. I can slip easily into a quiet camaraderie with them and allow inter-actions to unfold without anxiety. I suppose this makes me a misfit in the Western world and probably accounts for my inability to understand the wants and needs of a consumer society.

I thought Golden must be on to me when he arched a fine eyebrow and rumbled, 'Sally, you should have more confidence. You are kind and very knowledgeable. These ladies will respond well to your personality and wise words.'

What could I do? I had the wry thought that he was wasted as an under-secretary and would make a superb diplomat. I told him so and his rosebud mouth parted in laughter. But his eyes dared me to refuse as his finger wagged. I accepted his invitation/command.

We invited him to join us for sundowners at our camp. As usual I was dressed in my cold-weather evening clobber of jeans, Biro-sprouting shirt, vest and boots. In contrast, Golden was wearing a dark grey Savile Row suit and hand-made shoes. He was an erudite, sophisticated man born into a wealthy and powerful Shona family. He had attended an elite Anglican private school in Harare and was a graduate of Oxford University.

Night fell quickly. Jer piled wood into the drum and lit the fire. We relaxed by the flames as Golden regaled us with the news of the world in the wonderful manner of Africans. He was as articulate as a BBC newsreader, but his delivery was entertaining in the way of a great storyteller. We discussed logic. He thought it extraordinary that we lived in rough conditions with only basic equipment, and assured us that this wouldn't do for him. Oh, no! He was returning later to sleep in a luxury camp. Jer didn't wait for Golden to leave before he did so. A long day and a full belly are the perfect recipe for slumber. Our guest smiled at my husband where he lay slumped peacefully in his chair.

It seemed a good time to tell Golden the story of Horace. I hadn't been able to come to terms with the presence of the mysterious old man who had been visible only to Horace and to me – the man whom I saw as my saviour.

'Ahhh,' he breathed. 'The spirit of Africa came to save you. You have more to do before it is your time to die.'

There was wonder written on his features as he leaned forward in concentration. 'I'm telling you, Sally. The old man drew the elephant's attention away from you for long enough. He came to save you. I think you are a black person with white woman's skin.' Golden's face reflected the glow of the fire as he reached across to touch my arm. 'You are a very fortunate woman to have an angel walking with you.'

To say I was astonished is putting it mildly. 'Are you saying that I was right in thinking the man could be seen only by Horace and me? I thought the others were so focused on me and the elephant that they simply didn't catch sight of him,' I gasped. 'It can't be true, can it?'

He assured me it was and spoke of similar rescues by this

being, this spirit of Africa. His manner was matter of fact. I was emboldened to tell him also of the elephant that had saved my life at Savuti and changed my life forever. Again he showed no surprise and reiterated that the spirit of Africa was protecting me. At Savuti it had taken the form of an elephant. This time it had come in the guise of the old man. I discussed these events with Golden as if such happenings were commonplace, in a way that I couldn't speak with many white people. He suggested (cunningly, I thought) that I was being guided to work with both elephants and people.

Shortly afterwards, I observed a great shift in Golden's emotions. He became extremely anxious. His face glistened with sweat, his pretty mouth retreated inwards and his benevolent expression changed to a mask of terror. He was staring at something behind me.

'What's wrong, Golden?'

He shivered. 'It is *mshungu* [bad magic]! My mother-in-law is watching me from those bushes.'

Flabbergasted and puzzled, I turned around to see what he was looking at. It was a hyaena; standing very still, staring back at the man. Yet, Golden was seeing his wife's mother.

He whispered harshly. 'I don't have a good relationship with this woman'.

There was no doubt that Golden believed the woman was stalking him in the form of a hyaena. He left immediately. I know he was speaking the truth. I believed him. I knew he had viewed a human figure where I had seen a hyaena. After all, Horace and I saw a being where others had not. Regretfully, I understood that the schism between our worlds was too wide for frank discussion on such a deeply personal issue. Golden had already given me his trust by sharing his belief in a spirit of Africa with a woman from a culture very different from his own.

I recognised that I would never know Africa like an African does. It is a place where reality and *juju* (magic) all reside together in a strange harmony.

Since then there have been many times I have witnessed similar *juju* having an impact on Westernised, sophisticated Africans. Bridging the gap between Europeans and indigenous people in Africa is always going to be fraught with difficulty, because white and black concepts of the core aspects of life are very different.

Even so, I had been blessed to see and be rescued by the spirit of Africa. I hoped this awareness would stay with me so that I never again made a stupid decision that would cause the spirit of Africa to take charge of my life because it was not yet time for me to die. Unfortunately, this wasn't to be. In the months ahead I would test my saviour again and again.

A short time later, a letter arrived from Golden requesting information about the task he had set me. 'Are you achieving success?' he wrote. 'Are the villagers cooperating?' I knew damned well that his contacts would be keeping him informed and that he was aware I hadn't begun the task. Basically, his letter was a polite command. Golden had given me no guide-lines, and without parameters I needed to structure a program. But where would I start? A blank slate can be an onerous thing.

I decided to begin by touching base with a progressive project that had been implemented in parts of southern Africa and was beginning to have good results. It was the CAMPFIRE scheme (Communal Areas Management Programme for

Indigenous Resources). I had become aware of CAMPFIRE through Elefriends Australia, which sent funds to Zimbabwe to assist the operation well before we commenced our research with the elephants. CAMPFIRE was an ambitious plan adopted as a scheme for integrating wildlife conservation with rural development by empowering subsistence farmers to utilise the wildlife in their areas to generate funds for community development. The scheme was working well in some areas where the people had been open to discussion – protracted discussion. Communities in wildlife-rich CAMPFIRE areas were opting to allow safari companies to bring trophy hunters on to their lands to hunt on a sustained yield basis.

I believe there is a place for hunting in Africa. In a continent where people struggle to survive, the wildlife has to earn its living. The communal landowners are paid excellent money by the hunters who want to bag good trophies for their clients. These come from older animals. It is in the interest of the indigenous owners to maintain a good stock of ageing game.

In the areas where these methods had been embraced, I was told it was working well, even to the point where those who were once poachers themselves were now reporting poachers to authorities. Elders recognised the value of the wildlife and rejoiced in their growing numbers where previously there was none. They worked to increase the stock and to keep it healthy. It didn't matter that they treasured the creatures for their potential as hard currency. This provided hope for the continuation of Africa's wild heritage. And many of these were people who only recently were risking their lives as poachers in the national parks. Instead, their eyes were focused now on their own living banks, which was taking pressure off the game in national parks and off the anti-poaching patrols, who themselves were struggling to survive.

The people would be empowered if they utilised the wildlife for their own advantage in programs of sustainable development. It was clear that many local villagers watched and resented the white safari operators (and certain black government officials who own luxury lodges) pulling in foreign currency and living like kings. It was easy to understand why they wanted what the *mazungus* had; they were being bombarded by encroaching Western materialism.

The problem was that their motivation and direction were centred on the traditional belief system that children (the more the better), cattle and goats were their wealth. But these assets didn't transpose into hard currency. Children were born into relentless poverty; nevertheless, as a man's progeny grew, so did his stature. For this reason the concept of birth control was often anathema to men, despite their inability to provide for their offspring. Cattle were rarely sold. It was the number of cattle a family owned that decreed their status in the community. It didn't matter that often the domesticated stock were diseased and wasted.

It was very difficult to see the children suffering malnutrition in the midst of a herd which provided only milk that was itself limited due to the poor condition of the cows. It was a vicious cycle. All around the area of our study, overstocked landholdings were turned into arid landscapes, further degraded by the ubiquitous goats.

It was a great relief that my anthropological discipline was working well with the social behavioural study of elephants. I was hopeful that it would be even more useful for my interactions with the indigenous people. Previous work with island people in Fiji and with Aboriginal Australians had given me invaluable tools for my interactions with other cultures. Now I needed to acquaint myself with as much information about Matabele culture as possible before I entered their world.

I did this by spending time with Dingi, Bheki and the black guides Raphael and Dickson, who came from Matabeleland. They taught me some basic rules of etiquette. It was a privilege to be trusted by these patient men. I knew that none of them had escaped racially intolerant paternalism and condescension (even abuse) from the ruling elite – both black and white. They gave me confidence that I wouldn't commit too many social gaffes.

Even so, I arrived at the villages with my cap in hand and a stomach filled with the usual swarm of fluttering insects. I was only too aware that these people hadn't invited me into their lives. I breached their ramparts slowly and with deep respect, watching closely the way they behaved towards me so that I could emulate their greetings and actions. I soon learned that there is an intricate and lengthy process of introduction and subsequent greetings that requires patience and understanding. Most often the people responded with grace and gratitude to my diffident and sometimes clumsy efforts to understand them and their way of life. I tried to stand in their shoes and imagine how it must feel to have a woman from another culture intrude into my life, especially when this woman was suggesting I make changes so alien to my world view.

What I was doing also went against the grain from an anthropological point of view. The study of human cultures is just that. Anthropologists are observers who do not impose their own standards and beliefs on the social systems they are studying. They are there to learn about and chronicle the culture; not to inform. I found it hard to step outside the strict parameters of my discipline, but I was grateful for the tools it provided.

The process of gaining the confidence of the villagers was slow, as it involved complex codes of courtesy. Time was the key to gaining their trust. For instance, it was necessary to discuss the weather, their family, livestock and crops, and to wait for them to ask the reason for my visit. When this question didn't always eventuate during the first visit I had to return again, and again, until they judged it safe to communicate with me. Then our meetings were lengthy and amiable. I found the ground rules were to have flexibility, patience, humility and a good sense of humour. Laughter brought us on to common ground more quickly than anything else.

I learned much more from them than they did from me. I had already begun to understand that the lives of animals and humans are interwoven in rural Africa: that without co-operation from the local people (who in the final wash are the custodians of the wild) the future of Africa's wildlife is doomed. Intense population pressure had confined game to small areas of marginal land. Conflict between humans and wildlife needed to be addressed for the benefit of both. If they each offered cash flow to the economy of the country, the dual emphasis would validate their worth and grant them recognition from the government.

I had come to believe that many Africans have no emotional attachment to wildlife; indeed, they see the animals purely as a food source. After all, this was the order of things in Africa, and it worked well enough until the white man arrived. This is what I gathered from the men. Yet the women, the nurturers, seemed open to new ideas. Their opinions were often overlooked, due to time-honoured gender issues. These issues also affected my dealings with the men, but not with the children. The best way to reach the elders is through education of the children, who are receptive to new ideas. However, this requires time. Tragically, the rural people of Zimbabwe haven't been granted that time under the rule of a despot who has relentlessly brought the country to its knees.

Back then, there was still hope. I could see the women were eager to contribute to cottage industries that cashed in on tourism. Some were already creating jewellery, and making handicrafts to sell to tourists. Their husbands carved phenomenal sculptures out of wood and stone; but mostly these artworks were sold along the road for embarrassingly insignificant sums of money. I spoke to the women about the possibility of making soaps, woven mats and decorative items to supply the local safari operations, just as Neil was hoping to provide them with vegetables.

I began to wonder why my observations were necessary when I visited an already profitable business operating at Gwaai village near a gracious old colonial pub owned by Harold and Sylvia Broomberg. The philanthropic couple gave the land to the people of Gwaai for the establishment of a pottery run by the gentle couple who had healed Jessie and me on the night of Horace's charge. It had become a viable operation that now maintained an entire village. Initially, the idea was to create crockery for the safari lodges and camps nearby. This developed quickly into a thriving industry, with tiles being pumped out in vast quantities and freighted all over Zimbabwe, and beyond.

I learned much from observing the manner in which the dedicated foursome motivated the people of Gwaai. Their sensitive recognition of the villagers' spiritual and cultural beliefs was probably the prime reason for the venture's success. Each working day began with a meditation and prayers which combined Eastern and Christian traditions in wonderful harmony. These were followed by songs and dances that expressed the thoughts and concerns of the pottery staff. Work didn't begin until the actors were satisfied that they had routed bad *juju* and appeased the spirits; and when they worked, it was with enthusiasm.

Potters were excused for important ceremonies such as funerals, and they were not expected to return to work until they had completed these rituals in the traditional way. Very few exploited this. The entire village had benefited from the business, with the people gaining critical thinking skills and confidence that empowered them. I pray this is still the case; the wonderful people who created the pottery have been forced out of Zimbabwe since then, due to the civil unrest.

I soon realised that there was little I could do except report my observations to Golden. Setting up a soap factory and craft business was a full-time job. CAMPFIRE was now in touch with the situation and I simply didn't have the time. The elephants were my priority. Even so, I hoped to interest other qualified volunteers in working with the tribal people. They could use as their tools the standards and methods set by the philanthropists at Gwaai who had become our mentors – particularly Harold.

The gentle guru won our hearts long before he shared his secrets of communication with the elephants. Whenever we could get away, or were close to the Gwaai, we visited Harold and Sylvia to soak up some of their peace and knowledge.

Harold had lived with elephants all his life. He generously passed on invaluable information about their behaviour that extended well beyond an inviolable scientific paradigm and into a spiritual dimension. In time, he even entrusted me with his conviction that cross-species communication is possible. He told me that if I wanted to experience such a possibility, I needed to learn to think like an elephant. 'Then, my girl,' he said, 'you will travel more safely in their company.'

He led me through a process of visualisation until I thought I could imagine myself as an elephant. I was eager to start, but he insisted that we take a day away from the herd to restore our energy at the pub he ran with Sylvia, the Gwaai. The pub was both a watering hole and a sanctuary. A tall, tottering security fence surrounded the sagging thatched roof and bougainvillea-draped stone walls which reeked of the days of colonial rule, when Zimbabwe went under the name of Rhodesia. The Gwaai was an icon of those days.

White farmers and hunters became Rhodies again when they entered the gracious gardens where white iron tables and chairs were scattered beneath arching, flamboyant trees. The men lolled with their *vellie* (desert boot)-footed legs spread aggressively apart. Their wives sat primly with knees together beneath the gathered folds of dated, flower-sprigged dresses. They were faded, as were the women. They looked tired and worried. Their children played and screamed and cried like all children, beside the suspiciously green pool. Their parents quaffed imported beer (the men) and pink gins (the women), and ate stodgy English food. As the temperature soared above 35°C they scoffed roast beef with Yorkshire pudding and topped it off with heavy treacle tarts.

The bar held up lone, weather-worn, angry men who wore

revolvers on their hips and toted rifles. Blacks were still *muntus*, and the president was an arsehole. A Mashona barman, wearing crackling crisp whites and a red bandana tied at his throat, listened silently. His eyes occasionally flared beneath carefully deferential hooded lids. The Rhodies didn't see this, or they simply didn't care. 'These guys must be crazy, or stupid,' I thought. I saw a great bear of a man dabbing lavender essential oil on his ears and wattled throat. He said it kept the mossies away. He smelled of the sickly-sweet unguent mixed with bad body odour.

The walls were covered with trophy-sized horns and antlers, the mangy head of a moth-eaten lion, and cases lined with foreign notes and coins left by travellers. The atmosphere stank of stale beer and sweat – and lavender.

Harold tried to encourage the local people to use the hotel. They rarely came. Why would they? There was better company and *Chibunku* beer (dense ale brewed from sorghum) in the village.

The dinner bell rang and everyone moved obediently across creaking, achingly buffed parquet floors into the gracious old dining room. There was a set menu, except for a choice between meat and fish. The *maitre d'*, Diamond, was an ancient, proud man with a longing for the ways and days of old. He managed his waiters with a symbolic rod of iron that sometimes took the form of actual physical blows.

I was bemused when a waiter whisked away my plate before I had finished eating. My bemusement turned to alarm when Diamond swooped upon the hapless fellow like a sergeant major and slapped him across the head in time with a tirade of abuse. Jer said that my eyes flashed green ire as I watched the plate disappear through the swinging doors into the kitchen to be filled anew. I forced down another helping as Diamond stood by encouraging, and apologising to 'good Madam' for 'that very stupid boy'.

I thought Diamond was really a colonial white man in black skin, unlike his *mazungu* employers, who were liberal and fair. Harold and Sylvia are the kindest people I know. They loved their home and they cared for the people of Gwaai village. They offered sanctuary to all travellers, remaining impartial when tempers heated to boiling point. And they did, often, in a country still recovering from a civil war.

It was lunchtime and I was eating watery soup with manners that I hoped would meet with Diamond's approval. I watched Harold and Sylvia at the main table. Their heads were bowed as they gave prayers before they ate. With them were the couple who managed the pottery. Jer and I had just come from the anti-denominational (anti *any* particular creed or religion) chapel the Broombergs had erected in a secluded place in the garden.

We were still filled with the peace of the service that took place in the holy space each day. Our company had been eclectic: a black Catholic missionary nun, a Buddhist, two Hindus, three Jews and a couple of lapsed Christians. Harold guided us through a gentle series of prayers that encompassed readings from the Bible and the Bhagavad-Gita, and from the teachings of Sai Baba and Kahlil Gibran. He quoted great philosophers. Each of us was asked to share a thought, which we all did, although I felt inadequate in such fine company. This was how it was done each day.

The walls of the chapel rose only to waist height beneath a thatched roof. There were no windows. Except for some precious icons of various religions, and treasures from nature, the room was bare. I was amazed that baboons and monkeys hadn't swung inside and created havoc, as they did in hotel rooms if the doors or windows were left open. It seemed that even they respected the sanctity of the place.

After lunch we joined Harold, who was sitting at his desk in an office pocked with bullet holes. He had opted to leave a cavity in the ceiling where a mortar had impacted while he continued working as the war raged outside. He said being under fire wasn't so bad. His soft voice described harsh things. 'What could I do, my dears?' he asked. 'Life had to go on. God kept us safe.'

Sylvia nodded in agreement. 'One got used to it. We sent the children to South Africa, but we stayed to look after the Gwaai.'

I knew she wasn't referring just to the hotel. Harold's and her story has become legendary in southern Africa. I had heard it told by others in Botswana and Namibia, who also spoke of Harold's wild youth when he lived on his parents' farm before the pub existed.

It was said that on Saturday evenings he would drive his donkey cart across twenty kilometres of lion-infested country to meet with friends. When Harold was thoroughly drunk, and ready to leave, he would lie down in the cart and drop the reins on the donkey's neck. This was the signal for the faithful beast to take him home. In the morning his parents would open the front door of the farmhouse to find Harold and the donkey sleeping peacefully at the front door.

I looked at the lad who was now an old man, stooped and fragile. Jer gently assisted Harold to rise from his chair. I thought my expression must mirror the shining respect I saw on my husband's face.

CHAPTER 10

Elephant song

I began to try to think and speak like an elephant when I was with them. Jer chortled at the pathetic raspberry sounds I made, which were spectacularly ignored by the elephants. I wasn't prepared to give up. If Harold said it was possible, I believed him. But we were about to witness an extraordinary communication between the elephants themselves.

We arrived at a small grassed *vlei* ringed by heavy scrublands just before Skew Tusk led her family out of the trees. As usual, the matriarch greeted us with a staccato trumpet, shook her head and smacked her ears hard before she continued on. Sometimes she mocked us with a small rush, but she never charged us. This was the same treatment she gave arriving elephant families when they came into her range. While she often threatened other vehicles with formidable charges, she left us alone. I believe she was reminding us of her position as the supreme matriarch. There was no doubt she recognised and accepted our presence. Her dominance extended across the entire herd. All the other matriarchs deferred to her might, as she would have done to the matriarch before her when she passed on the ancestral information of her gene pool.

Skew Tusk led her family past us to a well-used plot of mineral salts beside a small spring. This visit wasn't about water. Within seconds, the cows were kneeling into deep holes, tusking clods of compacted soil up and out where great feet kicked them into powder. Immense bottoms wriggled and shivered with the effort. Tiny bottoms lifted above the heads of small calves who mouthed the soil as if their lives depended on it. And perhaps they did, for I noticed that some cows and several calves were scouring. Their legs were covered with the trails of loose green motions. It seemed that the elephants were visiting the local pharmacy to ingest the drugs that would settle their upset stomachs. Perhaps the adults had been far too long in a nutrient-deficient area, or had over-indulged in question-able fodder. We knew that they selectively chose to eat mildly toxic plants for reasons unknown. And sometimes after heavy rain the water-rich fresh tucker was a shock to their systems after too long on dry feed and could result in a bad case of gastritis. The symptoms were monumental tummy rumbles and loose bowels.

Skew Tusk and her sweet infant seemed to be unaffected. It was the younger cows who were looking much the worse for wear. The matriarch swung her head about in a frazzled manner. Perhaps the wise old girl was feeling decidedly frus-trated with her younger charges. She certainly seemed quite put out by the state of affairs. I noticed her fontanelle begin to quiver just before all the cows turned to look in the same direction.

Another family emerged from the bush, and then another, until there were seventy-four elephants socialising with excited greeting vocalisations and touching. No doubt they had arranged to meet at this place, at this time. We had seen these gatherings many times. The families all came from different directions, so we knew they hadn't been together earlier. We knew as well that they communicated with low-frequency sound waves that we couldn't hear. There are several theories about this. One is that low-pitched sound waves travel further – that they can bend and warp around obstructions that would block normal noise. Another theory is that the vibrations of the sounds travel through the ground and are felt through the elephants' feet: that they can even calculate the distance between themselves and the communicating animal. Although the sounds/vibrations were too low for us to hear, I had felt deep reverberations in my chest when we had been among a large group of elephants. Was I sensing their private conversations?

Skew Tusk padded about the herd, grumbling. She placed her trunk in the mouths of the other matriarchs. I wondered if she had called them from afar with: 'Watch out for the fat green leaves of the diarrhoea tree!' And then: 'We're going to the pharmacy for drugs. Do you want to come?'

The Gang of Eleven wandered in nonchalantly a little while later. They pottered about at a distance, stopped as usual by the head-shaking ire of the matriarch. She tolerated their presence only so far, except for Sabre who was permitted to join the cows. We thought he must be Skew Tusk's son. He boasted a strangely shaped tusk and their facial features were similar.

Sabre swaggered about sniffing the cows for a while. It was all show. For if one had been in oestrous, his chances of mating were nil. Whenever we had seen oestrous cows, there was always a mature male or two in attendance. If there were two bulls vying for the cow's favours it was certainly not a safe place for inexperienced youngsters. The fights could be savage. Sabre and the Gang of Eleven made themselves scarce at these times. They were too young, too small or too old to challenge a powerful lord.

When he finished his display of arrogance, Sabre returned to the Gang, who didn't seem bothered by the show of favouritism. He was a high-ranking male, probably because he was, presumably, Skew Tusk's son. Certainly her infant daughter, Cathy, was the leader of the smallest calves.

I was worrying that Sabre's tusk could make him a target for a poacher, when all activity stopped in the herd. They froze as one. The sight of eighty-five elephants standing utterly still and silent was almost shocking. I craned forward for a closer look and saw that fontanelles were fluttering fast. I felt the deep vibration in my chest. Then all hell let loose.

Led by the males, the entire herd stampeded in a tightly bunched throng. Now they were screaming and bellowing as they fled into the scrub. Skew Tusk brought up the rear. As she reached cover, she whirled about in the dust storm and squealed a terrible sound we had never heard before. She held her head high, and her ears stood straight out from her head. She was looking at us. It was almost as if she were telling us to flee, too. With a final blast she wheeled and disappeared from view.

The herd's panicked charge continued straight on through the heavy bush. We could hear branches cracking and wild trumpeting as the ground shook beneath 340 pounding feet.

'What in God's name is happening?' I asked. 'There must be a reason. Did we do something?'

Jer turned the Toyota for home. 'No, it's not us. They've been spooked badly,' he replied.

All the way home we discussed the strange event. We were caught up in the elephants' distress. Their fear had transferred to us. Jer's face was set hard. He drove like a madman and I urged him on, wringing my hands with concern. We called into Hwange Main Camp to check if anyone knew what might have happened. The warden, Frank Potts, settled us down with cups of tea and said he would investigate.

'It could have been lions or wild dogs,' he suggested. But I knew this wouldn't have caused a mad stampede. We had seen encounters between the elephants and dogs, and while they had reacted with rage to drive the predators away, we had never seen anything like this.

That night I was unable to sleep. I couldn't forget the elephants' terror. In the morning, Frank sent a guide with the news that one of the home-range bulls had been shot by poachers at the very moment the elephants fled. The gunfire had been heard by the anti-poaching brigade, who located the carcass an hour later. The bull's tusks had been hacked out of his face while he was still alive. The poachers hadn't wasted another bullet to ease his misery. The patrol leader shot the poor fellow when they arrived. They told Frank the bull had tears streaking his cheeks.

I cried for him and with shame at being of the same kind as the perpetrators. The bastards were cold killing machines. How could they be considered human beings?

We knew then that the stricken bull must have sent a low-frequency warning to the herd at the moment he fell. They heard his message clearly over a distance of at least twelve kilo-metres. It would seem they knew his death was violent and that they must escape to safe territory.

The elephants disappeared for ten days. When they emerged from the forest they were jumpy. Yet, they allowed us to be with them, even though one of our kind had murdered one of their kind. We have much to learn from these benevo-lent creatures. If the tragedy had been reversed, an elephant would have paid the price. They are inevitable losers when they come into conflict with humans.

Sadly, we knew the killing would continue. The poachers were small fry in the overall scheme of things, dying to feed their families while the evil overlords at the top of the chain continued to reap huge sums of money. Too many lives, both human and animal, had been lost in the killing fields. The need for the local people to empower themselves by utilising the living wildlife to provide good incomes was becoming urgent. I empathised with the poachers and their families, but I would never understand the brutality of leaving a dying animal in agony, or be able to think like an African struggling to exist in marginal territory.

We all worried that the poachers would kill Sabre. He was famous for the shape and thickness of his amazing tusk. It was always a relief to see him safely strutting within the ranks of the Gang of Eleven. Sabre was the elephant that would respond to my efforts to transmit a message, though one of us wouldn't understand the language.

This first happened at the end of a long session in the company of the Gang of Eleven. The morning had passed quickly, for although the shrinking waterhole was devoid of large animals, the birdlife was brilliant. A pair of elegant crested cranes bobbed and curtsied to each other in mutual admiration during an intricate mating dance. A Goliath heron loomed large in my binoculars, high-stepping his long, long legs through the reed beds as he stalked fish with dignity. His movements were stately until he made a lightning strike so swift that the action was over before my mind had caught up with the course of events. Only the lump sliding slowly down his long throat convinced me that 'His Eminence' had really stooped to kill.

Morning doves and glossy starlings swept down to drink and bathe in the water, catching the sun's rays in their iridescent green plumage. A crimson-breasted shrike tantalised me with brief glimpses of her vibrant beauty as she darted between the ground and dense bushes, gathering straw for her nest.

I was totally engrossed in the antics of a family of Egyptian geese when the Gang of Eleven arrived without warning, blaring excitedly and running quite fast in their desperate hurry to drink. Heads nodded with satisfaction as they waded knee-deep into the water, utterly unperturbed by our now familiar presence. Trunks lifted, coiling high into uptilted mouths before dropping back to refill – *slurp, hold, swallow, gurgle.*

The clique drank seriously for some time, their stomachs visibly expanding from the vast volumes of water they required to augment the 400 pounds or so of fodder they had probably consumed in the past twenty-four hours. Many waterholes in their territory had already dried up, but this substantial dam was on a wildlife concession adjacent to the boundary of Hwange National Park. The money to pay for the fuel had been donated by a local safari operator. The bore hole was now being artificially pumped to provide life-giving liquid for wildlife. The numbers of game swelled daily as animals crossed the invisible border in search of water.

More often than not the frustrated warden was unable to supply funds for fuel to run the pumps of artificial waterholes within the park, or to pay the meagre wages of the pump attendants whose jobs lay within his jurisdiction. Therefore, this precious reservoir would become the hub of increasing animal activity as the dry deepened. This changed the dynamics of our study. Unknown elephants began to make their presence felt. The home bulls saw these interlopers as a challenge. Tempers started to fray. But this was still early in the season and the Gang were confident and calm.

The water was deep enough to allow the elephants to submerge completely. It was the venerable Van Gogh who led the way in an exuberant, trumpeting rush. His great dusty grey body disappeared, leaving a widening arc of mercury-coloured ripples as the only evidence of his presence. For a moment his companions, with intense stillness, watched the place where Van Gogh had been. After all, it wasn't easy for an elephant to vanish. Then two shiny black fingers broke the surface to tantalise and taunt. Further to the rear, the curved hump of his back appeared. His trunk emerged higher. For a brief second the surfaced portions of the old fellow resembled that now infamous photo of the Loch Ness monster.

Rising like a breaching whale, he swept his streaming head out of the brown pool, tossing it back until his trunk plopped into the water behind. With one and a half ears held wide and pointed mouth at the apex, his upturned head momentarily took on the form of a reversed heart, until he abruptly whipped forward and cracked his fabulous nose, trumpeting a challenge to the Gang. They accepted the dare with a medley of screams and rumbles. Led by their urging trunks they thrust their heads forward and, with stiff ears extended, stormed into the deeper water, creating a large bow wave.

There is nothing quite like a communal elephant bath. Glistening, obsidian behemoths mound, roll and sink in a seemingly amorphous mass, glorying in weightlessness. How they must squeeze their eyes with pleasure at the wonder of floating their heavy bodies, miraculously transformed into supple, light forms caressed by a cool and gentle medium.

Van Gogh always swam and submerged alone, spending more time under water than the others, but usually one could see something of him above the surface – the tip of an ear, his square forehead, a wildly splashing trunk or the bulk of his solid rump appearing to bob like an inflated bladder. Four of the young males usually paired off to fence, spar and pretend to mount each other. This was certainly the only prospect for the smallest fellows to learn the ropes. On land their chances of sexual encounters were extremely slim.

Eventually, nine ellys, surely now feeling cumbersome, emerged a little shakily to stump close to our vehicle for a leisurely dust bath. I imagined dry, crackling sinuses coated in dust spores as they inhaled the stuff before blowing it in a red cloud over their backs. Soon their gleaming, black skin was cloaked in talcum-fine red dirt. And so were we.

Two young bulls (perhaps sixteen or seventeen years old) remained in the pool. One gave a good imitation of a resting hippo – standing quietly, shoulder deep – as he watched the other swing his head wildly from side to side, then stop before beating the water with his trunk, which sent geysers flying high. It was a tremendous treat to watch his fun.

Shotgun (so-named for the myriad small holes in his ears) obviously thought so as well. With a mighty trumpet he tossed his head, clambered out of a hole he had been exploring for mineral salts and charged straight back into the water. The caked red soil dissolved as he sank, and then there were three shiny black backs forming an axle shape. No doubt they were touching trunks under water.

During the next hour there was much coming and going between the water and the soothing dust bath. Any irritating insects and parasites were long gone from their thick hides. Only during these drawn-out bathing sessions did I ever hear a particular vocalisation that could best be described as an extended, droning groan. It was a sound of complete pleasure, similar to the long moan made by Roy the wart-hog when he scratched his rump against a stump.

Privileged as we always felt to share the company of the giants at play, there were elements of personal discomfort that made the pang of their leaving less painful. It was imperative that we remained quiet and still in close company with the elephants. Certainly, an elephant's vision is limited, but not so poor that they couldn't see and be disturbed by a flash of movement within a vehicle standing only a trunk's distance away. This meant that I had to endure cramps, biting insects and consequent itches with silent stoicism.

Obviously there were times when one had to react, but it always had to be in slow motion. And there was nothing quite like the agony of a full bladder when water was being hurled about with cheerful abandon. Once, amid a herd of cows and calves, nature's call insisted that I quietly squeeze the door open just enough to slide down beside the Toyota and wet the dust. I'm not sure that 'vulnerable' is a strong enough word to express how I felt. Psychiatrists have suggested that many women suffer from 'penis envy', which I have interpreted as women desiring to be men, to enjoy the freedom they perceive as not theirs. As one who delights in the glorious role of womanhood, I find such proposals have been cause for much amusement. But I *have* wished to be so endowed when crouched beneath a tree (for what seems an interminable time) with the prospect of ticks from above, ants and snakes from below, and the very real possibility of becoming lunch for a hidden predator.

Unfortunately, on this day the elephants were just too close for any relief. Eventually, as one, they ceased all activity. Their stillness and shivering fontanelles informed me that they were communicating, although my ears heard nothing. The low frequency sounds they were making were below the level of human hearing. Eventually, obviously agreed on a certain plan of action, they formed a single line to pad lazily away into the forest for further feeding. (The posterior view of elephants always appears to me to be comically similar to the gait of knock-kneed, overweight men in baggy trousers, shuffling along in bedroom slippers.) The animals were departing on my side. Young Sabre was bringing up the rear.

I decided that this was the moment to endeavour to make sounds of elephant vocalisation. My best efforts (to human ears) had come from cupping my hands around my mouth while I blew various types of loud raspberries. *Rrrrh-rrrrrh-rrrrrrrhHH!* As they departed silently, I craned out of the car window to rumble my farewell. It had been a long and special visit with the Gang on this day and I was feeling rather emotional about the gentle giants' extraordinary tolerance of our presence.

The first bulls in the line had already melted into the forest. Sabre's deceptive saunter was quickly closing the gap. My final raspberry turned into a groan of despair as I closed my eyes to visualise him turning around and responding. A resonant low grumble overwhelmed my imaginary efforts. It sounded just like mine. I opened my eyes to the astounding sight of Sabre doing an about-turn with his ears standing straight out. His trunk quested towards us in rhythm with a continual rolling greeting. For a moment he stood still, peering in our direction. Then he launched his grey bulk towards me with a jaunty stride.

Jer exhaled, 'Well, strike me pink!'

I was far too enchanted to be frightened as Sabre closed at speed. He ran to within a body's length of us and stopped. He reached out with his trunk. I looked deeply into a warm and lively amber eye. For a tiny moment we understood each other – this time without words. Too soon, Sabre remembered his original plan and turned away to follow the ten into a world we were unable to share.

My only regret about that magical encounter is that I have absolutely no idea what it was I said to the young bull.

Soon after our fantastic interaction with Sabre we had another encounter with a young bull. This time it was the elephant who communicated a funny and whimsical message to us. Inkosikasi (a large tusk-less cow) had recently given birth to a female calf. Her adolescent son, Frodo, was particularly jealous of the new arrival, constantly harassing his patient mother for attention. We thought Inkosikasi might have lost a calf between the two siblings, as the young male was about seven years old.

He was very upset that his long period of undivided mothering ended with the birth of his sister.

If an elephant can sulk, then this one did. Frodo began to vent his anger on us with noisy, clumsy efforts to charge us down. We always sat still until the inevitable end of his bluff caused him to pull up well short of his target. He would shuffle about within his dust cloud for a few seconds before creeping away with his head drooping to cast shame-faced, sidelong glances at the highly amused cows: until one day he approached us slowly with no pretence of a threat. He came close – right beside the car window – and fixed me with a soft brown gaze. I could swear that the youngster sent me a telepathic message to let him be a winner. Then he quietly returned to the herd.

In that moment I could almost see my son Lachy's hazel eyes asking a similar unspoken question when, as a young teenager intent on impressing older friends with his ability to ride a Vespa bike, he hadn't wanted his doting mother to coddle him or fuss. I recognised the need to cooperate with Lachy then. I could do the same for this youngster now.

I told Jer of my feelings, and he agreed to enter the pact. A few minutes later the youngster signalled his intention to charge. He trumpeted a shrill blast from his wildly waving trunk, ensuring that his audience would be watching the performance. With head bobbing and feet pounding, Frodo tore towards us in his usual feisty fashion. But this time Jer started the engine, and with the respect due a young fellow who had asked a favour, we turned and fled. He pursued us out of sight of the herd. He stopped. We stopped. For a second he watched us with the dignified bearing of the splendid bull he would become. Then he turned to stride away, holding his head and tail high and proud.

We followed slowly and halted at the furthest point where we could observe the family's reaction to his return. Frodo's stiff gait gave his motion the appearance of a strut. He swept his trunk slowly from side to side with ears standing at right angles from his head before sauntering up to his mother. She reached out her trunk and touched his mouth gently. He accepted her greeting with gravity. All fourteen cows and calves gave him their respectful attention for a golden moment. From that time on, he let us be.

We almost missed Frodo's bumbling mock charges; though he still pursued antelope, baboons, birds and wart-hogs who invaded his territory. However, his actions were more assured and he had become the highest-ranking calf. For him the rites of passage into maturity had begun.

Soon after Frodo's adventure we met another male calf who didn't have the protection of a loving family. It was a sleepy African afternoon in June. We were waiting beside the water-hole for the anticipated arrival of Skew Tusk's family, who were steadily browsing our way. The only sound was the soporific buzzing of insects: the only movement came from two small ducks floating mid-hole, and they were probably sleeping. Jer was slumped behind the wheel, his hat tipped over his face. Gentle snores fluttered his lips. Eventually, I too gave in to the ecstasy of slumber produced by stillness, silence and the womb-like warmth inside the vehicle.

I dreamed of a misty night harbour with glimpses of an oily sea picked out through the thick fog by the spotlight of a tugboat – a tugboat that continually emitted short, sharp blasts to warn other craft. I woke to a particularly loud boom from the fog-horn. There, on the opposite bank, stood a forlorn little male elephant emitting strange toots while his trunk weaved in constant motion.

'The vanguard has arrived,' Jer muttered.

Soon we realised that the herd wasn't coming – at least not yet – and this little fellow seemed to be quite alone. He looked strange somehow, but we couldn't work out why. With fierce intensity he evicted a baboon that had slipped down to the water's edge for a quick drink. The angry creature loped to the tree line; hurling screams of abuse over his shoulder at the cross little elephant who stood with legs spread-eagled and returned the profanities.

Satisfied he had won, he wheeled about abruptly and rushed back into the water with jerky movements. Sharp, short sucks of water blasted into his questing mouth, but more liquid seemed to slosh down his chest than went down his throat. Eventually, still with mouth agape, he threw himself down for a wallow. All the while he made staccato, blaring toots at regular intervals. It was evident that something was terribly wrong. He poked at his tiny tusks with his trunk, coiling the fingered tip into his ear cavities and mouth. He rolled, stood up, and rolled again. He charged out of the water in pursuit of imaginary beings, before screeching to a halt for a still second, and then the whole sequence was repeated. The poignant, abnormal pattern of sounds continued. We estimated his age at around nine, which was too young to have left the breeding herd.

I opened the car door to observe the youngster better. His eyes caught the movement, which precipitated an extraordinary attempt to get to us. We have no doubt that his intention was to destroy Jer and me. With all the strength of his small frame he tried to charge through the deep water that separated us. His coming created a wave. He was awesome in his fury. I turned cold with shock at the ferocity of his rage. The atmosphere had changed from one of sleepy indolence to one that was highly charged and volatile. I shrank from the wrath that was almost palpable, yet my heart ached for his suffering. The charge was doomed to failure because his mouth was wide open with the effort to roll an even louder series of blasts. He floundered in a choking mess of irate, distressed little elephant.

Tears for him filled my eyes and I longed to see my own children. His fear and loneliness triggered a memory of my six-year-old daughter's face when we were reunited after she had become lost in a department store. Lou's little face had crumpled with relief and the freedom to cry when I folded her into my arms. It appeared that this abandoned calf had no mother to offer him comfort.

As suddenly as he had seen us, he appeared to forget we were there. He stumbled out of the water, making no attempt to follow the shore to our position. Still bleating, and flailing his trunk in completely uncoordinated movements, he backed up and charged at invisible enemies.

'I think he's either brain damaged or retarded. He could only be eight or nine,' I said. 'Far too young to be pushed out of the herd. It would seem that perhaps they won't tolerate abnormality.'

Jer shook his head. 'I don't know. What about a head injury, or inflammation – possibly a tumour?'

'Hmm. Possible, I suppose. But do elephants reject sick youngsters? Mind you, if he behaves like this to his own kind then the herd probably had no option.'

We stayed with him until he rushed into the forest and we

could no longer hear his mindless blaring. The problem seemed to lodge in his tusks. He constantly touched and worried one in particular. However, we had observed Horace enraged by the pain of an abscess, and while he had been in pain, and enraged, he didn't display the distinctly uncoordinated movements, or regular toneless sounds of the youngster we named Tom Thumb.

A few days later we received a report from a game scout that a very young male elephant had been seen following the Gang of Eleven bulls, but always just out of their sight. He described him as 'One strange little guy – lonely and mean. He was pissed off. You know, he had a go at the Land Rover. I had to scram.'

We caught up with Tom Thumb soon after during a sandwich stop in our favourite glade within a stand of mighty teak trees. In game country thick with vegetation, we took our picnics inside Bluey. However, despite Jer's rude comments about me denting the bonnet, I sometimes sat on it while I ate lunch. Such was the case this day. Everything was hushed for the midday siesta. Even the tiny bees and mopane flies that sought the moisture of tender orifices were otherwise occupied. An occasional falling leaf was the only movement, which made the violent arrival of Tom Thumb all the more shocking.

I almost fell to the ground in my rush to reach the relative safety of the cabin. Jer had the engine started and we were moving within seconds, but Tom Thumb had connected with the rear bumper guard before our getaway was complete. Even such a small elephant gave us a frightening, lusty shove.

I was on my knees peering at him through the rear window. All I could see was his forehead and a straining back desperately trying to keep up with us. We 'gapped it' and the thwarted calf followed, screaming his rage and frustration.

This final encounter with Tom Thumb was the only time I felt fear based on a malevolence of spirit from any of the gentle giants. However, once again, our shock soon changed to sadness for his plight. We asked the rangers to watch out for him and report any encounters, but we heard of only one, and this was no more happy or productive than ours. Indeed, such was the likelihood of him threatening someone's life that it was decided Tom Thumb might have to be shot. We almost hoped this would happen, to ease the obvious mental and physical suffering of the sad little elephant.

There was never another sighting recorded of an elephant fitting his description. Perhaps he died of his disorder. I prefer to think he recovered and returned to his family to receive their protection until he was old enough to leave and join the ranks of contented young bulls. Maybe he even grew into a powerful and strong bull like the mighty male we named King.

CHAPTER 11

King of the elephants

King entered our lives on Bush Pig Road early in winter. The narrow sand track was covered in steaming piles of elephant dung and scattered broken twigs. Jer cut the engine and silence fell. The strong smell of droppings and the heavier odour of large game swamped the cabin; even overwhelming the scent of plum-laced smoke belching from Jer's briar pipe. Fed by the recent unseasonal rains, the surrounding bush grew thick, green and impenetrable.

We listened for a sound. The signs indicated the herd must be close. I smelled the heavy musk odour of elephant seconds before a deep rumble fractured the silence. Jer touched my shoulder and pointed behind. His gaze was fixed on the rear-vision mirror. Kathy and I twisted around to look.

A large grey block of bodies filled the road to the rear. The elephants had appeared en masse. There were several small calves with them. It wasn't a comfortable situation. Encountering a breeding herd on a narrow track bordered by thick scrub pumped the adrenalin as few things did. We needed to remain alert to the mood of the protective cows. I was glad we were in front of the herd, ready to make a quick getaway if there were an aggressive reaction from any of the elephants. For it was certain that we would never be able to breach the dense thicket crowding both sides of the road. This was quite different from encounters with the elephants on open savannah. I reached forward to pick up my camera from the dashboard – and froze.

Four bulls were standing quietly around the bonnet. Their trunks were raised above green-stained tusks to test our scent. Now we were completely surrounded by elephants. Starting from my toes, a surge of fear pulsed up into my throat – *ka-thump, ka-thump*. The beats seemed loud enough to be heard by Jer and Kathy, although I thought they were probably deafened by the sound of their own pounding hearts. Despite the inward quaking, I sat absolutely still. My companions were equally rigid. The young bulls loomed large over us.

Weaving trunks explored the substance of Bluey. One of them was delicately fingering every inch of the aerial with its prehensile tip. *It is. Yes, it is.* 'It's Stan,' I whispered with relief. 'And there's Laurel.' My heart rate started to slow.

Stan wore his usual woebegone expression. The Gang of Eleven was here and they knew us well. Holding the aerial in his prim little mouth that nestled between fat cheeks, Stan pulled the steel sliver back and down – then let it go. He surprised himself, and me, with the rebound that flicked inside the window to sting my cheek before the aerial sprang away to ping hard against his nose. He found this so amusing he did it again, and again, until I was forced to lean slowly in from the window to avoid being injured.

These elephants knew us, but they were unpredictable wild animals and we had unintentionally placed ourselves in a vulnerable position. We were just as worried about having broken our fundamental rule of not creating a compromising position for the elephants by threatening them with our presence unexpectedly at such close quarters. Under the circumstances the best we could do was sit tight until an opportune moment arrived to leave.

Jeremy never took his eyes off the mirror reflecting the family group behind us. I tried unsuccessfully to subdue thoughts of Horace. We were in a trap of our own making, with thick woodlands to either side of us and elephants ahead and behind. The breeding herd was moving closer. The cows on the track were keeping vocal contact with the rest of the family browsing unsighted in the adjacent bush. Skew Tusk was nearby. She watched us with intense concentration as she drew her infant close to her body with firm tugs from her trunk. I hoped Bette Midler was elsewhere.

Stan, Laurel, Popov and Renoir continued to wave their trunks about the vehicle; jostling and pushing for position so that our fragile hide rocked. Vast grumbles and 'huffing' noises mixed with the turgid stomach grinding of enormous quantities of poorly digested food. We could have reached out to stroke their massive legs. Then they were gone.

Kathy grabbed my arm with fingers of steel. 'Oh, dear God! Musth bull – coming this way,' she gasped.

The need for silence was shattered by the apparition bearing down upon us. He was a magnificent bull holding his handsome head high in the distinctive, grave posture of musth.

Oof, no! Is it Horace? Silently I apologised to the spirit of Africa. I had done it again!

It wasn't Horace. This huge bull had two perfect tusks aiming straight at us. But he *was* in musth. I could see clearly the typical signs of 'green penis syndrome'. His sheath was covered with murky green froth and dribbled a constant flow of urine between great legs that strode soundlessly ever closer. Swollen temporal glands streamed viscous fluid. His might reduced the status of the four males – who had now disappeared – to that of mere boys.

Kathy and I mewled nervous 'oohs' and 'ahs', in a strange mixture of fear at our defenceless position and pleasure at the bull's grandeur. He was a magnificent animal whose demeanour demanded awe and admiration. I thought that if I were an elephant cow I would find him irresistible.

A stench wafted before him, alerting agitated females to his highly desirable state. It was elephant world and our presence was disrupting the natural order of elephant interactions. The situation had the makings of a classic tragedy. We could cause the death of an innocent wild creature.

Long a reformed smoker, I suddenly needed nicotine so badly that I grabbed the pipe from Jer's mouth and took a deep drag. Before my throat and lungs had stopped burning, Kathy – an occasional smoker – had taken the pipe and was inhaling deeply. In this manner we passed the evil thing around. Unlike the first panicked snatches, we now moved our hands very slowly across our bodies. I hoped that any self-respecting elephant would surely give our stinking, hazy cabin a wide berth.

I should have known better. The breeding herd still blocked the road behind, although now they stood as still as the trees of the forest. The bush was too thick for us to penetrate. There was nowhere to go. The musth bull stopped three metres to the front. I was forced to bend down low to look up into his face. Every part of him spoke of pride and power. I shook with excitement and dread while praying to a greater power. *Ka-thunk-ka-thunk-ka-thunk*! I thought, *'It isn't Horace. I'm with friends inside the vehicle. We stand a chance.'*

His trunk began to curl into his chest. He was preparing to charge. I think we all had a similar thought: God helps those who help themselves.

'Enough, guys! We have to distract him *now!*' Kathy blurted out in a strangled voice. She crushed me against the door, reached over and began to beat the side of the vehicle. Charged by her electric energy, and startled at the change from silence and stillness to frenzied action, I joined Kathy in pounding the metal to add to the commotion. Jeremy was banging his torch against his side of the vehicle. He removed his hat, leaned out of the window and threw it towards the bull, who responded by lifting his face higher. Then he dropped it down and forward; his bunched, rippling shoulders adding impetus to tusks that were thrusting straight towards the grille.

With that we heard the sound of salvation. A vehicle was coming towards us. The bull paused, distracted by the noise to his rear. Startled, he stopped, raised his head and wheeled around to confront an open-sided Land Rover overflowing with shouting Italian tourists. I was astonished that I could hear their voices above the engine. Their vehicle was closing fast. Normally we would have been appalled at such an invasion, but this time they seemed like angels from Heaven.

Diverted from his plan of action the great bull lifted and swayed his right front foot with indecision as he inspected our noisy saviours. The bush around us exploded as the breeding herd took flight, away from the strident sounds of human beings and the throbbing motor. Dust choked the air. With a wild scream the bull lifted his trunk high and whirled away, angrily breaking branches as he ploughed into the bush.

Gasping ragged breaths of dust-filled air, we watched the furious guide rise from the wheel of the vehicle to face his charges with a tirade of words and gestures that would have shamed Mike Tyson. Shocked into silence, the tourists shrank lower and lower into their seats. Eventually the guide finished, turned, doffed his wide-brimmed hat in our direction, then hunkered down hard into his seat. He revved the engine, reversed and accelerated away with a grinding crash of gears. *This* game drive was definitely over.

Clients on African safaris are required to follow a strict code of conduct that is explained before each game drive. The guide usually demonstrates a series of hand signals that indicate when they should be silent. His vehicle is like a ship, and he is the captain. These rules also protect the game from undue stress. One noisy client can ruin for everyone the special pleasure of close observations of wildlife. In this case, seven disorderly Italian tourists had breached every rule in the book. Nevertheless, they had probably saved us and the elephant from tragedy. That night, their guide (who operated overland safaris) visited us in camp. With a grin and a wicked wink, he said: 'Saw you passing the pipe. Must be good *juju*, eh?'

'But it was tobacco!' I protested.

No one believed us. It's a strange truth that inklings of weaknesses in those who may have been perceived as idealistic idiots, humanises them for their critics. So I let it be, for what use denial when they wanted it to be marijuana. It pained me, but my silence in the face of their jokes earned Jeremy – who they saw as doubly dubious because he doesn't drink alcohol – and me a place among them. We became both less and more than 'those crazy elephant research guys'.

The next day we gave the bull a number – E180. As usual, we contravened the rules of science by giving him a human name as well. We named him 'King'. Everything about this proud male animal was regal. His ears and tusks were clear of imperfections. His conformation was strong and clean. On the rare occasions we saw him – after his three-month musth period – he always walked with majesty. At a later time, when we managed to take clear photographs, we were able to formalise his identity on our ear charts, though he was instantly recognisable as King.

Thereafter, whenever we encountered a gathering of bulls I looked for King. He was older than most of the home-range males and maintained an independent state. Except when a cow was in oestrous, he was rarely sighted – though he was always remembered, as each encounter with him was fraught with drama.

We renewed our acquaintance with King a few weeks later at the end of a long day of marking transects through the bush with Kathy and a volunteer. Establishing transects was tedious work. Kathy recorded each species of grass, plant and tree along a hundred-metre line over a range of different ecological zones frequented by elephants. She instructed. I wrote – *Combretums terminalia mopane ad nauseum*. Every few weeks the lines were checked to plot the habitat changes made by animals – particularly by elephants. In this way, a pattern was charted to establish long-term damage in an area considered by many to be over-populated with the largest of pachyderms. The work was not only precise and arduous, it was dangerous – in particular when we walked in heavy scrubland habituated not only by elephants but by buffalo and lions.

The transects were laid down on the privately owned concession bordering Hwange National Park. This meant that Jeremy could carry a large .375 calibre rifle, which was not an option in the national park except by the warden, professional guides, and the anti-poaching brigade or authorised personnel such as veterinarians. We all hoped it wouldn't need to be fired or, if so, only with a warning shot. I knew the responsibility of protecting us must have weighed as heavily upon Jer as the large gun, but he never spoke of it. I was concerned about the strain he must feel carrying the weapon, constantly alert to every small sound while he stood guard. Kathy and I were too busy to think much about the danger. Well . . . not *too* much.

The volunteer who had insisted on coming along became extremely nervous quite early in the morning. Rachel's startled screeches and jumps at every noise were driving us all mad. It was obvious she had expected more glamorous activity than holding one end of a string while Kathy and I stretched it along the ground and charted species of flora in a notebook. It was the string I had laboriously measured in the face of Dingi's amusement.

Eventually, the volunteer sidled up beside me and hissed urgently, 'I've got my period. I think lions will smell me.'

Kathy heard the comment. Her eyes opened wide with astonishment. 'For God's sake, Rachel, that's ridiculous!'

Rachel's pallid face quivered towards tears. I could smell the sweat of fear. She had moved beyond reason. I had been there myself and knew the terror would continue to mount until she lost her dignity. I didn't want that. 'We'll have to pull out,' I muttered.

Kathy wasn't having a bar of it. 'Bugger that,' she cursed. 'We're going to finish this transect. Go back and sit in Bluey,' she ordered Rachel, studiously refusing to look at the whining girl.

It was the first time I had seen her explode. Later I discovered that Rachel had made a play for Neil while Kathy was away at a conference. Even the serene Kathy had her limits.

Jer coughed and cleared his throat, but otherwise remained silent. The twitch in his left eyebrow said it all as he drew deeply on his pipe and stared into the distance. He insisted that the smoke kept the mopane flies away.

I was irritable and turned my ire on him. 'It's all right for you. You're a bloody man. What would *you* know?'

Kathy blinked in surprise at my snarling rebuke. 'Ja, well, that's true enough.' She scratched the top off a sting so that it bled. 'There, I'm bleeding, too. Those lions won't know who to munch first.'

She smiled dangerously. I felt very unsettled by her sudden explosion. The air crackled with tension. Jer's mouth had joined his eyebrow in barely controlled twitches. I hated him in that moment, but I knew I was projecting my irritation where it would do no real harm.

'Come on, Rachel,' I muttered as I took her arm and led her back to the vehicle for what I knew would be a long, hot wait, in dubious safety.

'What will I do if something comes?' she whimpered as I turned to go back to the transect.

'Hit the bloody horn!' I called over my shoulder.

A while later, Kathy looked down at me where I was stretching the string across stubbly grass with one hand and smacking flies with the other. 'Damn, I've just beaten a thorn in deeper,' I groaned.

Kathy wasn't interested in my thorn. She had just one thing on her mind. Wrinkling her nose with glee she chortled, 'What do you think Rachel will do if the ellys come?' This was the only real possibility, and potentially more dangerous than rampant lions pursuing women who had their periods.

'They'll hear the shrieks at Main Camp,' I shrugged, tired of worrying about the extreme sensibilities of the girl who had driven us mad with requests to come until we gave in. I was tired, anyway. We had been ploughing through thorns and thickets for days now.

I forgot her in my efforts to fend off the swarms of tiny sting-less bees invading my eyes and nostrils in search of moisture. I had learned early to wear pale-coloured shirts rather than darker hues, especially the particular shade of dark blue that attracted the insects to us like vultures to carrion. Even so, the annoying pests coated our faces. After a while I gave up swatting them away and accepted that I would inevitably swallow a few hapless individuals. 'An injection of protein,' Jer joked.

We were back in rhythm and working fast. Establishing transects was a job that had to be done. Once in a while, an unseen beast crashed away from our presence. Then we all ceased work to assume the posture of statues. The silence following the panicked retreat was worse. I asked myself what creature had been nearby and where was it now, before returning to work. We heard a heavy movement. We had flushed out an old buffalo that had one blind eye; the other wept constantly. His evil reputation had made him a legend in the area. The huge black bull took a one-eyed teary look at us, then beat a bush-smashing retreat. It was our lucky day. There is only one creature more fearful than a lone old buffalo bull – a *wounded* lone old buffalo bull. The locals called these males 'old *dagga* boys' in reference to the coat of caked mud that clings to their shaggy coats after extended sessions of wallowing.

Because of his injury, the real chance that he might return, and the fears of our volunteer who waited fretfully in the vehicle, we called it a day. We decided instead to try to locate the herd and spend a few hours in their understanding company; for they were indeed very tolerant of us.

'What now?' groaned Jer, when we arrived at the road. Music was throbbing from behind the fogged-up windows of the vehicle. Rachel was grinning inanely, a joint sagging between her lips. Rod Stewart was inviting her to come sailing which could have been a good idea, considering she was on the verge of asphyxiation.

'Out!' Jer shouted.

Now we had the man's attention. Silly women who complained all the time were one thing; polluting his beloved Bluey was another thing altogether. Rachel was giggling as he pulled her out. He looked around and yelled, 'Come and get her!' to any waiting lions. He then muttered an aside to us: 'Hop in. We'll drive out of sight.'

We did, but she was so stoned she just wandered along the track after us. 'He-he-he-he-he,' she crooned. 'I am sailing. I am *sa-a-a-aailing*.'

'Oh, for Christ's sake,' Jer growled. He reversed, jumped out and pushed her into the back beside me.

'I don't want her,' I laughed.

And then we all joined in: 'We are *sa-a-a-aailing*. We are SA-A-A-AAAAIILING, cross the *vleiiii*, cross the *vlei*.'

Everything was fine. We headed for the ellys, shouting idiotic words to favourite songs. We had sighted them browsing their way towards a favourite waterhole on our way to the targeted transect in the morning. That's where we were going. Like the rest of us, elephants are creatures of habit. We were almost certain we would find them at Mpofu. We did.

They were wallowing happily along the muddy edges of the pool. Some swam, while others took dust baths nearby. Safe on our knoll, we got out of the stuffy vehicle and watched quietly. Kathy was perched on top of the hood. Jer and I were standing beside the driver's door and Rachel was lurking, still giggling quietly, behind the open tray. She really was a very fearful person and even in her stoned state this must have seemed the safest place she could be without actually being inside the HiLux.

The evening light settled gently over the scene. It was bliss. We drank cans of soft drink and didn't care that they were warm. The liquid washed down delicious, locally dried taro chips. What could be better than sundowners and munchies while watching a glorious spectacle of romping, gloriously undignified elephants framed against a backdrop of fragrant blossoming trees? *Nothing at all*.

Each tiny spray of flowers merged into the next, forming a beautiful halo of swaying pink, gently tossed on a cooling breeze. Beneath them three delicate, dappled bushbuck moved quietly in the late afternoon shadows. The sky was beginning to blush into sunset. My heart sang a song of Africa. No one – even Rachel – spoke. What was there to say when nature was conversing?

Instinct (or a friendly nudge from a higher source) becomes a welcome friend in the wild. I responded to a feeling and looked behind us. It was King – coming fast and soundlessly. He was straight on course towards the hapless Rachel. She was looking at the glorious spectacle ahead with a silly grin of pleasure – just like the rest of us. The huge bull was moments from making contact.

Jabbing behind us, I shouted: 'It's King!'

I ran to Rachel, pushed her into the back of the car and scrambled on to the tray as Jer started the engine. Kathy was clinging to the top. The vehicle jumped forward just before King reached us. We bucketed down the slope straight towards the startled herd, hurling mud clods away from wheels that were sliding uncontrollably into the bog. King was still coming fast. *'Ka-thunk-ka thunk'* said my heart. Rachel was squealing.

The engine sound changed as the tyres gripped; just in time to surge out of the way of a mass of huge bodies that were throwing off their own flow of sludge and ire. Rachel and I clung to the struts of the open hatch in real danger of being flung out into King's path. He was so close that our vision was filled with the underside of his solid body and his thrusting tree-trunk legs. I didn't breathe again until Jer had driven the vehicle to a safe distance.

King stopped dead, shook his head, slapped his ears and trumpeted mightily. Within seconds he was cloaked again in dignity. As if nothing had happened, he turned towards the cows, lifted his face high and began a measured stroll in their direction. His grave approach invited the pattern of flirty, flighty behaviour so often observed when a handsome dominant male was in attendance.

Rachel packed her bags and left the next day. *Woohoo!*

* * *

The close encounter with King paled into insignificance a week later. The certainty of safety in our little home was threatened by both an unknown presence and the greatest of predators.

Once again the focus was food. Sausages sizzled on the grid we had formed out of thick fencing wire. This rested on top of a rusty forty-four-gallon drum salvaged from an old campsite. Holes drilled in the sides allowed heat to escape for warmth, giving us a multi-purpose tool. The spicy, delicious smell of Boerwurst sausages set my gastric juices flowing as I chopped fleshy red tomatoes on a table which 'Stevie Wonder' had assembled out of a few rusty nails and relatively straight pieces of raw timber.

I placed the rich red fruit into a saucepan with a bunch of native spinach purchased from the *shamba* (garden) of a local villager. While the selection of fresh vegetables was limited, the full flavour of organically grown produce convinced me that the wide variety of perfect-looking specimens found in modern supermarkets lose in taste and goodness what they gain in ascetically pleasing forms from overdoses of pesticides. We were thriving on this unadulterated tucker.

We had no refrigeration, so fresh meat was eaten only after a journey to the butcher shop in Dete; the closest village to our camp. The name 'Dete' translates as 'passage', which provoked certain individuals to call it 'the arsehole of the world'! I hadn't experienced a summer on the low *veldt* but was assured by friends who had endured the mindless heat, dust storms, insects and the diseases they carried, that Dete lived up to that aphorism. In winter it appeared as a sleepy, pleasant collection of mud huts where the most basic of supplies could be purchased. Very occasionally we made a full-day trek to the colliery town of Hwange on a major shopping expedition.

Meat was kept for a couple of days inside a polyurethane icebox buried in the ground. I loved rare beef, even raw (thanks to my Danish grandfather, who taught me to enjoy his recipe of uncooked minced fillet of beef mixed with egg yolk, olive oil and fresh herbs), but this meat needed to be cooked well to destroy parasites and human and insect dirt.

The carcasses hung in an open-air butcher shop and were hacked into irregular portions (sometimes peppered dangerously with tiny bone chips) on a bloody block by a machete-wielding butcher of immense stature who was, appropriately, named Samson. His blue and white striped apron was stiff with dried blood; his sandals were made out of rubber tyres. Samson would slap the gobs of meat into newspaper and present the parcel along with a paper bag full of fresh, orange-yoked eggs gathered that day from his hens. I could be sure that half of them would be double yolkers.

'The master must have much food, Madam. One who walks with elephants eats like elephants,' he would bellow, gleefully slapping his own elephant-sized thighs with his bloodied hands. I have never laughed as I did when I was with my African friends.

As I turned the sausages, I giggled just thinking about Samson. Above my head the purring Primus lantern hung from a low branch, casting a circle of golden light around us. We settled into our folding chairs and munched on an unrivalled feast – if we excluded the offerings of Shaddy, of course. Our dinner music was a haunting medley of hyaena whoops, jackal wails, and the intermittent shrieks and hoots of nightjars and owls.

Occasionally, we played a favourite tape on our tiny recorder. But batteries were precious and best saved for the BBC's *News of the World*, particularly the weekly round-up on Sunday nights.

This night, the unseen world was totally silent, which seemed strange, as it was never truly silent. As usual, Jer doused the lantern after the dishes were cleared. This was our time to discuss the events of the day and plan the next day's activities. Even our quiet conversation sounded obscenely loud in the unnatural hush. The darkness seeped over me like a shroud. The friendly unseen became the fearful unknown, and I kept looking over my shoulder. We drew closer to the drum and each other, but the warm coals couldn't ward off the chill we both felt.

Suddenly, we sensed that we were in the presence of evil. Together we reacted, turning our heads in the same direction to peer into the gloom. We froze and waited. I thought of Golden and his visitation. My cold skin prickled into goose-bumps. I felt sure that whatever was watching us wasn't an animal known to us. We could do nothing except cling to our hope that evil might be countered by good. There was nowhere to hide from the dense presence.

We sat motionless – waiting. I smelled a putrid odour. Somewhere in the silence, a low, grotesque rattle began to waver. It rolled on without pause, until I knew I would have to scream to cover the sound. And then the grumble began to lift thinly, like a violin bow moving harshly across the strings towards the highest pitch. Slowly it ascended to a thin screech of shocking intensity that filled my head with pain. It was a dreadful, grotesque noise. I have never heard its like since. I silently began to recite 'The Lord's Prayer' and grabbed Jer's hand. At that moment it was gone. I sucked in a deep breath as perspiration broke through my skin.

'That was gross,' I croaked. 'It certainly wasn't a hyaena. Do you think it was a leopard?' Or had it been Golden's mother-in-law? *Was she angry with me, too?*

174

There was no response from Jeremy, who looked pale and drawn, other than a perplexed shrug. Some things were better left unsaid. He took the flashlight and circled the camp perimeter, aiming the light beam wide and far, but he saw nothing. Then the air was rent with the sound of gunfire.

Jer shouted urgently, 'Get inside the hut. Now!'

I was on the floor in seconds. Jer barricaded the door with a tin trunk, then joined me.

'Is it poachers? Oh, dear God, don't let it be the rhinos.' Rob had seen Rose and her baby near Konondo in the afternoon. The few remaining white rhinos in Hwange were the last of their kind to roam free in Zimbabwe.

'There's nothing we can do. Whatever they're after is already dead. We will be too if the poachers see us,' he replied.

He was right, of course. We had no weapons with which to defend ourselves or the poor creatures under fire. Once again the air was heavy with silence. Suddenly a twig snapped outside. Jer drew me close and put his finger to his lips. Then we heard two more shots further away. Somewhere nearby, a baboon barked. The animals were once again going about their nocturnal business. We were safe. However, when sleep came it gave me little rest. I was besieged by nightmares as disturbing as the previous night's ghastly visitor.

We were on the road before dawn, heading for park headquarters to alert the warden to poacher activity. Close to camp we met a truckful of armed men coming the other way. It seemed they already knew. Dickson leaned out to tell us that a safari operator had radioed a distress call. It was decided the sound of the shots was located between our camps.

An hour or so later they found Rose. Her face and horn had been cut off. Her three-month-old daughter was keening beside her. The baby was sedated and transported straight to the Chipangali Wildlife Centre near Bulawayo, where she would be raised by a kind human. It was a dreadful irony. The poachers got away. They usually did.

We stayed at Main Camp until Dickson returned. I told him of the strange happenings before the shooting. His eyes clouded and he muttered evasively about predatory leopards, or lions. But I wasn't going to let it go. This time I was determined to broach forbidden territory. I needed an answer so that I could sleep at night.

'Do you think it might have been *juju*, the spirits of the wild, warning us of what was to come?' I persevered.

Dickson looked anxious and refused to answer. I backed off. The apprehension on his face mirrored the expression I had seen when Golden saw a terrible thing.

The unknown is always more frightening than real encounters with dangerous animals, when the threat has a physical form, where the protagonists can assess each other's potential for harm. Even so, I never found it easy when I locked eyes with a lion with attitude. Pemba, who lived with Marius, the game farmer who lent us his tent, wasn't an average lion. He was part of the family and had his own two-seater lounge chair in the living room of Marius's homestead. I always looked forward to our visits to the farm to take high tea with the family. Wilmarie was a fabulous cook and loved to mother us by preparing sumptuous spreads of traditional Afrikaaner cakes and rich pastries.

Shortly after Rose was killed, I asked the couple if they thought the spirit of the wild had paid us a harmless – if terrifying – visit. I really wanted them to laughingly agree.

Instead, Marius, Wilmarie and Jer exchanged furtive glances before Marius replied: 'Ach, man, I think it was a hyaena. You know, those guys make some terrible noises.'

'No, Marius,' I urged. 'This was the worst sound I have *ever* heard.'

He just looked at me, his brow creased. Wilmarie placed another cake on my already heaped plate and patted my shoulder, saying nothing.

Just then Pemba wandered in, breaking the tension. I could see that my companions were relieved. I wasn't. Instead, I felt like a chastened child. The great cat lay down on his threadbare throne. God help anyone who sat on his chair. The tea shivering in my cup was a dead giveaway that my thoughts had moved on. I thrilled to his presence, but I never got used to the company of the enormous lion that had the run of the place.

A wide verandah, scattered with settings of comfortable cane furniture and fat tapestry cushions, wrapped around the gracious ranch house, which was surrounded by a hectare of beautiful gardens. Something was always flowering there. A large concrete pond cooled the eye and slaked Pemba's thirst. He spent his nights in a large compound at the rear, but otherwise he roamed freely.

An elderly lioness with a disabled leg lived permanently in the compound. Marius felt responsible for her welfare after one of his hunting clients made a mess of the kill. When Marius closed to finish her off, he heard sounds coming from a bush nearby. To his horror he found two tiny, shivering cubs. He had chosen this female to hunt without observing her swollen teats.

Marius still cringed when he told us how it was his mistake.

He immediately wanted to make amends. He and his men loaded the unconscious female and her offspring into the tray to take home. Somehow, the mother survived with her milk flow intact. She fed the cubs throughout her convalescence, but there was only enough milk for the strongest. The female died. The male, Pemba, survived.

He was a happy lion. His mother was less fortunate. Her wild instincts had never dulled. She was fearsome in her rage whenever anyone approached the compound. The imprisonment of the lionesss was unfortunate, but her disability would have ensured her a slow death if she were returned to the wild. Her son couldn't be released because he was habituated to a life with humans, and had never learned to hunt.

Marius loved to tell the story of the time an overbearing government official came from the city in an attempt to elicit a bribe. Marius invited the man inside and offered him Pemba's chair. 'Ach, man, sit. You must have a beer,' he said.

The man didn't know about their pet. When he was settled into the somewhat smelly seat, Marius left the room to find his lion. As it happened, Pemba was already padding along the verandah on a mission to see who had come to visit. Marius crouched down out of sight of the visitor and encouraged Pemba to enter the room. Then he positioned himself outside the window to watch the drama unfold. The official's face turned ashen, then broke out in a sweat, when the lion sauntered into the room.

Roaring with laughter, Marius said: 'That guy lost it. And I mean he lost it: *everything*! It was *lekker*. I've never seen anything so funny.'

'*I* didn't think it was *lekker*,' Wilmarie protested. 'I had to clean up the doodies!'

I was sitting in the chair beside Pemba, trying to control my jiggling cup. I felt sympathy for the man when I dared to look at the enormous cat. His massive woolly head lolled over the edge of the settee. Pemba was watching me in the way that lions do. It is never a comfortable feeling.

'Man, when this big guy saw someone was sitting in his chair, he got mad. He snarled and charged. That's when the *munt* dropped his bundle. Ay-ay-ay-ay-ay! He was making squeaking sounds like a mouse.' Marius slapped his thigh between hoots of glee. 'This lion just jumped up and sat on the guy as if no one was there.' That official never bothered them again.

Marius and Wilmarie were incredibly supportive of us. They made our lives much easier with gifts of basic goods and food parcels. They had been the first guests at Farm 41 when they came to lend us a tent to use during the times when the elephants' movements took us far afield.

CHAPTER 12

The song of my son

The tent served as a shelter for my son Lachlan when he came from Australia to visit us. He was about to make his rite of passage from boy to man. I was married at seventeen, gave birth to my daughter Mary-Louise at nineteen and to Lachy at twenty-one, soon after the death of my father. It would be an early celebration, but I wanted to honour his coming of age with a happiness that had been missing at my own. I was eager for him to meet the elephants and to join us in a canoeing trip on the Zambezi. Also, I just needed to see him.

Within days of his arrival, Lachy won the hearts of our friends with his charm and with his music. Des or Jen, and guides who were off-duty, began to find excuses to visit our camp in the evenings for singalongs around the fire accompanied by Lachy's guitar, or to invite him to visit them when they were unable to get away from their clients.

Jer and I would leave at dawn, when Lachy was still sleeping, and return to find him gone. By the time we left for Lake Kariba I almost needed to make an appointment to see him. I was content that he was happy and occupied while we confronted some difficult times with the elephants. On the other hand, when we boarded the light aircraft we were all ready for a holiday together, although we had no idea of the drama to come.

'Howzit? My name is Garth. Would you please sign this form to indemnify the company in case of accidents?' Garth said as he handed an official-looking document to each of us. Jer, Lachy and I glanced at each other with wry grins.

My son joked: 'Bring on the man-eaters.' Our fellow travellers joined in nervously with dubious humour.

Thus began a canoeing trip that would provide extraordinarily beautiful scenery, great fun – and total terror. We signed the forms and listened to our guide describe the mechanics of paddling canoes. We took careful note when he spoke of the ways and dangers of hippopotami and crocodiles. He told us to beat our paddles against the sides of our craft before passing pods of hippos, to alert them to our presence. We learned that if one of the animals should capsize us, or if we rolled our canoe, then we must float without making any movement until we were rescued.

'There are plenty of big, hungry crocs,' cracked Garth. 'So, you must pretend you are a log.'

Oh, great! This is wonderful. I bring my beloved son to Africa for a break from his studies, only to expose him to death by any number of means.

'How often do people come to grief?' quavered Margaret, an attractive, fit-looking New Zealander.

All eyes fixed on Garth – thankful that someone had asked the question that had been on all of our minds. *Memories of Savuti and Ira.*

'I haven't lost anyone yet,' he chuckled. 'And this is my sixth season as a professional guide. You know, this is going to be one of the best few days of your lives. *Mushi* stuff. Trust me.'

Somewhat shakily, I joined in the laughter. I wasn't so sure that '*mushi*' would have been my choice of word to describe what I was now thinking might have been a bad choice for time out from the elephants.

Burdened with the responsibility of eight green, though intrepid, tourists, Garth and his trainee guide encouraged us to clamber into five canoes heavily laden with supplies. The Zambezi River stretched wide from our sandy shore to the reeds on the Zambian side. Before us loomed five days of paddling this great water-course armed with one rifle, the bare essentials of living, and group longings for adventure and freedom.

However, for now, I was absorbed in mastering the art of balancing in the fragile craft assigned to Jer and me. While I had little experience of paddling, Jeremy had been a champion rower in his school days. But sculling in an eight-berth shell with oars is quite different from bilateral strokes with paddles in a two-seater canoe with a partner who is a lightweight, both physically and in experience. His powerful slices into the black flow of water were far too strong for me to match. In fact, they were altogether too hectic for our small craft. We began to skew in wobbly circles, threatening to overturn at each stroke.

We continued to struggle as the rest of our 'fleet' drew away in what appeared to be an orderly, closely bunched group that hugged the steep embankment of the river. Canting dangerously, our bucking canoe entered the main current mid-stream in the 150-metre-wide flow. Jer threw his strong body into an attack on the surface with single-minded determination, as if to force the flimsy craft to obey his will. Instead, the canoe came perilously close to capsizing with each of his lunging movements. I was frantic that we would lose our precious film cameras and equipment. Struggling to remain calm, I asked him to take it more gently.

Then I caught sight of a huge saurian form swimming past my paddle. A malevolent eye watched me from a head that was as long as my leg. I forgot about the cameras. We were potential crocodile food and this was a monster. It was enough. I lost my temper. 'Bugger the show of strength. We're history if we don't take control.'

This was a mistake. My husband, his pride now hurt, renewed his efforts as if he could actually step on to the water, lift the canoe with me in it and walk to dry land. I was petrified.

'Ay, ay, ay, ay, ay! Stop paddling. Let her drift,' shouted Garth from just ahead.

And so we did, until our saviour crossed our bow and dragged us out of the current.

'Throw your right legs over the side of my boat,' he ordered, doing the same with his left leg over ours. His crew member was Lachy, who followed suit. With them paddling to the right and us to the left, our linked canoes made swift progress towards the main flotilla waiting quietly near the shore. I was mortified that we had perpetrated the first cock-up of the journey, though Jer wore an innocent expression. Apparently all of the canoes had been having teething problems of one kind or another. It was just that ours was such a public display of stupidity. Garth settled us all with some quiet words of encouragement.

'You know, guys; it's dead simple to paddle a canoe even if you've never rowed any boat. Let's unlearn some things and start again.'

Jer was looking down his Roman nose with a haughty expression, but he took the paddling more gently. Reluctantly, I entrusted him with the captaincy of our wee boat and the others gained confidence with some intensive tutoring. We got properly under way and soon realised that, except for sluggish by-waters, there was really little need for paddling. So long as we kept control of the steering, the canoes surged along with the current. We eventually became expert at braking where the stream gathered strength; even charting difficult channels between fallen trees close to the bank when there were birds to check out.

Renewed faith in an ability to remain safely afloat relaxed into a rhythmic flow, like the feeling of skiing when the going is good. Now I could lift my gaze away from the water, and delight in the extraordinary beauty of the Zambezi Valley. The river rolled fat and oily through lush floodplains studded with groves of wide-topped trees. I recognised acacia, teak, mahogany, ironwood and ebony trees. On the Zambian side the river flats ended at the escarpment of a towering mountain range that lifted brightly in the mid-morning light towards the soft blue sky. The montane forests constantly changed colour, from soft peach, through the spectrum, to deep purple. The mountains were like sentient beings expressing emotions.

Sometimes they appeared grim and sombre; most often they were swathed in a lilac, misty dreaming. I longed to go to their far-off place to explore their secrets.

Mist of a different kind signalled the presence of villages on the Zambian side. The border that separated the two countries was a thing of flux. It lay at the centre of the Zambezi, which had no certainties. When we paddled close to the Zambian bank, before we navigated a bend we were alerted to the presence of people by the smell and sight of smoke and the noisy chatter of busy voices. We weren't supposed to be hugging that bank, so we allowed the stream to sweep us past the curious eyes of adults and the reaching arms of running children. Several times, these 'sweet' kids lined up, turned their backs, dropped their shorts and expressed their attitude to us with a combined show of brown-eyes. Their hoots of laughter afterwards indicated it was done more for their own amusement than out of malice.

Many of these communities made a living out of poaching in Zimbabwe. Stinking racks were spread with mountains of drying meat disguised as swarms of flies. They stood as rank testimony to the illegal excursions by night across the Zambezi into Zimbabwe to hunt elephant and rhino for trophies and antelope for meat.

Late one evening, during our search for that night's camping site, we found a rough-hewn canoe hidden among the reeds in a small channel. Garth grounded his boat, jumped out holding an axe and slammed it angrily into the bottom of the poacher's get-away craft.

'Bastards,' he snarled. 'It won't be pretty if I ever get my hands on one of these guys.'

This time I agreed. These villagers weren't hungry. They

185

lived in a bountiful area of highly productive land. Maize crops and domestic stock thrived and water wasn't a problem. Their lot was quite different from that of the local people where we worked. However, I didn't allow myself to feel angry for long. I was on a holiday with my boy. I was determined to rest my mind, if not my body. Actually, my body needed a good workout after all the months of endless sitting about. New muscles rippled beneath skin that was already tanned a deep golden colour, giving the illusion of fitness. My face glowed with well-being. I was beginning to feel as healthy as I looked. When I proudly flexed my pectorals at Lachy, he exploded with laughter.

'Get out, Mum. Those tiny things are chicken's insteps,' he said, clenching his fists to expand indecently bulging boulders. 'Now, these are what I call muscles!'

Each evening we paddled into narrow side-waters where a land crew had already prepared camp. It was heaven – once we resolved a few irritations. On our first night the tents were arranged like good soldiers standing close together all in a row. Lachy shared the tent next to ours with an Irish playwright. Jer snores when he sleeps on his back. Usually I can control this when we sleep in the same bed by (sometimes not so gentle) suggestions that he roll on to his side. But this time the camp cots were set irrevocably apart inside the tent.

I whispered to Lachy: 'Find me a long stick so I can reach across and prod Jer when he snores.'

This was soon done, but nothing I did that night stopped Jer's heavy snores of exhaustion. He broke the sound barrier, once again attracting lions to check out the source of the intriguing din. I slept little, although the rest of the crew must have slept less. For when we arrived at our new camp the next night there were five tents standing close together – and one set fifty metres away.

The new arrangement brought relief to everyone else, but I wasn't prepared to face another sleepless night either. We folded the camp cots away and dragged our mattresses together on the floor. It was just as well we were used to isolation, as lions, elephants and buffalo all came to visit during the night. As usual, Jer slept, and snored, through it all. How I envied him his capacity to sleep when sleeping is the order of the night; and to be completely in the moment with the events of each day. In this way he mirrored our African friends. Perhaps they thought he was also an African with white skin in the way that Golden described me, for he was always treated as one of them within minutes of meeting. He helped pave the way for me – a woman doing the work of a man and probably considered highly suspicious by some.

In this way, Jer made my life much easier, but very often he wasn't with me, or able to help when my life was endangered. And this was the case soon afterwards. Our flotilla lingered too long, mid-stream in the Zambezi, revelling in a glorious sunset. Darkness drops like a heavy blanket at this latitude. It is suddenly there. Flocks of carmine bee eaters were winging their way into their nests on the banks of the river; hippos were honking to each other as they left the water to disperse for the night's feeding. Garth broke the magic spell. 'Let's gap it.' He pointed to the tiny entrance of a channel. 'It's getting dark. We must get into the stream now-now or we won't see our way to camp.'

I was sharing Garth's canoe that day; sitting high in the bow with my legs crossed. We led the fleet into the shallow stream which was only three metres wide between two-metre-high banks on either side. Holding a forefinger to his lips, Garth twisted around and whispered to those in the canoe that followed closely behind, 'Pass this down the line. We must be absolutely quiet – not a sound.'

Turning back to me, he mouthed softly, 'Pull in your paddle. I'm it.'

I knew we had stayed too long when I saw the concern etched into his thin face. But I wasn't sure what the immediate problem might be. The canoe moved quickly in response to Garth's urgent stroking. Claustrophobia closed in as we shot ahead. The fragile craft was lying very low between the tall banks. There was no one ahead of me.

Close, so close, a hippo bellowed. The canoe adjusted to Garth's startled response. My belly was filled with heavy-winged moths. There was a movement atop the bank. It was hard to see in the looming darkness. The shape of a huge creature was running hard along the edge. Moths beat their wings high into my throat. It was a hippo and it was panicking. The enormous creature ran ahead of us. Pounding feet drummed the earth.

Garth drove the paddle into the muddy bottom to stop the canoe. He held it there. The hippo turned and ran back. It stopped; then wheeled to run again; turn and run; wheel and return; over and over and over.

I had uncrossed my legs ready to jump out and run. They were hanging over the prow. The water was shallow. Suddenly I felt a great pressure on my legs; as if strong hands were physically pushing them up and into the canoe. I pulled my knees in close to my body just when the enormous animal jumped into the channel. *Moths' wings thrashing!*

The hippo hit the water right in front of me; grazing the bow in a desperate surge forward, across our path, and up the other side. The incredible rush of power and the immense weight of the creature impelled its massive body up the steep bank. The heat of its body, the shock waves of its passing, hit my face like a punch. *Moths in the bowels!*

We clung to the sides for our lives as the canoe tipped first one way, and then the other. A dank odour of muddy places remained when the hippo crashed away into the bush. My skin crawled. *Oof . . . have the moths hatched from my body?* I knew the hippo would have hit my legs and then attacked us to defend itself if I hadn't drawn them into the canoe.

Garth touched my shoulder. 'Sorry about that. Let's move on quickly.'

By now there was no light at all. Somehow, Garth navigated through the black cotton-wool darkness that was pierced occasionally by an unknown call or the heavy sound of movement. Ten terrifying minutes later there was a flickering orange glow that guided us into a small beach and a welcome fire. My men were out of their canoe before us.

Lachy's youthful face had turned to that of an angry man. He grabbed Garth around the throat. 'That's my mother who almost got killed!' he growled, holding his other clenched fist to Garth's face.

Garth pulled away. He strode to a small table by the fire and poured several shots of brandy; he kept one and handed the others to us. Jer clinked my glass with his and then drank the alcohol in one gulp. I was astonished. The tension eased with a communal hug that included the rest of the party. It turned into a wild night. The playwright acted out scenes from his works. Lachy's deckchair collapsed when he was mid-story and he stayed where he was amid the wreckage on the ground, continuing to talk as if nothing had happened. When I encouraged him to turn in, he levelled me with a heavy gaze and bellowed: 'Get me another beer, wench!'

My son had become a man. His statement reminded me of the male calf who had shown off for his family. I paid Lachy the due the elephant mother gave to her son and crept away to bed early. I was more shaken than I had shown to the others. They didn't know that some unseen force had been with me when the hippo rushed and that it had forced me to pull my legs close to my body just before the animal flung itself into the channel. I knew this as certainly as I had known the elephant at Savuti had been more than he seemed. I said a prayer in gratitude and wondered how many more times the spirit of Africa would come to my rescue. I was pushing my luck.

I might have been lucky, but Garth began a battle with malaria during the night. His face was yellow and his body racked with rigours when I covered him with my sleeping bag in the morning. He was raving beneath the layers of coverings, but nothing warmed him, as nothing would ease the heat when the cycle of cruel fever returned. The Zambezi Valley is renowned as a 'hot' malarial zone, but Garth had developed dangerous side effects from taking prophylactics over a number of years. He had only recently stopped taking the toxic drugs.

'My liver's stuffed. Christ, my head hurts,' he groaned. When I asked him what we should do, he moaned: 'Set me on fire!'

None of us knew what to do other than organise a speedy evacuation to Harare. We had prophylactics, but it would have been idiotic to use them to try to treat a man with liver complications caused by the drugs themselves. Yet, if it were cerebral malaria, he might be dead within twenty-four hours of the first symptoms appearing. Jer asked Garth's right-hand man to radio for help. The tents were dismantled in a rush and we were shuttled by road to the airstrip at Ruckomechi Camp, where a light aircraft arrived to take Garth to a hospital in Harare.

Pip and Henry had come to the strip to help when they heard the radio call. They were old friends who owned a rustic camp nearby, deep within the Mana Pools National Park. They had no guests and asked Jer and me if we would mind the camp and their Siamese cats while they took the flight to Harare. It was a golden opportunity for them to get away and a wonderful chance for us to luxuriate a little longer in paradise.

The cats wound around our legs, squeezing their exotic blue eyes closed with earnest imprecations as they called constantly for Pip and Henry, who treated them like their children. I attached leads to collars studded with tiny bells, and took them for a walk around the camp. Their voices sang constantly until they were locked safely away for the night in Pip and Henry's *rondavel*.

Jer was in the office tent attempting to get through on the radio to Harare to see how Garth was doing. The news was mixed. He had cerebral malaria; however, they had arrived in time to save his life. Henry said that Pip was at the hospital donating blood. Her group was the same as Garth's. The medical staff had drained the parasite-infested blood from his body and was replacing it with a healthier supply. It seemed he would make it. We relaxed, taking turns to bathe in a huge bathtub surrounded by a reed *boma* which opened on to the river. It was total indulgence to lie in the bubbles under the stars in a safe place, sipping chilled wine as I watched a pod of hippos make their way from the water to the night's grazing on

191

land. A friendly elephant, fondly named Bill, habitually came into camp. He stood quietly beside the candle-lit table while we ate and accompanied us to our small *rondavels* when we retired.

An urgent call woke us in the morning. 'Madala, come quickly. A terrible thing has happened in the night!' The cook was dancing about outside, wringing his hands. We hurried with him to Pip and Henry's *rondavel*, which was set further back from the main camp.

'Modem, you must stay here,' he pleaded as he opened the door. 'It is a bad thing.'

Touched, yet determined to see for myself, I followed the men into the silent room. Blood was smeared across the floor beneath toppled furniture. The trail led to a shattered window. A strong gust of air tinkled the bells on a collar hanging from a sharp sherd of glass. The cats were missing. One of the guides read the story from the spoor: larger pad marks intermingled with small paw prints upon the trail of blood in the room. Only the large spoor left through the opening and reappeared on the ground outside. There were marks showing that an object had been dragged beside the larger animal. A leopard had taken the cats by hurling its weight against the window to get to its prey. The domestic cats had no chance. The predator must have been watching them for some time to know that the usual human presence was missing. I shivered with dread at the intent and amazing daring of the leopard.

Our hearts thumped with a different kind of trepidation when we met Pip and Henry on their return. They accepted the sad news with grace, but we all felt in some way responsible for their loss.

* * *

We returned to camp and to personal tragedy. It was always difficult to make contact with our children, because the lines into the radio phones at the safari lodges were often disabled. Frustration set in often, driving us to make the long journey to the post office in the town of Hwange to call the kids on public phones. Hwange is a mining town, and communication services were kept running. Our family wrote often, but letters sometimes took weeks to arrive.

Once again the phone was down when we returned via the lodge. It didn't seem so disappointing when we were handed a bag of mail. Jer and I took this treasure to the lounge area and settled into plush chairs to catch up on news. Lachy chatted with some guests while we read.

Shockingly, Jer jumped up and shouted: 'No, No! God, no!'

He staggered outside. Lachy and I ran to him. My strong, calm husband began to weep with terrible racking sounds. It must be shocking news. Lachy took the letter out of his hand. I read of the agony of Jer's sister, Jay, and her husband, Colin. Their only son, David, was dead; killed in a shooting accident. Jer had loved him like a son. He had been the only male among the ten offspring of Jer and his two sisters. We mourned the loss of a wonderful young man. My husband was consumed with guilt. He hadn't been there for Jay, Colin and their girls; or for his daughters Jenny, Jackie and Kate, who would be dealing with their own grief.

A week later, Jer and I were sitting on a pontoon at Lake Kariba, an artificial dam where the skeletal white limbs of flooded dead trees thrust high above the silver water. It was a grey day. We were speaking of David; he was alive in our memories. Silence fell as a magnificent Marshall eagle swooped down to perch on a limb; so close that we could have touched it. The brown eyes of the great bird watched each of us in turn above its proud, hooked beak. I thought I saw David's face through my tears.

The eagle stayed with us for a long time. Jer was transfixed. When the bird left, it circled around our heads three times before disappearing. Unaware of my experience, Jer spoke later of seeing David in the eagle. He felt he had been forgiven and life could return to normal. And so it did when we settled back into Farm 41. Lachy's holiday was almost over and we planned a farewell party.

I watched the guitar hum beneath the fingers of my son. His haunting hazel eyes never left those of the pretty girl whose cheeks were smudged with tears as he sang a ballad of lost love – his own composition. Our friends had come from many different camps for the *braai*. Everyone was there. Kathy and Neil; Josh; Aubrey and his wife, Siti; Stevie; Des and Jen; Rob and others not yet introduced; even Harold and Sylvia and Marius and Wilmarie were having a rare night out. Dickson and Ekaim came with their brother, George, who lived deep within Hwange National Park. He was here, en route to a visit with his number one wife and family.

Lachy was surrounded by the young guides who swayed their bodies to the rhythm. He put down the guitar and swung the pretty girl into a wild dance around the fire. It was heaven. I thought there could be no one happier on the planet. My dreams of my child being free to realise his passions were fulfilled.

Jer returned to the drum to tend the sizzling T-bones and Boerwurst sausages with a long fork created from a wire coat hanger. Marius was bossing him, but Jer ignored him. Des was throwing in his two bits' worth as well. Eventually, Jer grumbled: 'Back off, boys. This is an Aussie barbecue.'

Marius and Des raised their eyebrows but left him in peace and headed to the chiller box for another drink.

Jen caught my eye and winked. She was working beside me as I rotated the foil-wrapped potatoes in the coals with home-made tongs. There was sweet satisfaction in making do with the few tools we needed to make life easier. The meal was simple and the beer was tepid; yet, this night, both tasted better than haute cuisine consumed in the elegance of a fine restaurant.

Stevie Wonder had volunteered to make *sadza* (mealie meal porridge) in a huge pot. 'This is *real* food,' he mocked. 'Africans know what is good for them. Look at these muscles.'

And I knew my Matabele friend was getting drunk. Ekaim had propped himself against a fallen log on the ground. It seemed that he was heading in the same direction when he twisted around to beat hard on the log and call to Lachy, 'Man, where are the drums?'

Lachy immediately disappeared into the hut, only to re-emerge a minute later with a bongo drum, hand piano and set of marimba pipes. He began to play an African rhythm. George and Ekaim jumped up and began a vigorous Zulu dance. Their strong legs lifted high and wide before they pounded them on the earth and Stevie deserted the *sadza* to join them. Their deep voices harmonised, and their bodies shook in a wild and powerful dance. Joy, pride and male strength powered every thrust of their legs. Shoulders shimmied, heads were tossed back, and bottoms were thrust out. It was sensuous and hypnotic. Even Wilmarie joined the rush as we all tried to follow their movements – except for Jer (who was singing along as he turned the steaks), Sylvia (who was smiling her pleasure from the comfort of a chair) and Harold (who had taken over the stirring of the *sadza*) . . .

The spell was broken when Jer called, 'Tucker time!'

Teeth were tearing at the steaks when two honey badgers suddenly appeared, running hard towards the party. 'Holy mother of God! Bugger up high. Now-now!' shouted Aubrey as he scrambled into a tree. It was every person for themselves as our guests jumped on to chairs or headed hastily for the hut. Jer and Lachy joined me on the table.

'Throw them the bones,' Marius yelled.

The fearsome badgers swung their glowering heads and uttered deep growls as they made small, threatening rushes. Each animal gathered its trophy with large paws tipped by vicious long nails. The honey badger is considered to be one of Africa's fiercest characters. They are single-minded and have a tendency to go straight for the genitals of an enemy. It is said that one day an elephant was walking along a narrow trail when he encountered a honey badger coming the other way. The elephant stepped aside!

Remembering this story I surveyed the scene and burst out laughing. Every man, with the exception of Lachy, was holding his hands protectively over his genitals. My son didn't know the ways of honey badgers. He was squatting beside me amid the salad bowls enjoying the sight of the stocky pair that had flopped down to eat. They held the T-bones delicately between their paws. Their incredible self-assurance made a mockery of those people who remained perched high. When the honey badgers finished their meal, they peered myopically one last time at the scene and lumbered away into the night.

Kathy got down quickly from her chair and stood with her hands on her hips. She began to make Shakespearean bows; fluttering her hand down as she turned around and dipped to each man in turn.

'My heroes,' she mocked. 'Ladies, let's give these brave knights some applause.' Her tilted eyes were shining and her glossy hair swung. Then she bent over to hold her stomach as chuckles bubbled into a crescendo of hooting laughter.

Aubrey descended from his perch looking less than amused. 'Is it? You can bugger off, too,' he muttered. 'Those guys were on a mission. I wasn't going to spoil their fun.'

Alison now seized the opportunity to run into Lachy's arms. He winked at me over her head and explained, 'I didn't know, did I? Greenhorns do what their elders tell them.'

Soon cans were popping as he took up the guitar again. He speaks now of how the accompaniment of hyaenas and jackals, and the calls of night birds and insects, lent a rhythm to his music that has continued to influence his work.

Sleeping bags were scattered through camp when I emerged from the hut the next morning. Only the older couples were missing. The wisdom of age had led them home soon after the badgers retreated. Shaddy was taking time out from his job to join the party. He volunteered to cook breakfast and was already tossing pancakes crammed with savoury mince splashed liberally with rum, or liqueur-laced lemon butter sauce. They were delicious. The fillings topped up the alcohol residue from the previous night's excesses.

Before long, Lachy was caught up in a game that required him to hold a stick aloft and keep his gaze on the top, while two others spun him around for the count of ten. The inevitable result was a graceless staggering fall accompanied by screams of laughter. As the game progressed, Shaddy was called upon to create even more of the potent crepes. Rob told me later that he kept falling asleep over the wheel all the way home – drunk from six pancakes.

Aubrey and Siti returned to Bulawayo. When I think of Aubrey I see the colour ginger. His eyes and his freckles were ginger, and his shock of hair was mottled silver/ginger. He relished teasing people, to 'ginger them up'.

Aubrey was a fine raconteur, exuding charm from every pore. During our meal I had watched him tuck into fatty spare ribs, liberally doused with salt, and hoped that a third heart attack would wait for another time. His penchant for pork crackling, fatty biltong, salty food, and generous shots of Scotch had undoubtedly contributed to his heart condition. The other factor was a lust for dangerous living. He headed both the Hunters Association and a major conservation body.

In the beginning I found this a conundrum; but it soon became evident that the purest form of conservation often sprang from the heart of a hunter. Aubrey had progressed from wild days of mindless hunting in his youth, when he said his greatest atrocity was to shoot eleven lions in one night, to becoming a concerned and active manager of wildlife. By manning the controls of the hunting body he was in a position to set boundaries and limits that ensured sustainable growth in a country where population pressure insisted that animals must earn their living.

CHAPTER 13

Spartacus and other lions

I was invited to attend a conference in Kenya at the same time as Lachy left for home. I boarded a flight for East Africa in Harare as my son boarded his aircraft for the long and tedious journey back to the east coast of Australia.

It was in Kenya that I met my friend Salim who took me deeper into the life of lions. He was my guide when I escaped Nairobi for the Masai Mara and the Serengeti. The national parks of East Africa offer wide views of plains game at every point. This was quite different from game viewing in the scrublands and forests of our home territory in southern Africa, where each good sighting was a triumph. For me there was no comparison. I far preferred the mystery and wildness of the south, where sightings were often hard won. The satisfaction was greater when the search had been long. But for tourists on short visits to Africa, the entire congregation of game could be ticked off quickly where the savannah was sparsely treed and throbbing with wildlife.

When the conference finished, I left for a short safari in the Mara. We stayed in solid *rondavels*. The sense of security they provided enabled me to have some desperately needed uninterrupted sleep, though my inner alarm clock still woke me at 5.30 am. A subtle lifting of black allowed light to frame the window. By 6 am a small group of us were away, driving directly east. I stood in the minivan with my head poking through the skylight, inhaling the scent of foliage and the odour of animals carried into my face on the wind. There is nothing gentle, no pastel hues, about the birth of an African day. Each morning a great red orb juts above the horizon thrusting vigorously, arrogantly, into prominence. Sunset is equally climatic. The day is not so much drawn to a close as erased by an explosion of colour. My eyes smarted with tears which had nothing to do with the heady draught whipping tendrils of hair across my face.

Salim's wide shoulders were forced into a well-worn, shiny brown, polyester safari jacket. His grizzled greying hair was cut hedge-like into a topiary shape. It looked like the crest of a cassowary. He lifted his elbows wide as he hunched low over the wheel. Partially obscured by Elton John-sized reflective sunglasses, his glowing face wore a dangerous expression as we hurtled across the savannah.

Early, I had feared our safari would be Kenya's answer to an hour in the Louvre. I was wrong. I came to believe that Salim possessed eyes like flies, seeing fore, aft, and to the sides instantaneously. If he raced like a Formula One driver, it was to move faster between sightings in order to give his clients optimum viewing time with their photographic prey. He seemed to sense where to encounter one marvellous moment after another.

We were watching two zebra stallions test each other's strength in a fierce display of rearing and savage back kicks. Our eyes were riveted on this contest taking place to the right when Salim threw us off our feet with a sharp turn to the left. I clung tenaciously to the back of the seat in front as the vehicle careened over rocky ground towards a green line of trees that snaked along a river course.

'I have seen a *li-on* running fast,' Salim shouted over his shoulder. 'Man *simba* is only running to eat, to fight, or to make the loving.'

Then we saw a dark-maned, tawny body break from the tree line on the other side of the shallow rivulet. Salim changed direction and bore down upon the water. The tyres bucked across the narrow, rocky stream, shooting into the soft gravel too quickly to lose traction. By now Salim's elbows were level with his ears as he urged the van up and out of the water.

The lion was well ahead, maintaining a fast pace. When we drew level with him, I expected some reaction to our noisy presence; but his huge, black-maned head remained steady above the powerful thrusts of his shoulders. His gaze never wavered from the front, looking hard along his nose, which he carried high. It was obvious he was following a powerful scent. Bubbles of white froth spattered the fine black line of his open mouth. He was magnificent.

A group of pale gold bodies crouched ahead. Salim closed on a lioness and three sub-adult cubs, their lean bodies still faintly dappled with dark spots. 'Ha! There is the wife. *Simba* is hurrying very much to make a honeymoon,' he chortled.

He was wrong. The lion checked for a few seconds, ten metres to the side of the spitting female. Without a sound, he cast an urgent glance at the frightened family before returning to his original path. Salim engaged the gears to follow, but before we could move, two more males pounded around the van and fell in behind the leader. Their demeanour, too, was acutely alert, unlike the usual lion-manner of running, with head held low in an almost laborious swinging motion from side to side. All three tails were held stiffly out behind, the black tufts at their ends constantly twitching with irritable jerks.

Now I was doubly intrigued. Apparently we had been followed by these younger, golden-maned lions in our mad chase across the savannah. As befits such proud creatures, lions are generally aloof in the company of humans, but most indicate an awareness of our bothersome presence – if only to turn away in disdain. This trio behaved as if we didn't exist. Furthermore, it was unusual to maintain such a pace for so long, with such deep intent. Even Salim was scratching his amazing crown in a bemused manner.

We pursued the band across the dry terrain for another ten minutes. The lions' stomachs heaved with effort as they passed close to wildebeest, zebras, and Grant's and Thompson's gazelles, which simply stood and stared. With speed as their foremost strategy of defence, such calm indicated awareness that they were not the quarry. The lions actually blundered on to a resting juvenile wildebeest, flushing the frantic youngster out of the flaxen grass. This easy meal was also disregarded.

Then 'Black Mane' slowed his pace, opened his mouth wide, closed his eyes and roared. The mighty sound forced the air from his overworked lungs, sending strings of foam down his shaggy chest. Another series of bellows caused his flanks to

202

shrink and expand until the coughs diminished into silence. His young *askaris* remained silent, slightly to his rear.

Just ahead, a young lion with a half-grown pale mane faced the oncoming trio. His body was rigid with tension, his mouth drawn into a rictus of threat, or fear. He held his ground in the face of the formidable rush. Within seconds, Black Mane was upon him.

Deep growls and explosive snarls shook the morning. In a grotesque parody of mating, the attacker came over the back of his victim, forcing the youngster into a crouch. Yellow teeth sank into the back of the vulnerable neck before Black Mane freed himself to spit fur from a face creased with disgust. He shook his head with revulsion – even using his paws in the process.

All the time the sinuous bodies of his *askaris* closely circled the arena, adding to the spine-tingling chorus of roars and grunts. Billows of dust soon rose. Disregarding his neck wound, leaking thick rivulets of blood into his beard, the interloper used his front legs as levers to spin around on his bottom and keep his adversaries in his sights. Surrounded by a moving wheel of tawny bodies, the youngster earned our respect and sympathy as he fought for his life.

With growing horror I observed my reaction to the terrible battle. Every part of my being throbbed with excitement. I bit my tongue to stop from expelling a great battle cry. The awesome power emanating from the heavily muscled bodies of the warring lions activated a dormant, primitive instinct. I wasn't alone as a voyeur to blood lust. Later, my companions all admitted to having similar reactions, though they didn't last. I was soon overwhelmed with admiration for the courage of the solitary young nomad, so gamely facing his adversaries, and by despair at the inevitable outcome.

There was a strange sense of order in the method of combat. The three attacking lions took turns to lunge into the ring and engage with 'Spartacus'. I could have sworn that Black Mane communicated the strategy to his comrades. While one launched his assault at the head, the other concentrated on the hindquarters. Meanwhile, Black Mane worked on the wound he had already opened. After each assault, all three rejected the enemy's flesh with distaste. Sorely wounded and weakening fast, Spartacus never attempted to retreat although it was obvious to us that he was doomed.

When the end came, it was quick. For the first and only time, the males struck together. While the front and rear were engaged, Black Mane once again bounded up and sank his great canines into the large back wound. With a surprised expression, Spartacus dropped like a rock. His spine was broken. He was paralysed from the neck down, but lifted his head to watch his assailants depart.

Led by Black Mane, the panting band strutted stiffly a few metres to shade, where they gracefully flopped down. Careful to avoid acknowledging their victim by even a glance, they closed their eyes with apparent pleasure and proceeded to clean every part of their bodies. I watched the dying cat watching them with an extraordinary expression of longing. Tears cut a path through the grime to my mouth. I tasted the bitter salt.

The victors completed their grooming by licking each other with affection. Then they rose and turned away to retrace their route. Spartacus watched them leave, his body already hidden beneath black waves of flies. The faces of two jackals bobbed, and fell, as they tacked a wary course closer. A hyaena waited for us to leave. Its ugly head was lunging forward and up – thick black nostrils sniffed the heady stench of impending death. I couldn't bear to witness such an ignoble end to this worthy combatant. Before I could speak, Salim moved away.

The van fell in behind the stately procession of victorious males. No one spoke. There was nothing to say. The odds had ordained the outcome – the fittest had survived. This was the rhythm of life on the African plains. We followed the trio – still curious about the chain of events. The fight had taken its toll on them. Their pace was slow, and each paw lifted and hovered before splaying heavily into the dust. Shaggy heads hung low. As we approached the place where we had seen the lioness and cubs, a lithe form emerged from a copse of bushes and swayed provocatively towards Black Mane. We could see two tawny faces peering through the leaves where their mother had stashed her adolescent cubs.

Black Mane drew himself up to his full height as the female stroked her body along his length. When her tail snaked enticingly under his mouth he curled his lip in a terrible grimace to test her allure. All tiredness was forgotten. He was smitten. With a terrible snarl he wheeled upon his companions, who retreated hastily to flop down in the shade of a spreading thorn tree. They commenced a pride-saving regime of intense grooming. Only occasional wistful glances at the courting couple hinted at their state of frustration.

Now I understood. The lioness was coming into oestrous and this was Black Mane's territory. Had Black Mane been a stranger he would surely have killed, or chased off, the sub-adult youngsters. So it was reasonable to assume they were his cubs, and that this was his domain – for now. The young male had caught the irresistible scent of the female and taken his chances. I wondered, had he been a less worthy rival, would he have survived the encounter by turning tail and beating a rapid retreat?

In the evening, Salim drove back to see what had become of Spartacus. Dust hazed the red glow of the setting sun behind a surrealistic scene that could have been painted by Dali. Hundreds of vultures were writhing over the remains. Squawking and screaming obscenely, they wielded their greasy wings as weapons, hopping upon each other to strike with cruel, hooked beaks that sprang from cadaverous heads. Their bald, snake-like necks swayed grotesquely as strings of meat slithered into gullets. As some clumsily lifted aloft, others swooped in to take their places. And in their midst lay the bones of a noble warrior. Engorged, and too heavy to fly, many of the birds lined the branches of nearby trees like sentinels of death outlined against the blazing sky.

However, new lives were being created nearby. Black Mane was covering his prize every fifteen minutes to ensure the creation of a new generation of lions that would fight, and love, and die in the manner of their kind – if our kind permitted.

That night, Salim joined us after dinner. I anticipated these evenings with relish. He was a fine raconteur – a never-ending source of fantastic and frightful stories of encounters with wildlife. Some of them were tall tales indeed, but the yarn I am about to retell did happen as it is told. I know this – for Salim has become quite famous among his peers and the safari operators as the anti-hero of this adventure.

This story needs to be told using Salim's appealing manner of speech. I am not being derisive. He is a man who speaks many African dialects and also communicates well in a number of European languages. I speak only English fluently.

Salim fed a stick of wood into the fire before he settled on to a canvas stool to tell us his tale. In the beginning he spoke to the flames . . .

After a particularly long day driving through boggy terrain in Tsavo during the time of the long rains, Salim felt very tired. Immediately after dinner he left his equally fatigued charges to retire to the tiny staff hut he had been allocated behind the lodge. The night was black under glowering, dense clouds. Salim hunched for protection beneath an oilskin coat he held high over his head and above the paraffin lantern he carried to light his way. He hurried through gusts of rain along a narrow path separating the staff quarters from those of the guests and from the main building. His objective was the last of the tiny beehive structures that were staggered either side of the glutinous track.

Finally home, the relieved man ducked beneath the sheltering porch that channelled away a sheet of water streaming from the conical thatched roof. Pausing only to remove his mud-caked boots and to hang his raincoat upon a protruding branch, he pushed open the stick-and-daub door.

The lamp illuminated a small round room just big enough to take a single trundle bed set off to one side. The only air came through a circular vent in the cone of the ceiling where the roof wore an elevated small hat. As he had done many times before, Salim decided to leave the door slightly ajar to promote a 'healthful sleeping'. Even so, the atmosphere inside was muggy and oppressive. He removed his clothes, blew out the light and lay down upon the blanket. Sleep came quickly to one 'such as Salim, who is working harder than a lion making babies'.

He woke with a thudding heart. The rain had stopped. A rank, gamey stench lay upon his nostrils. Deathly afraid, he swivelled his eyes towards the doorway looking for a break in the darkness. There was none. The door was shut. Salim relaxed. It must have blown shut and the stink must be coming from a passing hyaena.

'I am thinking that this is a very good thing. To have died without a face because I have left open the door is very bad.'

With the instinctive knowledge of all great story-tellers, Salim paused. As if on cue a distant hyaena whooped. Now Salim curled back his lips, exposing his shining teeth. From his throat issued a maniacal giggle in response. Our Scheherezade opened his eyes very wide, stood up, then stalked away from the fire as if to find the fiend. We sat and waited, our eyes straining to see into the darkness. When he eventually returned he was adjusting his fly. Salim had taken a comfort stop at the critical moment where suspense ran high and the audience was captivated. His comic timing was superb.

He made his way back to his stool by the fire, facing our semicircle of chairs. We all leaned towards him, silently waiting for him to resume his tale. Africans know the value of silence, never seeming to feel compelled to fill every pause in conversation with incessant chatter. Of course, the delay only served to heighten our anticipation.

Salim continued. 'So, . . . The door is closed. Now I am feeling too hot. The blanket is making the sweating on my back. I think – maybe I will step outside, for I am needing the piss.'

Looking at me (the only woman present), Salim gave a small bow, his hands held in the prayer pose. 'So sorry, *memsahib*, but it is necessary to speak of such things for this is the way of it.'

I nodded, careful not to allow my notoriously mobile face to erupt from hardly controlled twitching into a delighted grin.

Reassured, his voice a stage whisper, Salim hissed: 'I am

beginning to move. I stop. Some other big thing is moving upon the ground beside me – inside the house!'

Salim's body was rigid. His eyes swivelled from side to side. We were there with him.

'Salim is lying very still without the breathing.' Tapping his fingers hard against his chest, he continued. 'This heart is drumming very loudly so the thing that is lying beside me must hear it. I tell you, my friends, I am frightened too much.'

Now Salim was lying on the ground as stiff as a board. His face was twisted with horror. The man had forgotten the actor within the play. And so had his audience.

'Now the creature stands and I know the greatness of his body. I am thinking, is this animal re-ally a *fisi* [hyaena]? His breath is very loud. It is smelling very bad. It is hot against my face. Old Salim is trying to become the bed-place. Now I want to be inside the blanket to make me safe.'

I watched with fascination as Salim inched his hand down his leg until he made contact with an imaginary cover that he slowly hauled up and over himself.

'I am pulling the blanket over my head when the rain is returning. Salim is wondering, what is this terrible thing sharing his house? And then it makes a loud roaring. I am telling you I am passing the urine in the bed!'

This time his gesture of respect to me was just an aside. 'Once again I am being sorry, *memsahib*.'

Salim the actor was still down on the ground – curled into a tight ball. He was so involved with the drama that I could only hope he refrained from a need to relieve himself on the spot.

'I am smelling of the urine. This old man is shaking so hard. He is thinking that his hour has struck. This animal is a *li-on*. I am sure that the *li-on* will be finding and eating me. He is very angry. He is shouting. Oh yes, he is a very mad *simba*. He wants to get out of this prison he has entered to hide from the rain. I am telling you – this *li-on* he is shouting and shouting! And he is running round and round, but he cannot find the escape. He is jumping at the wall. He even jumps on to Salim on the bed, but he does not know that there is prey lying there crying with the frightening. Now I am having a big accident! So the *li-on* smell is like perfume unto the smell of poor old Salim.'

Aware of the beginnings of another deferential apology, I pre-empted the prostrate figure on the ground, 'It's all right. What happened?'

Still clutching the invisible blanket, he continued: 'My friends are coming to see what is wrong with this loud *li-on*. They have heard him shouting from inside the house. I know these men are thinking it is the will of Allah for Salim to be eaten by *simba*. I too think this. Because just this day I have wounded another *li-on*. My shame is very great. I speak to Allah from my heart. I tell him that the hurting was an accident and this thing I will never do again.'

With his hands held in the prayer position, Salim rose on to his knees from the ground. His face shone with holy benediction. 'Allah heard my prayer. Praise be to Allah,' he whispered with devotion.

I watched, entranced, as he leaned forward to touch his head to the ground. This was more than acting. Salim was renewing his pledge of gratitude to his God. We waited quietly.

Soon he rose to his feet. 'Now this man is not breathing. There is hurting in my body where the *li-on's* feet having walked across my breast. I am wanting to shout out to these people for *hatari* [help], so it is good that the strangling of my voice is stopping my shouting or that *simba* would have known me. I can see no thing from beneath the blanket. I tell you this because the rest of this story belongs to my friends who had climbed on to the roof to open the door with a big stick. They say that *simba* saw freedom with his night eyes and jumped outside. For me, all I could hear was his shouting.'

Salim paused, nodded his head earnestly and announced mournfully, 'I tell you, that old *li-on* was so happy to get out of prison, and away from the smells of Salim, that he just ran away too fast.'

We laughed with Salim, who dripped with sweat from the energetic re-enactment of his fearful experience. He sank into his chair with a deep sigh and gratefully accepted a well-earned cold beer.

'That *li-on* cost Salim very much. This body was broken by the dancing of his feet. My family was very poor for one season.'

I imagined that his ribs and lungs must have taken a terrible hiding. But I was still curious about his mention of wounding another lion earlier that day. He believed that he had commit-ted a sin, which had created the trouble. And this was another story.

Before dawn on the morning of Salim's *li-on* he had set off from Amboseli Lodge with eight tourists crammed into the Kombi van. It would be a long day of steady game viewing en route to Tsavo, where they would spend the night. It was Salim's duty to find the species most sought after by his charges. He was very good at his job, having an acute knowledge of the wildlife, although I suspected he felt no sentimental attachments towards wild creatures. Those feelings he reserved for his cattle.

On this day, like so many others before, all his charges desired a good sighting of lions. 'It is no good that Salim finds wild beasts of the sunlight times,' he sighed. 'They only want *simba*. I am looking for these *li-ons* everywhere. It is not good for me. They are all sleeping in their beds where I cannot see them.'

Salim took to the ground to flop out upon his back in perfect imitation of a languid, sleeping lion. We waited breathlessly while the man/lion appeared to doze, with occasional twitches of his face and swats of his hand/paw to shift swarms of imaginary flies. I could almost hear them buzzing.

In his own time he stirred, settled back into his chair and continued his tale. 'The monkeys were not happy. Oh, I am begging your pardon,' he offered, 'but these people are being like the chattering monkeys. I am telling you, even when I find for them a cheetah mother and her children they are not happy!' Once again he gave a deep sigh of disappointment.

'We are stopping for the lunch under a kind fever tree. This friend is standing alone on the plain with much shade to keep us cool.' He became the tree with arms stretched straight out from his shoulders to show us the wide canopy. He turned full circle. Then he returned to his seat wearing an expression of disgust, 'Two *sahibs* are sitting on top.' I imagined that the hatches of the Kombi van were open, with these men on top; their legs dangling into the van. I had done it myself.

Salim continued. 'The people are eating. They have full mouths. They chew some and they are making moanings to tell Salim that they want *simba*. They chew more. This is not good. Their bellies will be groaning, too.'

Salim rubbed his stomach and belched with force. 'Food is sacred. It is a worship to eat in silence. Do you think that Salim

could eat? No, his belly can only think, where are these *li-ons*?'
His re-enactment was so powerful that I felt my own digestive
tract was in turmoil.

With an effort he put aside thoughts of eating. 'I am telling
these monkeys *simba* will come out to eat when the sun goes to
sleep. Let us go home for the sleep to prepare us for later.'

Salim raised his hands into prayer position before his chest.
'I am saying in my heart to Allah, "Allah be praised. Please, sir,
find these hiding *li-ons* when the night is coming".'

For a moment he sat with eyes closed in this reverent pose.
By now his audience was leaning far forward, drawn deeply into
his world. Somewhere nearby, a hyaena giggled. A nightjar
screamed as it flew low over the fire. And Salim burst out of
repose into action. On his feet, terror apparent in every part
of his body, he shouted: 'Get in! Get in!'

He was so intense that I looked for a place to get into. He
made movements of pulling legs from above with incredible
urgency.

'There is *simba*. On the roof!' he shouted. 'Salim is talking to
Allah. Allah knows the *li-on* is sleeping in the tree. Allah is
waking him and telling him – this man Salim needs you. This
was very good. And it was very bad. It was good that Allah was
hearing my prayer. It was very bad that my prayer was not a
good prayer.' His eyes were huge with the memory.

'I am pulling inside the people who are shouting. *Simba* is
shouting and shouting. He is very big. Salim is standing on one
of the people for the closing of the roof. The hand of the *li-on*
is inside.'

By now Salim's face was pouring sweat as he struggled with
an invisible hatch. We watched it close. The terror-struck man
fell back, clambered into the seat of the spectral van and

started the engine. Now Salim was straddling a chair facing backwards, using the top as a wheel.

'*Simba*'s hand was shut inside the roof. This van is driving too fast with the man *li-on* jumping and shouting on top. The monkeys inside are shouting. Salim is shouting. I am telling you, this van wants to fall over.'

With this, he rocked the chair from side to side so violently that it collapsed. Without pausing he leapt to his feet, indicating with outflung arms what could only be a swinging lion lurching every which way atop the vehicle. It was not difficult to imagine the van careening across the savannah filled with nine terrified people all peering up at the roof as it groaned under the weight of a hapless lion trapped by one leg.

'*Simba* came with us for long and far. It is a bad thing Salim did. This *li-on* was very sick when he fell down. The hand was not good. He was not doing the walking.'

Salim's posture was now dejected. For a long time his chin was low on his chest. Then he rose, bowed, and left us to ponder his story.

Not another word was spoken of this. But we understood why Salim felt the world of lions took its revenge that night inside the conical hut as the rain poured down.

CHAPTER 14

Standing on shadows

My return to Zimbabwe coincided with a visit from Aubrey. He was leading a group of Earthwatch volunteers who were conducting an elephant count in the western corridor of Hwange National Park, which lies adjacent to the territory our herd habituated. The results of the count would be very useful to our research.

Aubrey found us at Konondo Pan after he had organised his crew into separate units at hides beside a number of waterholes within the national park. They would stay at these sites for seventy-two hours, catching sleep between shifts of six hours. We had volunteered to count with Aubrey on the following night of the full moon, at the closest hide to the boundary between Hwange and the concession.

He burst out of his Land Rover, clicked his heels together

hard, and saluted us with an arm-shuddering motion.

'Sergeant-Major "Sore Bum" reporting for duty. Can I come with you today?'

Jer and Kathy were in the cabin while I was setting up my camera equipment in the back of Bluey. I pushed the sliding window open as the Ginger Man approached wearing a face-splitting grin. He took my face between ridiculously soft hands, for one such as him, and planted the usual big kiss straight on my mouth. 'Howzit, Beautiful?' Then he planted another on my cheek. 'And this is from Siti.'

He looked skywards for a moment. 'And this is from the pooch,' he said, placing another kiss on the other cheek.

'Stop!' I laughed. 'It's enough already.'

Jer was out of the cabin and on his way with his fists up, but his eyes were screwed up with good humour. 'Get away from my wife, you rabid old dog,' he growled. And then the two men were embracing awkwardly.

Kathy was the next recipient of Aubrey's mock ardour. She screwed her eyes tight and wiped her face with pretend disgust. 'Ugggh, how does poor Siti put up with this slobber?'

As usual, the air crackled with Aubrey's energy. He climbed in beside Kathy, clapped his hands with pleasure, looked around and asked, 'What's the mission today?' Then he turned to include me in the conversation through the open window dividing the cabin from the tray. 'Can I throw my bedroll on your floor tonight?'

'Of course you must,' I said, delighted that he wanted to stay in our simple shack when he had an open invitation to stay in the extremely comfortable accommodation at the lodge. We told him of our progress as we waited for the herd to arrive. We had passed them earlier, browsing their way steadily towards the pan.

It was the height of the dry cold season, when many elephants come out of the park to drink at the artificial water-holes that lie in the home range of our herd. They didn't welcome the presence of strangers in the area. The herd reacted to the strange elephants with stubborn ill humour, as if their land were being colonised by hostile invaders. Individual family units came together to withstand a common enemy.

Within the mass of the herd, individual matriarchs kept their families close together, but when it came time to move it was Skew Tusk who organised the logistics. She led them all into the clearing. With immense dignity she then stood still – on guard as the elephants filed past her – as if she were counting them until they were all safely lined up on the banks to take their fill of water. Only then did she join them. And the Gang of Eleven came behind her quickly, looking nervously to their rear.

After a time the elephants relaxed, but not for long. Suddenly three huge bulls broke from the tree line and paused to assess the situation, with up-stretched trunks questing forward. The herd faced them as one, vocalising loudly. Their ears were held high, wide and stiff. The youngsters and calves were herded within an encircling mass of adult bodies.

Unfortunately, we were parked between the opposing forces. Jer started the engine and drove quickly to the edge of the pan when Skew Tusk signalled her intent to rush the bulls with a mighty trumpet and a wild, ear-flapping snap of her head.

'This is more like it!' yelled Aubrey. 'Eee-ee, we've got some action! Go get 'em, girl!'

The Ginger Man was incorrigible. Yet, it was exciting to watch the gutsy cow take on three mighty males. She thundered towards the stationary bulls. Dilingane and Bette Midler

217

broke ranks to follow her, then more cows, then some of the Gang. Their muscle power was almost frightening, but not to Aubrey, who was jumping up and down and shouting, 'Get the great woolly muffs. Kill the bastards! Yoo-bloody-hoo!'

Skew Tusk and her enveloping cloud of dust were drawing close when the bulls decided to flee. They withdrew into the bush as she closed. She was screaming, but she braked to stand still in a very stately posture. Her head was high; her ears rigid with indignation and her body puffed up like a cobra's head. The cows who were following assembled in an admiring cordon. Her mouth accepted their patting trunks with pride.

During the drama, the rest of the herd had moved beside us. I felt humbled by what I perceived to be their faith in us, until Skew Tusk returned to show us a thing or two. We were also on the receiving end of her ire, and were forced to skulk away to a safer place to discuss what had happened.

Later, all was calm when we returned to the herd, who stayed at Konondo for longer than usual. It seemed they were determined to keep the strangers away. My shoulders began to ache from the long sessions of filming them swimming, coating themselves with dust and digging for mineral salts.

It was mid-morning when Skew Tusk finally gave the marching orders. Once again she stationed herself beside us as the herd filed by before throwing us a half-hearted warning that seemed more dutiful than rebuking. My heart swelled with admiration for the old girl and with warmth for the Gang of Eleven, who shuffled hurriedly behind at the distance required for courtesy. Skew Tusk ran a tight ship.

'Time for a toot,' Aubrey said. 'It's my shout for lunch at the lodge.'

We ate toasted cheese and tomato sandwiches and drank

Malawi shandies on the manicured lawns where Horace had served me notice. Aubrey left to monitor his study group when we adjourned to the research bunker to collate data. We had arranged to meet Aubrey, Kathy and Neil at our camp for a *braai* that night, which turned out to be an evening with the elephants as well. They arrived when the sausages were sizzling and stayed in our company until dawn.

The next night we took our sleeping bags and supplies to the platform in Hwange for a moonlit tryst to count other elephants. Or so we thought. Instead, we would come to understand how the beautiful, shy bushbuck earned its reputation as a creature of fierce courage.

Warmth departed with the day. I pulled on a thick tracksuit, parka, mittens and beanie and poured tea awkwardly from a flask with fat, furry fingers. The cold air in the hide became thick with the soft mist from our mouths as we whispered about the day's sightings. Our discomfort disappeared when animal activity commanded our attention.

We sat in darkness, amused by the mutters and shrieks of baboons fussing towards sleep in a large teak tree on the opposite bank. These easily recognised sounds intermingled with the stirrings, murmurs and calls of unknown creatures arriving to drink. At 10 pm there was a brightening on an unsighted horizon. The moon appeared with a whimper, and grew and grew, until it became a full-bodied orange orb magnified to our sight by the haze of dust. Now, cold white light radiated the sky and landscape, exposing the open spaces around the waterhole. The moon was reflected in the silver water.

A lone elephant ambled slowly away towards the anonymity of the tree line. I marked 'one' on my Earthwatch spreadsheet.

Before the light came, I had recognised the unmistakable sound of deep draughts of water being sucked into an elephant's trunk, like a cistern flushing, as the liquid surged into his stomach. I detected the distinctive odour of elephant and the heavy, sweet, grassy smell of copious droppings, but I had no idea how many grey ghosts might be drinking in the darkness. Our silent presence hadn't stopped his arrival. I doubted he was one of our home range bulls, but we needed to check. Even through the binoculars I was unable to recognise him without seeing his head, and he was moving away. His large, baggy bum obscured his ears.

A pearl-spotted owl whistled its bell-like call all the way down the scale. A nightjar screamed as it flew low over the black, brown and white-banded quills of a waddling, crested porcupine single-mindedly following an ant trail.

People often ask if we became terribly bored with the tedious hours of inactivity while waiting for elephant arrivals: not for one moment was I ever bored! Instead, I often wished I had four eyes with which to observe all the fascinating doings of lesser beasties such as termites. Their massive earth mounds are the most entertaining and architecturally perfect cities in the world. And while everyone hopes to see lions, during daylight hours they are mostly sleepy and inactive. Now, *that* can be tedious. Granted, a hunt (successful or otherwise) is a fantastic spectacle.

At 2 am a delicately spotted bushbuck arrived. He picked his way forward with the typical hunched gait of a creature with hind legs longer than those in front. His maleness was indicated by small, slightly spiralled horns and a sturdy build. He stood almost as tall as an impala buck nearby, so I was able to estimate his height at about a metre at the shoulder. The moonlight was bright enough that I could pick out white spots on his rump. It was always a treat to see this shy antelope, whose nocturnal habits made sightings elusive.

A dark cloud passed in front of the moon. The sudden velvety blackness was almost tangible; seeming to press against my face. A baboon sentry barked an alarm – or was it one of the antelopes? I found Jer's hand as, sightless, we responded to the frenzy of thudding hooves. Close by, an evil sound scoffed at the panic. When hunting hyaenas vomit their obscene signals of death, hairs raise on the vulnerable necks of all living things. It is a sound straight from Hades. The hyaenas' timing was impeccable. Panic prey and it might make a mistake; panic prey that has suddenly been plunged into total darkness and that chance becomes a certainty.

The fleeing hooves receded from the baying of Cerberus's pack. The foul odour invading my olfactory senses told me the hyaenas were milling about close to the hide. I felt sorely tempted to break our rule forbidding spotlighting of animals engaged in nocturnal activity. Some poor creature was barking its distress as it struggled and splashed in the water.

Then the heavens turned on their own spotlight, illuminating the landscape as suddenly as the cloud had obscured the light. The curtain lifted on a formidable scene. The bushbuck was baled up three metres in from the water's edge. Coughing loudly, and stamping his front hooves, he directed all of his energy towards three spotted hyaenas engaged in a series of lunging forays that always pulled up well short of the buck's furious legs. It was hard to judge whether they were repelled by the deeper water, or by the threatening attitude of their prey. They shrank away from his most defensive moves. However, they were by no means the only predators.

The lone small crocodile that lived in the shallow water slid in behind the bushbuck, hardly rippling the water. I doubted the feisty fellow would have noticed if the crocodile had created a bow wave in its charge. All his attention was focused on the mortal battle with the hyaenas. Coming in a final surge, the snout of the overly optimistic croc lifted out of the water and lunged at the buck's vulnerable stomach. This was a chance sent from the crocodile god, for such a small croc hadn't graduated to larger prey. The buck dropped his hindquarters below the water line. A minor whirlpool swirled. Suddenly the buck took a great, plunging leap closer to the bank and the swaying, bobbing hyaenas. He was free, but his stomach was torn. Blood dripped into the water. The croc waited his time further out in the pool, while on the edge, three slobbering mouths growled and giggled with excitement. Now the buck stood side on to the opposing dangers. Hunched over in pain, he renewed his splashing stamping, thrusting his horns from side to side.

My heart was in my throat as I remembered my six-year-old self struggling to escape a group of children who held my arms while another beat my stomach with a stick. As the new girl in the frontier town of Mt Isa in far western Queensland, I was being punished.

'To hell with the count,' I whispered to Aubrey. 'We can do that on the next full moon.'

He said he would stay.

Jer and I made the forty-kilometre drive back to camp in silence. My mind raced with memories of my own childhood ordeal and thoughts of the brutal attack on the hapless buck. At home I huddled inside the sleeping bag, hating the distant calls of roaming hyaenas.

Before dawn I woke to the clinking of a spoon stirring in an enamel mug, dressed quickly and joined Jeremy by the small fire. I must have looked as mournful as he felt. He nodded towards Bluey and muttered, 'Let's go.'

We drove across a plain bathed in the gentle rosy light of dawn, oblivious to the animals scattering as we passed. I expected to see no sign of the previous night's drama when we arrived at the waterhole, but I was wrong. The bushbuck was down, but not out. He was closer to the water's edge, but still on his feet.

Aubrey took the flask of hot coffee I offered, but he refused a rusk. His face was drawn from exhaustion, but he wouldn't have missed a second of the drama, he said. Like us, he was astounded that the wounded bushbuck had managed to keep both the hyaenas and the crocodile at bay for four hours. Surely the pugnacious fellow would collapse soon? He still stamped his feet and thrust his horns, but was twisting his body with increasing exhaustion. His tongue lolled out, and his barks and grunts sounded hoarse. I felt nauseous. *Someone should wring his neck . . .*

On the opposite side of the pool, a small herd of sable antelope drank as if all were calm. Bottoms up, heads down, the baboon family stretched along the water's edge slaking their thirst, but their eyes watched the bushbuck. Flocks of quilleas dropped in dense waves to drink. They landed en masse in nearby trees, crushing their shape with the weight of a thousand birds. The drooping branches sprang back with an audible whoosh when the birds lifted to fly. Or was it the sound of a zillion wings in flight?

An old buffalo plodded heavily down to the water; shaggy head hung low under the weight of his formidable boss. He paused briefly to peer in his short-sighted way across the pool at the frantic scene. He drank slowly. The old bull then sauntered to a well-used wallow, eased his bulk into the delicious mud and rolled with evident pleasure. And all the time, a struggle to the death was being enacted nearby.

In the strengthening light I could see the struggle was almost over. The life was gone from the buck's eyes and his exhaustion showed in laboured efforts to toss his horns and to bark. It was ghastly to watch. There was no dignity in the end of such a fine creature. However, fate had a plan that would deny the tormentors their prey.

A towering series of roars and bellows rolled across the savannah. Following the direction of the hyaenas' altered attentions, I turned to look behind. A large male lion was running fast – straight towards us. His body began to bunch for a spring. With one great bound he was upon the bushbuck. The hyaenas scattered, howling in frustration. The lion crouched low over his prey, grasping the buck's throat in his jaws. Except for the buffalo that was lumbering away slowly, the waterhole had been vacated. The crocodile had discreetly withdrawn to the middle of the pool.

Looking from behind, across the lion's heaving back, I saw he was desperately thin. Panting hard he lifted his shaggy, dark-maned head to survey the stage of his triumph. His lower jaw was hanging loose; the bottom teeth protruded over a flaccid lip. It became apparent that a strange sort of justice had prevailed. I imagined the events that had led to the lion's dilemma. Perhaps he had attempted to hobble a giraffe, only to collect a colossal kick from a powerful hind leg. His terrible injury assured an untimely death for the starving animal. But, for now, he would eat – albeit painfully. His flanks strained as he dragged the body out of the shallow water. With a baleful look in our direction, the lion flopped down across his meal.

I experienced a perverse sense of satisfaction that such a noble warrior would sustain (however briefly) the life of an equal adversary, and not fuel the stomach of the sly croc or provide breakfast for the grumbling hyaenas that swayed and weaved at a safe distance. As we passed them, I gave in to a childish desire to thumb my nose at their frustration. The six-year-old girl also felt triumphant.

We left Aubrey sleeping like a ginger fox in our lair and drove to the lodge to lead the Earthwatch teams to their designated hides for a last morning of game counts. When Aubrey woke, he was recharged. It was time to gather his crew for the return trip to Bulawayo, but he took a detour to the platform to view the scene of the night's battle. We followed him.

A satiated lion was dozing under a low bush, oblivious to the flies invading his ruined, blood-caked mouth. Beneath a blanket of vultures were the few remains of the bushbuck. Even now his spirit appeared to continue the fight: his horns seemed to butt at the foul spectres of death as they enacted a tug of war over his head.

Before he departed, Aubrey passed on a message the warden had received from Ekaim's brother, George Ndlovu, who lived and worked in the national park. A bull elephant had been hanging about his encampment. The bull was in great pain, crippled by a poacher's snare embedded deep in one leg. We needed to check the situation, and it was a wonderful opportunity to spend time with the Ndlovu family.

George was a pump attendant. He lived next to the artificially watered pan he maintained with his number two wife, Memory, and their toddlers. His number one wife remained in the distant village with their school-age children. She attended to their small plot of vegetables and tended their cow and goats. It was a domestically satisfactory arrangement for them all.

Every three months, George made the long journey to see his number one wife and their children. This required two days of travel in rickety buses each way, leaving him with only three days at home. It was the way of things for all the national park staff. They seemed not to mind. George considered himself a fortunate man to have a job at all.

Whenever we were in the vicinity of Ngweshla Pan, we set up our tent in the small compound next to George's concrete *rondavel*. There was a toilet and shower and a thatched open-sided shelter, which made our camping luxurious. But more than that, we enjoyed sitting by the fire sharing stories with George.

He seemed to know when we were coming, for we always found him standing at the crumpled iron gates wearing his best uniform that Memory had pressed into impossibly sharp creases with a coal-heated iron. It didn't matter that the shorts were frayed, or that the long socks were threadbare above highly polished worn boots.

George's pride in his appearance matched the dignity of the man. And even though I always asked Jer to stop so I could splash water on my face and hands, brush my hair and put on lipstick just before we arrived, it was hard not to feel scruffy when the gentle giant gravely clasped my hand in the African handshake.

As on every other occasion, George was there to meet us when we arrived to discuss the problem of the elephant. His

I could never relax on the water after my close encounter with the hippo while canoeing on the Zambezi River. I was an intruder in their world and made it my mission to tread quietly through wild Africa.

On the eve of our wedding.

Skew Tusk's infant daughter, Cathy, gleefully chases birds. When calves play, the world is perfect.

A wide-eared greeting from Sabre. I feared he would be targeted by poachers after his massive right tusk. Sabre and I shared a rare moment of understanding.

Within minutes, individual families would come from different directions to Konondo until the entire herd was gathered in a frenzy of joyful greetings – as if a time had been arranged. The tuskless cow, Inkosikasi, is content with our company.

We had great respect for feisty, unpredictable Bette Midler. She was a lovable rascal. Here she keeps her calf close as she decides whether to send us packing. Seconds later she trumpeted mightily and charged. We scrammed.

Skew Tusk, Tunny and Dilingane forget their dignity to revel in a mud wallow at Mataka. The elephants themselves humbled my belief that I would quickly identify individuals.

A family group
having a chat about
their latest triumph.
Once again the
cows had dug deep
to break a water
pipe in search of
clean water.

Sweet-natured Tunny
was always the first cow
to greet us when she
returned to the herd.

I will always remember
the first time I saw
Dilingane. Everything
about her was beautiful
– flawless ears, perfectly
matched tusks, a fine
conformation and a vivid
personality. She was the
loving peacemaker of the
herd.

Far left: Kathy Rogers (nee Martin) mentored my induction into the research project with the patience of a chameleon. Together we shared extraordinary times of joy, awe and sorrow as we entered the complex world of elephants. Our mutual passion to help the herd grew into a treasured friendship.

Left: Harold Broomberg. The gentle guru of Gwaai.

When I thought I might die, or simply needed a Band-Aid, I fled to Jenny Delange at the safari camp she ran with her husband, Des. Their kindness and concern for 'the crazy elephant guys' was humbling.

Far left: My son, Lachlan Anning, loves the rhythm of Africa.

Left: Jane Williamson came to the rescue the night of Jer's collapse.

Bheki cared for our needs in 'the days of joy'. He welcomed us home when we returned in 2006.

Tenzi the Elder (left) and Steve (centre) surprised me with a giraffe's head in the freezer. Janaman (right) created miraculous cuisine from simple ingredients in a tiny oven.

Every time we visited George Ndlovu at Ngweshla, he taught me more about Matabele culture and the ways of the wild. The nights were magic when we sat by his campfire as elephants trumpeted at the pan.

Memory Ndlovu was the 'number two' wife of George. We had no common language other than the understanding of being mothers. That was enough.

Calves test the food in their mothers' mouths. In this way they learn food choices. But this youngster habitually took water from his mother, which was unusual behaviour.

With the typical proud posture of a bull in musth, King strides majestically towards a breeding herd.

My hands were shaking when I took this photo just seconds before Tom Thumb charged. I was sorry for the sad little elephant. But even youngsters have immense strength.

Elephant bliss at Mpofu Pan. Skew Tusk (left on the bank) sifts for mineral salts.

The breeding herd came quietly into the acacia grove. After years apart they remembered us and blessed us with their trust, despite the escalation in poaching.

A rare night out in the wilderness.

Aubrey Packenham recognised a kindred spirit when he met my ebullient daughter, Lou Anning. The cheeky elder statesman and the wild child brought a refreshing lunacy to our campfire.

A Himba village near our safari camp at Hoanib in Namibia. Traditional ochre-covered Himba people resist change to follow a subsistence lifestyle caring for their cattle and goats.

A lioness chases hyaenas from the carcass of a poached bull elephant. His low-frequency, infrasound distress call reached across several kilometres to the breeding herd, although we didn't know then why they suddenly froze before stampeding in panic. It was the exact moment when a ranger noted the time he heard the gunfire that was inaudible to us and the herd. It was the greatest of privileges that the elephants continued to allow us to be with them despite such human atrocities.

Jer and Rembrandt at Farm 41. The Gang of Eleven visited our camp often. Once, a young bull in search of water flopped his trunk into the flow when I was taking a bucket shower.

We broke our journey from Australia to Zimbabwe in Egypt. Stricken with the 'Pharaohs' Curse', for a while I quavered with apprehension. A week later, any lingering doubts were banished when I met the breeding herd at the waterhole.

A storm gathers over the elephants.

A herd of springbok took flight when I surprised them while walking at Hoanib River Camp in Namibia.

Hippos are territorial animals. I was lucky to survive (while canoeing a backwater of the Zambezi River) when I inadvertently came between a bull and his pod. But the hippo was simply defending his home.

After I saved the yellow-billed hornbill, Effie, from a jackal, she became the camp mascot.

The white rhino, Rose, was killed by poachers. We found her calf crying beside the body. Rose's face and horn had been hacked off.

Giraffes sometimes chew bones for their minerals. However, this bull I named Predator always had a bone clasped in his ageing mouth.

Below: Unique social carnivores, wild dogs (painted wolves) are a highly endangered species. Sadly, when they enter farm holdings, the dogs are shot as vermin. This pack drove the kudu antelope against our tent. Within minutes it was consumed.

The sable antelope fought bravely to protect their young from the reign of terror of huge packs of spotted hyaenas. Once, I intervened.

Breakfast in the teak forest with friends. Rob (kneeling), Aubrey and Jer watch Shadrick cooking his legendary pancakes. Behind Jer, Stevie Wonder is probably hoping for *sadza*.

Settling into the hut that Stevie Wonder built for us at Farm 41. A shovel thrust beneath the door was our only protection from large predators. The camp was a safe haven until we discovered that an Egyptian cobra shared our home.

Lachy and Lou welcome me back to Australia.

Observing the Gang of Eleven from my favourite tree hide at Mpofu. It was here that I had close encounters with various wild animals – and one deadly boomslang.

With Cleophis (left) and Bellamy at Sikumi a few hours before our reunion with the breeding herd in June 2006.

deep voice softened with concern. 'You are home. Welcome to this house. The tea is coming soon.'

The little ones couldn't contain their excitement for long. Encouraged by Memory, they peeped from behind their mother's skirts with huge eyes and took hesitant steps. They knew we would have gifts for them of sweeties, balloons and fresh fruit. Their young mama was more reticent. As usual, she looked to George for his approval before she curtsied to accept the meat and provisions we offered. I had given up trying to stop this practice. I understood she did it out of habit.

It was different when the men left to look for the elephant. Now we were two women alone together. Memory giggled and chattered freely in Ndebele as she told me her news. Neither of us understood a word the other was saying. It didn't matter. We were women admiring each other's hair and skin. Memory's hairstyle was magnificent. She braided wool into her tight curls to make intricate patterned designs. I think mine was interesting for her because it was soft and loose, could be combed and had red undertones. She loved to brush it and weave it into tiny plaits. I thought we differed little from apes consolidating friendships, or from me as a mother tickling my children's backs while they groaned their delight.

Each morning and evening, George walked a hundred metres to the pump to top up the fuel – when there *was* fuel. His only protection was a strong pair of legs that were often put to good use in wild runs from dangerous animals back into the safety of the compound. The black rangers patrolled their territory on ancient pushbikes, which I thought incredibly brave. But George was a simple pump attendant who didn't qualify for such an expensive item.

I woke at five o'clock the first morning to a guttural whisper from beside the tent. 'Come, my friends. The wild dogs are here to kill a kudu.'

Sounds of chittering and whistling merged with the screams of a terrified creature. A great weight dipped into one side of the tent. I fell out through the flap into strong hands that hauled me quickly away from the canvas. Jer was right behind me. He flipped the switch on the torch. Its white beam lit up a scene of horror. The pack had an adult kudu bailed up against the canvas and were tearing the antelope apart while it still stood. I prayed that shock masked its pain. The kudu's haunted eyes stared fixedly ahead towards nothingness. Its tongue hung from a yawning mouth as it groaned the death rattle. When the dogs disembowelled the kudu, it fell down dead. Within minutes there was nothing left except the victim's steaming essence. The pack of nine then licked each other's bloodied faces. They fawned and skittered for a few moments more before peeling away, their tails wagging behind distended bellies. We were ignored, as being of no account.

My hand had been to my mouth throughout. Now I bent and retched, while Jer and George walked away to light the fire. When I joined them I observed that George was clean-shaven, immaculately dressed and calmly drinking tea from an enamel mug. In contrast, Jer looked like a wild man. His cheeks had heavy stubble and he was barefoot and shivering in the bitter cold of dawn, dressed only in a kanga he had hastily donned when George called. We could only think that George must have been up and about when the dogs arrived.

We recorded the sighting for our friend Josh, the wild dog researcher, who had still to witness a wild dog kill. I knew he would bemoan his bad luck at the same time as he cheered our good fortune (if it could be called that!). For this was our second experience of Africa's most efficient killing machine in action. On the other hand, Josh was witness to some aspects of elephant behaviour that we missed seeing.

After breakfast, Jer walked with George to the waterhole. Then they came running back. The lame bull elephant had arrived and was mad with pain. We drove the vehicle within viewing range, but not so close as to alarm him. He was standing beside the water worrying his grossly swollen right front leg with the left. Just above his foot the skin ballooned on either side of the deeply buried snare. Pus pulsed out with every movement.

Once again I felt sick with shame that human beings had calculatedly set a trap they knew would cause agony to an innocent creature. I smelled the stench of decay. He was dying from the foot up. We radioed Mike, a vet we knew who was de-horning rhinos on the western boundary of Hwange. There was a heavy silence before he replied wearily that nothing could be done 'for the poor old bugger'. He would tell the warden to put the bull down.

To soothe his agony the elephant moved deeper into the water. He stayed there all day and we waited with him until the warden arrived. Unfortunately, the bull had to be driven out from the water on to the plain before the merciful bullet could be shot, to ensure the waterhole wouldn't be polluted by his decomposing corpse. I felt like Judas when the men forced the elephant to place weight on the rotting foot for his final forced journey. Frank's bullet was straight and sure. The elephant was dead before he hit the ground.

'I won't be as good to the *munts* who did this thing if I find them,' he growled. 'They'll get bullets in the balls!'

Frank's expression remained dark while his men hacked out the elephant's tusks to take to a central repository for sale as culled ivory at auction. 'At least the poor old guy paid his way,' he said.

I didn't envy Frank his job. The government ran the national parks on a shoestring. Much of the warden's time was spent pleading for money to pay the staff, and I knew he had gone without in order to provide for others. His onerous job didn't make him easy company and he was a solitary man. We admired him, but we didn't know him.

Everyone was spent by evening and we decided to stay with the family for another night when the rangers left. Ekaim had come with Frank to help him dispatch the wounded warrior and he also stayed to visit his brother George. What a pleasure to sit peacefully around the fire in their company, in a treasured ritual of storytelling, cultural exchange and special silences. During previous visits, George had taught us something of his Matabele heritage and we wanted to hear more this night. It might help expunge for us the taste of an agonising death.

Other elephants surrounded us in the darkness, cracking branches and rumbling their own messages. Sometimes they came too close, which sent us running to the ablution block. Even then, George made a dignified retreat, never hurrying or appearing concerned. I was lurking in the shower receptacle long before he had completed the stroll to his *rondavel*.

We popped corn and toasted marshmallows over the fire for Harmony and Loveless, before Memory took the children to bed. George stayed with us, cradling a mug of steaming *rooibos* tea in his huge hands. Only his bulky outline could be seen framed against the night sky. He told the story of a day when he was relieving a ranger.

'One time, when the sun was just saying good morning to the day, I was riding my bike to fix a pump. This man was knowing to stay in the middle of a road. You see, there was *li-on* spoor walking before me – many, many feet are saying too many *li-ons*. The road was made of bumps and holes. I could not push the peddles hard to make a fast journey.'

He stopped and looked into the darkness carefully. 'I saw a thing that was not good. There were four father *li-ons* sitting upon an *mpofu* [eland] carcass on one side of the road. On the other side of the road there were four mother *li-ons* and their little ones. They had hungry bellies. You see, those daddies, they are too selfish with the meat.'

His shining white square teeth flashed a grimace. 'The mother *li-ons* were just sitting there, waiting for their husbands to finish. Their children were very hungry – and George was there in the middle,' he said.

'Were you frightened, George?' I asked.

'Aa-a-h no. *Re-ally*. I just stopped and stood beside my bicycle,' he replied.

'Was your heart beating fast?' I asked.

'Aa-a-h no. If it had been beating loudly the *li-ons* would have known my fear.'

He nodded gravely. 'A father *shumba* charged. He was shouting. He stopped near this man. I did not look into the eyes of the big father. To look into the eyes of *li-ons* is very foolish. It is asking a question of their courage. I stood with the *li-ons* for long. When they took some more food I pushed my bicycle like this.'

George walked backwards, pushing an imaginary bicycle ahead.

He continued, 'This man was thinking his ancestors were calling him. I could not stop to listen. There was just the going to fix the pump. This was my job.'

He paused to swallow a mouthful of tea. His eyes were downcast, looking at the fire and into his memories.

'The *li-ons* were sitting down. *Su-are*. They did not want to eat this man. But their heads were up and they were all looking. I just got back on my bicycle and rode to the pump.'

'But you had to return that way, didn't you?' I asked.

'Ahhh, *su-are*,' he replied. 'I was thinking much about those *li-ons*. All day. Too much. The drinking of water did not wet my mouth. It was dry.'

George pointed at his lips as he re-created the motions.

'When I was finished my work I came back. The father *lions* were sleeping. *Su-are*. The mothers and children were feeding. I lifted my bicycle into the air and made the walking – far around them. I am telling you it would not have been a wiseness to question their courage again. This family was making a meal. They did not want to lose their food to George.'

'Why didn't you ride your bike around them?' I asked. 'It would have been faster.'

'*Re-ally*, Mama Ndlovu, I lifted the bicycle of my friend because there were prickles in that *jess* [thick bush] that would hurt his tyres. These things are too much money.'

'I think you are a very brave man, George,' I said.

He replied, 'Ahhh, no. Thank you too much.'

I asked him which animal he feared the most. He rubbed his chin as he considered my question. His all-encompassing attention always rested on whoever was addressing him, as if that person were the most important being on earth for George. His courtesy was engaging and flattering. I thought he would have made a wonderful diplomat, but his grace wasn't studied. He was a born gentleman.

After long deliberation he replied that the only creatures he truly feared were venomous snakes. I would remember his response a few days later, but just then my thoughts were focused on the larger species of mammals. I reworded my question and asked George which of the Big Five – elephant, rhino, lion, buffalo and leopard – he considered to be the most dangerous animal. This time he replied immediately that, while he didn't fear them, it was the Cape buffalo he respected most for its tenacity and intent to kill.

'You see, my friends, when a buffalo charges he doesn't stop – *su-are*! You must run away. Ahhh . . . but this is not a good thing to do because that buffalo, he runs faster than a man. That animal thinks. You are needing to think better. If you see one resting in the shade you have to run away quickly. You seek to find a giant tree to climb.'

Ekaim nodded his agreement. 'Friends of mine have been gored to death by buffaloes,' he rumbled in a matter-of-fact voice.

George stood up and walked to a large camel thorn tree. Resting his hand against the trunk he said, 'This is the friend you want to see when the buffalo is chasing you. You must climb very high and wait. *Su-are*. Sometimes that buff will be with you a very long time.'

George shook his head with amazement. 'You know, even when that old man leaves you, it is a wiseness to wait long.' Buffaloes are very clever, he stressed, and will find a bush where they will hide and watch and wait. Tapping his head he said, 'But this head is too smart. This man doesn't come down early. Not before the buffalo has forgotten me.'

George leaned forward, his face grave. He explained that lions and elephants give warnings. 'With the *shumba* it is good to stand like the statue and never meet his bold eyes. When the *li-on's* body relaxes, you walk backwards. You must never show him your back. Or do the running. You see, running will tell him you are the prey.

'With the elephant you must also keep stillness. His eyes are not good and he can be distracted. But if his eyes are on you when you have caused him bother, he will charge. And he will not stop if you run. The tree will not be big enough to save you from an elephant. When he is very angry he will kill the tree and the person who is hiding there.'

George laughed. 'Then he will sit on you!'

He told us that some men had become too confident with wild animals and had died as a result. He shook his head sorrowfully as he spoke of a ranger who stopped his vehicle next to a waterhole to show his clients 'where mother elephants and their children were drinking'. The ranger got out of the vehicle and led the group towards the family. The female warned him with a curtailed charge.

George's eyes grew wide and hard. 'He mocked this mother. That crazy guy just kept walking at her, even when she was shouting and shouting, "Stay away from my children!" He did not listen. She killed him.'

He shook his head with disgust as he told us how the clients saw the elephant kneel upon the man and drive a tusk through his chest. 'They were very frightened and ran to the jeep, but they were not bush people and they did not know how to start the motor. They sat there, very much frightened, until some person came by.'

I jumped as an elephant trumpeted close by. Ekaim stood up and shone his flashlight in the direction of the sound.

George continued, 'You see, Madala, that elephant out there eating does not chase us away. It knows we are weak and very small, but it is leaving us to live. We do not threaten his spirit to stand on his shadow.'

Ekaim returned to feed a stick into the fire as George continued. 'The mother elephant left the body of that man and took her family away to a safe place. She did not hold bad thoughts about those frightened people.'

He sighed. 'These animals are just like you and me; they are wild creatures protecting their children. And then these government boss men want to come and shoot the mother and all her family – to punish them for the death of that man who asked the mother to kill him.'

The tragedy had been reported widely throughout the world, he said. 'Many visitors are reading this thing in the newspapers. For very long they did not come to visit us. Everyone suffered. Even my friends' jobs were taken from them. There was no money when the visitors did not come.'

Over the years, Jeremy and I learned much from George. We enjoyed his stories, both frightening and gentle, all told with a soft, melodious voice and in a quiet, thoughtful manner.

In a way, George's lion story prepared me for what was about to happen. For a while after witnessing the misery and death of the bull elephant my optimistic nature deserted me. I began to wonder if there were any hope for the wilderness. Whether Shakespeare had been right when he said there was a time and season for all things. I stayed close to camp pondering whether the time of the wild creatures in Africa was drawing to a close and our efforts were akin to breaststroking uselessly against the current. It was evident that humanity was swamping the last retreats of Africa's creatures and forests.

My friends made a plan to jog me out of my gloom. Neil arrived in camp. I was delighted when he introduced me to the long, lean fellow who unfolded from the passenger seat, doffed a battered bush hat, shook my hand and offered me a wonderful invitation. 'Would you care to come on a mission to find a Mozambique nightjar?' he asked, without preamble. And then, 'If you would like?' in a deferential way.

'I *would* like,' I grinned, before he decided to keep his own company.

I had been hoping to meet with Jim, who was an expert on the world of feathers and flight and something of a legend in Zimbabwe, both for his knowledge and his willingness to lead safaris despite his reclusive nature. Each time he had blown through the area I'd expressed my disappointment to Neil at missing him, so I guessed my friends had used my burgeoning interest in birds as an excuse to organise our meeting.

We set out on the evening of a brilliant winter day when the hot sunlight stipulated light clothes. Jim parked the vehicle beside the bush track and led me along the bank of a dry riverbed. I felt safe walking there with him. He was one of a select group of professional guides with the credentials, and the weapons, to lead tourists on walking safaris. Round metal spectacles perched primly on his beak-like nose. I found myself lifting my legs high and carefully in empathy with his manner of walking. He stopped often to strafe the surrounding bush with a wary gaze as he smoothed back his long black hair so that it peaked behind his head like the crest of a stork. Indeed, he looked like a stork. I giggled to myself at my tendency to reverse anthropomorphism by bestowing humans with the habits and looks of animals and birds.

'Is it, Mama Ndlovu?' he asked wryly with an arched

eyebrow, and I knew he didn't mean 'Are there any munchies out there?' He'd seen I was giggling.

An embarrassing blush spread slowly from my throat to my hairline. It seemed he had the acute sensory perceptions of a bird, too. *Bugger!* I felt silly. I was in danger of betraying Neil's trust in me at the same time as I squandered a precious opportunity to learn from Jim. Jim's encouragement of an embryonic birdwatcher was a privilege – especially in suggesting we seek the nocturnal birds which are always there, though rarely seen.

Jim stepped out again, with me tagging meekly behind. It seemed he forgave me, pointing out and identifying every bird we saw, even the many varieties of little brown jobs whose similarity made them impossible for a novice to recognise – unless the birds trilled their signature song during a sighting. Invariably the plainest birds made the sweetest sounds of all. We hugged the edge of the bank, keeping clear of the dense, thorny vegetation. Birdsong and the hum of insects filled the air. Tiny lizards scurried from the path where they had been crouching low to capture the last heat of the Kalahari sands. It was the arena of the god of small things – until I sensed the presence of a predator. Jim's back locked at the same moment.

A lean lioness bounded up the bank directly in front of us. Her startled face mirrored my shock. We froze as she dropped to her belly, growling and spitting. Black-backed ears flattened, behind a glowering amber gaze. Her tail was flicking hard. Everything about her indicated an imminent charge.

I knew that Jim would shoot only to save us. I also knew that the first shot would be over her head. With a steady, slow movement he drew the revolver from its holster. Another lion roared close by; adrenalin surged. I focused on the gun. It promised security, but we were in trouble. Moths fluttered in my stomach.

Jim put back his hand indicating that we should back off. Slowly, slowly, we began a silent shuffle to the rear. I watched his knobbly knees, huge compared with his thin legs. That was all I wanted to see until the lioness gained my attention with a series of roars that mimicked the call of the unseen lion.

She bunched her flanks. Again we froze, watching her only with our peripheral vision. My body was trembling. I remembered what George had said. She would sense my fear if my heart raced, but how could I stop its wilful thumping, or the rancid sweat of fear? The moths' wings were gathering strength. I heard George again. We mustn't challenge her further by staring directly at her. Nor should we face away from her. Her body eased a little when the other lion roared again. It sounded very close.

Jim backed off once more, lifting his lanky legs with care. I aped his movements from behind. Again the lioness bunched and wriggled, preparing to charge. Jim lifted the revolver high – aiming it above her head. There was comfort in the thing of steel. Another lioness bounded forward from the bushes, stopped beside the other and glared at us.

Just then I backed into the wide trunk of a tree and seized the chance to move behind it and out of sight. Jim joined me. We were hidden from the lionesses' view, but this meant we couldn't see what they were doing. As if there were nothing untoward happening, Jim indicated the tree and whispered, 'This is a *Terminalia sericea*.'

At that moment I didn't care about the tree *or* the cats. My attention was riveted instead on an enormous lizard spread upon a branch above our heads. The reptile returned my gaze for a few seconds, and then scurried down the trunk. Its long, curved claws screeched the bark as it passed by. I shuddered at the memory of being run over by a two-metre goanna in western Queensland and wondered that my mind could drift when I stood between lions and a monitor lizard in Africa.

We skulked in hiding for some time before Jim risked taking a look. I peeked out from behind his back and saw that the lionesses had the large reptile in their sights. They seemed bemused as it swept its rudder-like tail languorously to sway steadily into a thick bush.

'Is it?' Jim whispered. He seemed pleased at the strange sighting. Putting his finger to his lips he indicated that we should retreat further. Pointing behind me, he put his mouth to my ear and hissed, 'Head for those bushes. I'll cover you.'

He joined me seconds later. The cats had forgotten us. Their backs were turned, and their golden bottoms expressing intrigue were held high above their crouched front quarters. Their heads were buried in the thicket of the lizard's retreat. The threat to us was over.

By now it was almost dark. Shadows hugged the crisp night air and goosebumps of fear turned into goosebumps of cold. We made fast progress back to the vehicle, ignoring the shredding thorns that swiped at our bare legs. Just as we pulled away, a Mozambique nightjar landed on the road in front and settled into the dust to fluff and bathe. Jim braked hard. We had a wonderful sighting of this solid bodied nocturnal bird, after all.

Once again, Jer was elsewhere when my life had been endangered. But there was another night when we met a lioness on the path and he was beside me; along with an unseen friend.

It happened during one of our sojourns spent looking after the safari camp while Jen and Des took leave. On this occasion there was little time to lap up the opulence. We soon became involved in the problems of an unhappy Italian couple who had come on safari in a last-ditch effort to save their relationship.

The woman, her exotic beauty accentuated by her sadness, would share her misery with me at breakfast. Both she and her partner began drinking at lunchtime. This continued through the game drive and on into a dinner punctuated by abusive shouting and gesturing. We didn't understand a word. By now they were smoking hand-rolled cigarettes that gave off the sweet smell of marijuana. Even the waiters were bemused by their wild ravings, loving every moment of the drama.

Casting surreptitious glances at the couple, the entire staff lined up in their crisp white uniforms, as they always did, to dance and sing a rollicking blessing of the meal. The Italian couple were in full flight, apparently quite unimpressed with the melodious requests to God for harmony. They ignored the performance, too engrossed in throwing napkins at each other to care what was happening, and too drunk and stoned to notice the effect their tirade was having on the other clients, who were patently unamused by the drama. I asked Shaddy to make very strong coffee and attempted unsuccessfully to get the sozzled woman to drink it. Jer encouraged the swaying man to go to bed.

Suddenly the woman pushed the coffee out of my hand, jumped up sobbing and ran into the surrounding bush. Jer and the staff set off in hot pursuit. The man gesticulated wildly one more time before slumping into unconsciousness. The inimitable Jabulani found a new role to perform. Eyes gleaming with excitement, he swung the limp body over his shoulder and carried him to his *rondavel*. I followed. We eased him on to the bed and locked the door from the outside.

A swaggering Jabulani and I returned to the other guests who had by now joined in the salacious enjoyment of the proceedings along with the goggle-eyed staff. Perhaps it added spice to their safari. I settled them by the fire just as the elephants arrived. Usually the big guys stayed out of camp until the lights were extinguished, but not this night, on which there was a stoned, frightened woman running around in the darkness. At any moment she might stumble upon one of them, or fall into the mouth of a lucky predator. So could my husband, or one of the others searching for her.

Smiling with false confidence, I escorted the reluctant guests to bed, suggesting that they could watch the elephants browsing on the trees outside from the safety of their windows. I knew they were too excited to sleep and promised to tell them when the woman had returned safely.

For ages I waited with Jabulani and Shaddy by the fire. Our ears tracked the distant sound of men's voices communicating during their search. Then I heard a short scream from behind the staff quarters. The three of us ran there. We stopped and listened hard. I followed the sound of racking sobs behind the vast trunk of a rain tree. She was perched on the lowest branch and literally fell down at my feet with relief. It was like saving a drowning woman. She slobbered into my shoulder and clung to me so tightly I couldn't walk. Just then, Jer and the others appeared.

Back in camp, Shaddy made her a hot chocolate and she calmed, slumping into sleep. We put her to bed in an empty *rondavel*, taking the added precaution of locking her inside. She wouldn't be going anywhere for the next few hours.

Jer paid each guest a visit to assure them that the performance was over. He doused the paraffin lamps on their doorsteps. A ghostly blue aura hung above them. The elephants had gone and we felt safe to call it a night. Jer lit the way with a lantern to our own hut. It was quite far from the rest of the camp and was never an easy walk to make at night. No fences protected us from whatever might be in the vicinity. I don't think I ever made that trek without holding my breath. We had gone only a few steps when Jer paused.

'Hold on. I want to find a flashlight,' he muttered, twisting me about to return to the bar.

I pulled against his hand. 'Why? We've got a lantern,' I grumbled. I was fractious with exhaustion.

He replied in a harsh tone I have come to respect. 'Don't argue. I'm getting it!'

A few minutes later we returned along the path with the torch. I felt particularly anxious, but I put it down to the preceding traumatic events. We were almost home when a deep grunt stopped us. Could it be Roy? It wasn't. Swinging his great furry head lazily, a lion strolled across the path in front of us. We froze. He froze. The lantern surrounded us with soft light which only served to tell him all about us. Thank God, Jer had gone back for the flashlight. He switched it on and shone it straight into the eyes of the lion. I was back at Savuti with Nigel. This time the lion snarled once, squinted and bounded away. I shuddered to think of him earlier possibly watching the Italian woman as she floundered about in the darkness.

I didn't wait to see what would happen next. I bolted to the hut, closely followed by my husband. There was no conventional latch to hold the door shut here, either; this was a shovel job as well. I hoped it would hold if the lion decided to investigate further, but these thoughts didn't linger long. We felt shattered and sleep descended as a blessing.

In the morning, the Italian couple appeared at breakfast separately. They had the grace to look embarrassed. His face was haggard; hers was pale and even more beautiful: a Renaissance vision of tragic, heavy-lidded misery. They ignored each other as everyone else chatted in forced high spirits. I thought it doubtful the couple would resolve their problems. They had been saved from tragedy in wild Africa, but I think their relationship was doomed to end in gentler territory.

Paradoxically, I noticed that the other couples were showing each other more affection, and I found myself touching Jer more often. Peace returned to camp when the Italians left.

We kept the presence of the lion as our secret. I asked Jer why he had insisted on returning for the flashlight when there had been so many nights we had walked that path with just the glow of the lantern to guide us home. He looked puzzled. 'I don't know, Sal. I just knew we needed it.' He hugged me close. 'Sorry if I was rude. There was no choice.'

He held me away and looked deep into my eyes. His eyes widened in amusement and the same thought came to each of us.

'Instinct, I suppose,' he teased, as I said, 'It was the spirit of Africa.'

CHAPTER 15

The good, the bad and the chocolate thief

A few days later I was to recall George telling me of fearing snakes above all creatures. I would taste that fear and understand the feelings of dread, which were very different from my respectful wariness of warm-blooded predators. Snakes were always there, though rarely seen. It was too easy to forget their lethal presence while walking through the bush and even more so when we sat in tree hides far above the ground, in apparent safety.

It was blissful to sight elephants drinking, swimming and wallowing, but especially so when observed from hides that were secreted high among the branches of tall trees that lived joyfully beside spring-fed permanent waterholes. If trees re-incarnate, these must have earned good karma during previous lives; their roots were secured in tiny wells of plenty in a thirsty land. The trees camouflaged the vehicle beneath drifts of foliage.

With equipment strung around our necks and shoulders, we clambered up primitive ladders constructed from single planks nailed directly into the trunks. I always apologised to the trees for the intrusion as I climbed up into hides that were basic platforms encircled by rough slabs of timber. Smooth, wide planks were set horizontally as top rails.

I learned to be wary of the company that might be waiting above. Wisdom decreed we should broadcast our arrival to alert any creature tenants of our presence. Respectful of the silence of the forest, of the animal empire, we devised warning methods involving throat clearing and elephant-speak. In this way we confined our jarring human disturbance to the immediate vicinity. Our sounds weren't always heard and we had some close encounters.

One day I lifted my head above the floor to meet the shocked stare of beady brown eyes just an arm's distance away. The vervet monkey and I looked at each other with horror for an agony of seconds before the old man 'wokked' a harsh warning, and bounded up into the branches. He spent the next hour abusing us with a steady stream of invective – watched by his admiring family.

The youngsters in the troop played hide and seek with bright-eyed glances; peeping around clusters of leaves, and bobbing and ducking their heads whenever they caught my gaze. I mimicked their actions and they followed mine. The game was no different from many others I had played with human babies, who also found it very jolly.

One young male gathered the courage to scream at us in a higher tone, as if his voice were breaking. Perhaps it was the first time he had vocalised as an adult. He appeared to shock himself with his own daring, for mid-shout he fell from his perch into the hide, landing ignominiously on his stomach. His body continued the momentum, sliding almost to our feet. We burst out laughing at his human-like expression of horror before he made a hasty, undignified retreat.

Another morning we flushed out a pack of baboons – but not before they coated the platform with fetid calling cards. What was worse, we were unable to avoid smearing our hands, cameras and boots with the evil stuff. The stench of baboon faeces must surely classify as the foulest smell of the animal kingdom. We would have made a hasty exit to the water to clean ourselves and the hide except that a solitary buffalo bull lumbered in to the mud below us for an extended session of laborious wallowing. The resulting film of his groaning pleasure was almost worth the olfactory ordeal.

Most of the close animal encounters in hides happened at my favourite platform in a camel-thorn tree above Mpofu waterhole. Mpofu translates to 'Place of the Eland'. I think this was a misnomer, for I caught just one fleeting glimpse of these notoriously elusive antelopes at the waterhole.

There came a day at Mpofu that an intruder joined me and a close friend who was visiting from Australia. Celia's fortitude had been tested already that morning. She was in need of rest after a rugged few hours of exciting elephant activity. Before dawn we had nibbled a lean breakfast of rusks and dried fruit at a pan in the company of the Gang of Eleven. Celia and I sat in the tray with our backs to the rear doors; Jer was behind the wheel, ready to move out in an instant if the mood changed.

The bulls were jostling for the right to hog the closest source of fresh water where it flowed from a bore-pipe. Rembrandt's stance was defiant. As usual, he held the prime position where the sweet stuff emerged, well after he was replete. His wide face looked a picture of innocence as he kept the tip of his trunk clamped firmly over the pipe. Thousands of twitching muscles were busily beating off questing reaches from the other elephants. Rembrandt played with the water while his friends grumbled and shoved their discontent.

Eventually, bored with the game, Rembrandt broke away from the group and ambled amiably to the back of the vehicle. The trunks of the others surged upon the liquid gold, but it was Van Gogh who took up the stance of dominance as the second highest-ranking bull in the gang. His stay was always brief – just long enough to stamp his position in the pecking order – for he had a kind heart.

Rembrandt was in a happy mood. He draped his trunk along the top of the canopy. This wasn't unexpected, as he had discovered through experimentation that it was possible to span the width of the vehicle with his tusks. The distance between his widely spaced tusks towards the tips equalled the width of the vehicle. The first few times he tried this exercise we took evasive action. Eventually, his sociable attitude won our trust so that we judged it safe to stay with him in what was surely a compromising position – although Jer remained ready to start the engine for a quick retreat. Rembrandt's faith in us was an honour.

This day, like all the others, the bull gently eased the ends of his tusks around either side of the tray where Celia and I sat with our backs to the door and to him. For a long time he remained there, rumbling his contentment. His acceptance and trust of us were glorious for me, but not for my companion. I understood Celia's reaction when she broke into a heavy, shuddering sweat. People who live more conventional lives are bound to fear elephants during close meetings – just as I had in the beginning. It isn't just a question of courage; there is recognition of one's minute place in the universe. Hadn't Horace reduced me to the semblance of a worm so that I knew my smallness?

I tried not to take for granted the good grace of any wild creature. Yet I did permit familiarity where the elephants gave me their trust, even though I often continued to question their good intentions.

Eventually, when Rembrandt took his leave, we drove to Mpofu, to restore Celia's strength and to rest during the hottest part of the day. I had almost run out of film. Jeremy left us to snooze while he returned to camp for more cassettes. All was quiet. Celia and I settled into ancient fold-up chairs Jer had found abandoned in the ruins of a deserted farmhouse; what joy even broken things brought where the living was hard. The chairs looked very jaunty after I stitched up tears in the canvas with red cotton. Stevie hack-sawed nails to size to fill the holes where screws had been. Delighted at our lucky find we had hoisted these treasures up the tree to make long waiting periods more comfortable. Our outdoor theatre was now complete. We never knew what the performance would be or what creatures would play the roles. It didn't matter if nothing much happened on the stage – it was enough to be there.

We also cherished these moments of rest at the hide as opportunities to decipher our haphazard notes scrawled during wild waves of elephant activity. Sometimes, I would feel compelled to put aside such work and doze, do yoga or meditate. The platform was large enough for stretching exercises, which released the tortured knots of tension that seized my neck and shoulders after long stretches of immobility in the close company of the herd. During those encounters I was seldom aware of discomfort. When they were over, my numb body often woke into an agony of aching muscles – the painful after-effects of twisting into unnatural contortions while capturing fast-moving events on film and paper.

On the day Celia and I rested there the wild was still. I drew my hat across my face and dozed. Occasionally, the heavy silence of early afternoon was gently stirred by the hum of insects. I recognised the quiet snuffles and pungent odour of a wart-hog family nuzzling for tit-bits in the mud below. The tranquil moment was short-lived. There is no way to describe instinct. It just *is*. No thought of danger preceded the goose-bumps or slow chilling erection of the hairs on my body. Some inner force, greater than my conscious self, took me over. I have learned to heed the warnings I receive from my intuition, instinct or a spiritual force – for they share the same energy.

I slowly lifted my hand and drew the hat off my face and placed it on my chest. Without moving my head I swept my gaze around the hide. Celia was out of sight behind me, and so silent that I suspected she had succumbed to sleep. Our still and video cameras were set ready for action upon the wide rail in front of me. A flicker of movement shadowed across my peripheral vision. A hissing noise whispered once. The thing detached itself from the rail and slid with sinuous grace down on to the floorboards close to my boots.

Keeping still, speaking in a soft, steady monotone, I warned Celia not to move. Her soft exhortation to God assured me that she was awake and aware. Hardly breathing, I watched the snake glide closer, thinking of my bare legs, exposed between my shorts and socks. I doubted the snake was a harmless tree species. Something about the egg-like shape of its head suggested otherwise. The top of its body was a luscious shade of green with each scale clearly marked.

Previous experience with snakes in Australia had taught me when the distance between the reptile and me was great enough for a speedy retreat, and when the only option was simply to stand and wait. This was definitely an occasion to sit and wait. Besides, a tremendous snort below indicated the arrival of an elephant. There was nowhere to go. I hoped my companion would remain immobile. We sat as still as statues.

The muscles of the snake's body tightened and bunched before it lifted its head to sway close to my legs. There could be no doubt that this was a venomous creature. I knew. It is odd what comes to mind during moments of self-preservation. My thoughts were racing – jumping about like a mad monkey from the immediate danger and the knowledge that the closest source of anti-venom was in Bulawayo, several hours away by road, then back to the past in the lecture theatre where the professor of theology had explained the Hindu pantheon. The snake was the symbol of the Hindu god Shiva, the giver and taker of life. The mantra 'So Hum. So Hum,' came to mind: 'God and I are One. We are One. Shiva and I are One.'

The symbol of Shiva flicked its forked tongue to determine its onward course. I chanted silently my song to God. But it seemed the snake must surely feel the hot vibrations of my shallow breathing beaming a signal of fear. Clutching my hat against my breast with locked fingers I closed my eyes, hoping to find a calm space; to control the adrenalin surge; to contain the olfactory signals my wilful, overheated body was sending to the reptile. A picture appeared in my mind's eye of our much-loved little silky terrier burying her face under my arm whenever we attended the veterinary clinic. She worked on the premise that if you can't see the frightful thing, then it isn't really there. Perhaps this would work for me.

A quiet expulsion of air from behind me broke the spell. I dared to look. The snake was slowly retreating towards the edge of the platform. Effortlessly, elegantly, it slid up and over the rail and on to a nearby branch. *Thank you, God.* Living on the edge can habituate one to surging adrenalin. Sadly, it can also make one begin to crave the addiction – to taste the bliss of having survived. In this state of euphoria I saw a golden opportunity to film the snake at close quarters. Creeping nearer, I bent to pick up the video camera I had left on the ledge. I used up the last of the tape on the snake, leaving me with a superb series of images of reptilian grace.

Celia still hugged the rear of the platform, apparently horrified at my temerity. Her cockney accent returned with a vengeance, as it did whenever she was excited despite having lived half her life in Australia.

'Cor blimey, Sal! What are you doing? Don't be so bloody stupid,' she said. 'I'm having a heart attack!'

I laughed. 'It's all right, Celes. We're safe now.'

But I did move back a little. She had reminded me that photographers can too easily forget the danger at hand while training the eye on the lens. The remoteness of the creature through the frame creates a false sense of security, as it seems to be imprisoned there. But I felt sure that this snake wasn't interested in me. Not anymore. By the time Jeremy returned, he was unable to leave the vehicle until the seventy elephants flanking the water moved away. And somewhere close, the snake slithered about its business.

* * *

That night I described the markings of the snake to Ross, who was a guide and amateur herpetologist. He snapped his fingers with regret, 'Man, you had a boomslang there. Why didn't you grab it for my snake house?'

My answer was a series of wry facial expressions.

Ross, otherwise known as 'The Angry Ant', had been known to brake violently during game drives before calmly descending from the vehicle to capture venomous snakes. Once, he took a long black mamba by the tail, bagged it and then continued the drive quite oblivious to the condition of seven horrified tourists, who thereafter saw nothing except the ripple of the loosely tied hessian bag on the front passenger seat.

Dark, sharp-faced, whip-thin and hyperactive, Ross wore his youth as a burden, tempting fate with an aggression that bordered upon mania. When his rage was ignited by opposition, authority or disappointment, I feared for his safety – even for my own.

Twice, I confronted unacceptable behaviour from him with reasoned argument and faced the full force of his uncontrolled rage. One time the herd had been fidgety and alarmed for several days following a confrontation with poachers. Slowly we had regained their confidence, and we rejoiced when they joined us at their favourite acacia grove. We deemed it wise to sit quietly, forsaking cameras, fearful of startling them with clicks or whirrs.

After an hour we heard a vehicle approaching at speed, but expected it to halt at the sight of the elephants. We were wrong. The driver – easily identified by his trademark baseball cap worn back-to-front hunched low over the wheel as he rammed the accelerator to the floor to charge at the elephants. All hell let loose. They turned tail and thundered away into the thick bush. Confused, frightened cows shepherding their terrified babies were the last to leave. Equally confused, I turned away from the sorry sight to see what in God's name Ross was doing. I felt hot with rage when I saw his mouth agape in grotesque glee. Slapping the wheel with satisfaction he screeched to a halt beside us; tyres spewed more dust into the floating red pall left in the wake of the herd's retreat. For a moment there was a heavy stillness. I glared into his close-set black eyes set on mine with a familiar 'death stare'.

Ross cut the expression of glee from his face, looked grimly from Jer to me and then defiantly shouted, 'Howzat?'

Before I could follow my instinct and slap his face, he spun the wheel and roared away. Figuring that quiet, reasoned discussion would be the best approach, we waited until our fury had subsided before confronting him. He stabbed an inverted middle finger at us then stormed away to his hut, where he loaded his rifle and shot the thrush that woke him at dawn by pecking at its reflection in the window. Jer and Des sorted him out in their own way. I noticed the Ant had a black eye the next day. I didn't ask any questions.

After that, we maintained a kind of truce with the surly man-child. He took possession of an Egyptian cobra found inside our hut by Lovemore, who sometimes collected our laundry. It was essential to have all of our clothes ironed (even my delicate underclothes) to destroy the eggs the putzi fly lays in search of a host. If these parasitical insects are transferred from clothing and burrow into moist areas of skin they develop into maggots that eventually hatch from disgusting boils.

Equally shocking was the presence of a snake that must have decided our pile of dirty clothes made a lovely warm bed where it sat on the floor awaiting Lovemore's collection. I was crouched over the early-morning fire, clutching a cup of hot coffee in frozen fingers, when I smelled diesel fumes and heard the sound of Stock's tractor chugging down the track. He sat like a statue behind the wheel with an unlit cigarette hanging from his lips. He was drunk, as usual. The tiny form of Lovemore stood behind Stock wearing a wide-brimmed Stetson he had been given by a grateful guest. The crown covered half his face, dwarfing his small frame even further. Stock turned off the engine. He attempted to focus on me with the questing movements of a blind man.

'Would you like a drink of water?' I teased, knowing he would refuse.

I think his veins would have closed with the shock of anything less than pure alcohol. Lovemore bounced on to the ground and disappeared into the hut to collect the laundry. Within seconds he retreated back through the door shouting, in a perversely deep baritone 'Mama! Mama! There is a terrible thing – he is wanting to bite me!'

Jumping up and down on the spot, looking for all the world like an African leprechaun, he pointed repeatedly in the direction of the hut and bellowed, 'You must come and get this bad snake from the master's pants!'

Resisting the impulse to crack a joke about being more terrified of the snakes in the trousers of men than of the snakes in the bush, I clenched my jaw and resolutely marched towards the hut. Stupidly, I looked at Stock to see if he would help. He had fallen asleep over the wheel. I was it, then.

I well knew how much Africans loathe this spectre of myth and magic; but I didn't much like them, either. Certainly, I had been forced to dispatch snakes in Australia, but there I had some knowledge of what behaviour to expect from the local species, which I didn't of the boomslang that had come into the hide at Mpofu. Thrusting my chin forward with determination, I attempted to present a facade of confident ease to the trusting little man who followed at a safe distance. I peered around the doorway at the offending pile of clothes that was now strewn wide. I saw a section of tail emerging from the leg of a pair of khaki trousers and quickly decided that this was not a job for 'the Mama'.

Jeremy was away collecting firewood, but I felt sure he too would prefer to hand over to an expert the extrication of our visitor. Posting Lovemore as the lookout behind a tree that stood by the hut, I called Ross on the radio.

'Jolly good. I'll be there now-now!' he shouted with delight.

As he was fifteen kilometres away, 'now-now' took about twenty minutes; and that was good going in his decrepit matriarch of a Land Rover, which he had purchased from a group of nuns who ran a nearby mission. The ancient vehicle was aptly titled 'Chariot'.

Jeremy returned with a load of dead wood to find me filming a prancing Ross as he waved his snake-catching apparatus before the swaying hood of the bemused cobra. Meanwhile, Lovemore's hat was peeping from behind the tree trunk where he had remained since I asked him to watch the snake. I was immensely relieved to see 'Chariot', Ross and the snake disappear in a black fog of exhaust fumes, especially so when Ross discovered the cobra had lived in a burrow beneath our humble abode.

The only other snake we flushed out of the campsite was a puff adder, which was similarly transported to Ross's snake house. Strangely, 'The Angry Ant' always released the snakes back into the bush when he had completed his observations. In the safety of the wilderness grew an embryonic conservationist, even if it were cold-blooded reptiles that he admired. Perhaps in controlling such emotionless creatures he was exorcising his personal demons.

As a child of the Australian bush I developed a healthy respect for poisonous snakes. I learned early to advertise my presence by singing, whistling or crashing about when moving through long grass. However, a goanna once caught me unawares as I stood very still, looking up into a tree at a bird's nest. The metre-long reptile must have mistaken me for a tree trunk, as it ran straight up my legs, over my head and down the other side!

Another time I was washing clothes in the wash house of my family's isolated cattle property when I tripped on what I thought was a hose. The 'hose' rose before me to chest height. I still wonder at the high jump I made on to the platform of a tank stand to avoid the reptile's strikes. My children were infants at the time, so the decision was made to lay thallium bait in an overturned tin of condensed milk under the floor of the homestead. The snake took the bait a few days later. It was a deadly, three-metre-long western king brown – a particularly aggressive variety with lethal venom that is injected into victims (again and again) through long fangs. If the snake had bitten me I would have died before we could get to the nearest town of Charleville, 150 unsealed kilometres away. The ferocity of this Australian snake is infamous: similar to the legend that has been built around a particular snake of Africa and its capacity to attack without provocation or warning – the black mamba. I began to harbour a fear of encountering one of these snakes after hearing some of the stories recounted avidly around campfires.

Jen's freckles stood out in contrast to her ashen skin when she told me of her encounter with a black mamba a week before we had arrived in camp. She was prone to understate rather than exaggerate facts, which made the story even more frightening. One very hot day she had felt compelled to wind up the window of her small truck before stopping to watch a herd of sable antelope cross the road.

'I know it sounds silly,' she explained. 'I just had to do it.'

With her attention locked upon the beautiful scene in front, she heard tapping on the glass beside her. What she saw there was extraordinary – a black mamba attacking the window in an effort to get to her. With each strike, the fangs of the frenzied snake slimed the glass with bursts of venom. Horrified, Jenny gunned the engine forward among the startled sable. In the rear-vision mirror she watched the enormous snake slide and skip after her, with the major part of its body sweeping up off the ground in a grotesque pattern of swaying, forward-thrusting jerks. She was horrified at the calculated intent of the aggressive reptile.

When she arrived back in camp, Des measured the height from the ground to the venom residue on the window and estimated that the mamba was over three metres in length. The story was given more credence by the fact that thereafter, no matter how hot the day, Jenny always drove with the windows closed. She reminded me of this when my own predilection for hanging out of car windows brought me grief from an infinitely smaller creature.

* * *

The iridescent dark green insects slammed hard into my head. Jer was driving fast, with me leaning out the passenger window scanning the bush for elephants. Too focused to be concerned, I brushed the shimmering beetle bodies away, but my throat and left eye were burning.

Just then, we found Bette Midler and her family wallowing in the mud beside a round waterhole; *blissful moments*. For a while I was so captivated by their fun that I ignored the irritation. Bette accepted our presence for a while before she surged out of the mound of muddy bodies in a powerful charge. She never bluffed. As usual, she was shouting her displeasure and her family was already retreating in the opposite direction.

We returned to camp. The shaving mirror reflected a strange swelling beginning on my throat and at the edge of my left eye, and my vision was blurred. Jer decided we should go to Des and Jen's safari camp to see what to do. Normally I would have let the stings run their course, but eye problems aren't to be taken lightly. We placed the insect bodies in a jar for identification. They looked evil even in death.

When we arrived, I showed Des my cache of insects and the marks from the stings. He shook his cheetah head. 'Shame, man. You've taken a hit from blister beetles!'

'Should I worry?' I asked, unable to hide my anxiety. 'Surely there must be an antihistamine lotion that works?'

Looking concerned, he replied, 'Afraid not, Sal. These little critters give me the creeps.'

Leaning closer, he peered into my eye. 'Yah, I can see the beginning of a blister forming. It's going to get much bigger . . . then the thing will burst and release a liquid that acts like acid.'

He sat back, screwed his eyes into slits, bared his teeth and made claw hands at me; I felt far from amused, or reassured.

'Man, that stuff will start a series of new blisters where it falls and hits the skin. Ay-ay-ay-ay-ay! I think you should gap it to Bulawayo for medical attention. You need some good *muti* [medicine]. Mustn't mess with your eyesight, eh?'

'That's revolting,' I said. 'It sounds like something from a sci-fi horror story.'

Jer agreed with Des. 'We'll head off in the morning at first light.'

Jenny moved into full mothering mode, and insisted that we stay the night. Tutting and fussing, she led me to the most luxurious *rondavel*. 'Try not to worry, little one. Have a lovely long bath and come up to meet the guests. That will take your mind off things.'

Her expression of dismay mirrored mine as she looked at the now pendulous bags of acid hanging down my cheek and throat, which seemed to grow as we watched. Feeling a little frightened, and upset at the sight of the rapidly expanding blisters, I immersed myself in the water, in the ultimate luxury of the sunken, square stone bath. The bath was surrounded by a line of flickering candles arranged by my darling friend. Normally, this fabulous treat would have filled me with delight. Instead, I struggled to keep my throat above the waterline, where the blister swelled like the horrible gobble under the beak of a marabou stork. Both blisters burned hot.

I dressed for dinner in one of Jen's beautiful dresses. I hadn't worn a dress in months. Fortunately, it had a lace collar that was loose enough to button high up, but not so tight that it pressed upon the blister on my throat. I didn't know how I could cover the other one, which swayed horribly beneath my eye. My reflection in the full-length mirror reminded me of some alien being. Jer returned to find his wife sobbing on the bed. 'I can't appear looking like this. I'll put people off their meals,' I hiccupped.

He hugged me hard with one arm as he patted the tears beneath the 'thing' with the other hand. He was careful to avoid touching it, lest it burst. 'You look beautiful to me,' he whispered.

He pulled me into a sitting position on the side of the bed and began to drag on my boots. Unfortunately, Jen's sandals were too big for me.

'Come and have a drink, darling girl. That will make you feel better.'

I peered again in the mirror and burst out laughing. The blister jiggled horribly. I looked like Little Orphan Annie, wearing heavy boots without socks beneath the lovely, feminine dress. I let my hair fall forward to droop across my eye, and we set out arm-in-arm to face the stares.

As it turned out, the guests were very polite and made no comment on the strange sight. I suspected that Des and Jen had briefed them before we appeared. After dinner, I retreated outside to sit on the *stoep*, aware that the blisters were now swollen hard and probably about to explode. I could feel intense heat emanating from them. A man came and sat beside me. His name was Howard, he said. He was a senator in the Zimbabwe government. For a time we talked about the challenges he faced as one of only two white senators. My fingers kept straying towards my eye. Howard took my hand. In a quiet voice he asked, 'Would you let me help you? I'm a reiki practitioner. I believe in healing with the energy of the universe.'

Recalling my amazing recovery at the hands of the couple from Gwaai the night of Horace's charge, I blurted out: 'Yes, please!'

For a few minutes he placed his hands above the blister hanging from my eye. His stomach gurgled and grumbled intensely as he concentrated on channelling energy. Soon I felt the area become cooler. When he had finished, Howard found Jer and said: 'She should go to bed now. In the morning it will be *lekker*.'

I added some fervent prayers to his affirmation as I slipped into sleep wondering at the depths of spirituality infusing the least likely of beings in mysterious, magical Africa.

As soon as I awoke the next morning, I rushed to the mirror. Relief swept over me when I saw that the blister beneath my eye was greatly reduced in size and my vision was no longer blurred. But the blister on my neck had burst and three more were forming around it. 'Bugger!' I shouted, waking Jer with a start. 'I forgot to ask him to heal the blister on my throat.'

The oversight convinced me that Howard had indeed worked a miracle. Within a week the only sign of a problem near the eye was a red mark, while the blister on my throat, which Howard hadn't been aware of, had caused real damage. We chose not to make the long trek to Bulawayo once the threat to my eye was over. Instead, I placed Elastoplast beneath the new blisters on my throat to catch the acid before it could touch my skin when they burst. But it was months before those lesions healed. Even today, my throat blooms red whenever I am nervous or have a fever.

'You know, I never thought I would say this, but I don't want to see any elephants today,' I said to Jer the next morning back in camp. 'Anyway, if they see these blisters they'll scream and run! I need time just to hang out and relax.'

I was thinking as well of the wicked box of Belgian chocolates Jenny had given me. 'You need a treat to help you get better,' she had fussed. 'A client gave me two boxes. I'll get fat if I eat them all.'

It was a generous present. Good chocolate was impossible to find outside the cities in Zimbabwe. Sweeties were confined to boiled lollies that refused to melt in my mouth and sherbet confectionery made from the tart fruit of the baobab that was too tangy for my tastebuds. I clutched the precious box and salivated at the prospect of soft centres and truffles. I needed to get out of my head space, in which thoughts of snakes and evil green bugs jostled for position, and what better way than through my stomach?

Jer said he would take a chair, a few chocolates and a book to the waterhole. 'Make sure you push the shovel under the door,' he insisted, as he left me in the hut, where I planned to take a nap.

The door to the hut didn't have a handle, and the shovel was one way to secure it. But it was a hot day, so I ignored his warning. I popped a soft-centred chocolate in my mouth, placed the remainder on top of our food box and collapsed on to my sleeping bag. I dozed off thinking of the treat that lay in store when I awoke.

Instead, I opened my eyes to see a wart-hog boar lying beside the bed slobbering and grunting with relish! His hairy wart face and immense curved tusks were coated in chocolate and he was snuffling into the empty box.

'Get out, you rotten swine!' I yelled as I hurled a book at him. The wart-hog jumped with fright. All four legs left the ground at the same time as if each one were attached to a pogo stick. Without thought for my safety I leapt off the mattress, grabbed the shovel and hit him on the rump. Screaming like a pig in a slaughterhouse, he lifted his tail high and tore away into the bush. I followed, shouting insults so loudly that Jer heard me and came running.

'What the hell is going on?' he called.

When I told him my precious chocolates had disappeared down the throat of a wart-hog he began to laugh, and laugh, until I threatened *him* with the shovel.

'I told you to put that thing under the door,' he howled. 'Serves you right. You're lucky it was a pig in a poke and not a lion in your den!'

He pulled from his pocket a squashed chocolate wrapped in cellophane. 'Here, Squirt. Have this. It's the last one. I was saving it for later.'

It was a cherry ripe, which is my least-favoured flavour. But I accepted his offering and ate it very slowly.

CHAPTER 16

Jer's health scares

Kathy came to visit that evening clutching a jar of cream she said would minimise the scarring caused by the blisters. It was an old Zimbabwean remedy, she said. I was less impressed when she suggested that Jessie might assist further if I let her lick the wounds! I admired the devotion Kathy and many of our friends in Africa had for their Jack Russell dogs, but there was a limit. Even though I had observed wounds on my own dogs heal very quickly when they licked them, I thought it was to do with getting rid of dead tissue. The acid from the blister beetles was getting rid of enough tissue already, and I wasn't about to lie down and let Jessie work close to my eye or on my ravaged throat. I declined the offer.

Jack Russells seem to be the favourite breed of dog in white

African homes. The genes of their ancestors have mutated into a different-looking animal from those who take out Grand Champion ribbons at dog shows in other countries, but they are nonetheless feisty Jack Russells. Like Jessie they all tend towards shorter legs, wiry coats and long bodies. Legendary stories are told of their prowess in chasing large game that is bluffed into retreating by their brave aggression.

Jessie came from a litter whelped by the adored bitch of Pebbles Williamson, who lived with her seven Jack Russells (sometimes dozens when there were pups) in a cottage near our research room at Hwange Safari Lodge. Pebbles was eccentric in the way of many white women who live in Africa. She was careless about her appearance, yet draped herself with an odd mixture of expensive gold jewellery and cheap baubles. Every month or so, she dyed her old-fashioned, shining bob of hair a different colour, or streaked it with shades of purple and mahogany.

Despite her languid, 'who-cares' attitude, Pebbles' capable efficiency kept her in employment when women of a certain age in Africa are often overlooked. She organised safaris for tourists, who were captivated and astonished by her peculiar way of speaking – 'Daaahhhhhhhling, how are YOOOooo?' – and by the many dogs she allowed free run of her office. She worried constantly about her future, and with good reason. In a country without social security, impoverished widows needed to work until they dropped, and to squirrel away enough money to maintain them in their retirement.

At any given time, there was always one bitch on heat in Pebbles' household. This drew the unwelcome attentions of the local villagers' male dogs – a lean and mean breed with the alert, ear-pricked attention (and appearance) of Australian dingoes. They were generally known as Kalahari dogs and appeared to have a common ancestor.

One day, a Kalahari bitch on heat came to Pebbles' house. Perhaps the female was searching for better genes for her pups, or for a better life. She took up a position under a tree outside the secure yard where the male terriers were fenced and began quietly to starve. Unable to satisfy their desperate desires, the males barked and moaned continuously.

Incensed by the ruckus, the management was threatening Pebbles with dismissal if she didn't get rid of the Jack Russells, the bitch, or both. She found us in the bunker and asked Jer if he would help her son, Bloat, who was coming to capture the female and take her to a distant village. If the rescue mission failed, the bitch would have to be shot. Soft hearts prevailed and we suggested a plan to bring Jessie along to quieten the female when we attempted to get her into the vehicle. Kathy said that Jessie would either hate the strange female, or decide to be her new best friend. Within seconds she was licking the cringing animal, who accepted her ministrations without complaint. This was a good sign.

Bloat was standing by with a rifle, but we all hoped to make a clean capture. Gripping a lasso behind his back, Jer approached the bitch slowly. He crouched low, and held his other hand forward and down in a submissive gesture. Without warning she bit him and ran off. Bloat had no choice. He shot her. I rushed to Jer to tend the deep and ragged wound.

'Oh my God, Daaahhhhhhling,' Pebbles drawled. 'That ungrateful bitch deserved to die.'

She looked accusingly at her innocent son and growled in a voice gruff from cigarettes, 'Bloat! Why didn't you take her out straight off?'

He rolled his eyes at us in a long-suffering way.

'Get real, Ma,' he muttered. 'It was you who wanted to be the Good Samaritan.'

Pebbles ignored him, and I became annoyed with her. It was unfortunate that our efforts to return the dog to her regular territory had failed: that she was dead. What was worse was the possibility that she may have been carrying rabies. Jer was required to begin a series of rabies shots in Bulawayo. These he christened the 'lilac torment' because of the colour of the serum in the gigantic syringes.

Undeterred by the endeavour's unsuccessful outcome, Pebbles called upon us a few weeks later to assist in eradicating another pest. This time it was elephants.

Apart from the Jack Russells, and her three strapping sons who were all professional guides, Pebbles' great love was the garden she had managed to generate despite the incursions of a multitude of creatures intent upon eating her efforts. She was the widow of a legendary game warden who had delighted in peeing on her most treasured plants during competitions with his friends as to who had the furthest-reaching, highest-arching and strongest flow. This became their excuse for imbibing enormous quantities of beer. They needed, they said, to gather the resources for the challenge ahead.

Bloat told us that his father also wanted to rile his wife. 'And why *wouldn't* he?' he said with a big grin. 'My mother's a doozy bird.'

Pebbles screwed her tiny nose at him, but she acknowledged the intransigence of his father's peeing exploits. 'Daaahhhhh-lings, that's why I keep these bloody plants alive, to show that man a thing or two – even though the stinker has left me.'

Everyone knew of the intense love they had shared, despite

their eternal bickering. It was deep enough to bear the burden of sarcastic humour.

By day, Pebbles' garden was protected by her 'dog-and-garden' girl. By night, it was up to their mistress to defend the ramparts. She set traps by surrounding the entire plot with an intricate cluster of tin cans, cow bells and bottles that were attached to lengths of string and rope. These served as primitive alarm signals whenever the line was breached. With the first clunk or smash, Pebbles would be out of bed. She was often seen running through the garden in a scanty nightdress waving an unloaded revolver about as she trilled, 'Daaahhhhh-lings, the garden has intruders.'

Pebbles contained her sanctuary well, until the elephants discovered the delectable scent of oranges and grapefruits that bowed the branches of their spindly hosts. The first night of their invasion, Pebbles enraged the management by shooting bullets over the heads of the bulls. This certainly sent them packing, but Pebbles was in danger of following behind. Guests were woken by the sound of shots being fired. Some even feared, they later confessed, that they were the targets of bandits after their belongings or even themselves.

The next day, Pebbles appeared in the doorway of the research room wearing heavy metal bangles that banged together as she gestured wildly, and an expression of troubled innocence. She was transparent, but I played along knowing she would dig in if I didn't. As usual she headed straight for Jer. 'Daaahhhhhling,' she crooned. 'You have to help me find a way to stop your beasties from stomping on my garden.'

Seeing his doubtful expression, she tottered over to me and folded me into an ample bosom strung heavily with amber and Venetian glass trade beads. *Ouch!*

'*You* tell him, Susie,' she cajoled.

Not for the first time, I said: 'Pebbles, my name is *Sally!*' She never remembered names, which was why she called everyone 'Daaahhhling'.

'Oh, never mind, daaahhhling. Tell him anyway,' she begged.

And so I did, for she was hard to resist.

That afternoon, Jer and several friends began to dig a moat, with Pebbles working hard beside them. Her bangles jangled, and from her thrice-pierced ears swung chandelier-length earrings. The dry moat stretched along two sides of the house until it reached high security fences that spanned the rest of the garden, dividing it from the lodge proper. The moat needed to be wide and deep enough that an elephant couldn't step across, or down and up on to the other side. When it was done, Pebbles rushed about restringing the cans and bottles along the perimeter. I jumped to her commands like a good child obeying her mother.

We stayed on for a *braai* with an interested group of friends who had come to see if the defensive strategy would work. Not a thing came near the moat that night. I suggested gently to Pebbles (one didn't dare to offer advice any other way) that it would have been easier simply to plan a party each night, as any self-respecting wild creature would have preferred to avoid the loud and awful renditions of rugby songs and bawdy laughter. There were no complaints from the management this time because they were all at the party. Even some of the guests at the lodge came to play.

The next night we worked late in the bunker. At 11 pm, we crept quietly to Pebbles' house to see if there were any action before we drove home to camp. Three elephant bulls were standing at the moat; each swayed a front leg backwards and forwards in frustration. They had already set the alarm system jangling. We watched as one tried to step down into the ditch, with embarrassing results. He slipped forward on to his face and was forced to balance by pushing his bottom high, until he could manoeuvre back out. He broke wind and squealed with the effort. The other bulls watched with amazed expressions, until he made it out and upright on to four legs. The three of them departed quickly.

Pebbles must have been sitting at the window watching them, for, as they left, she opened the pane with a dramatic flourish, stuck her thumb up at their retreating backs and shouted, 'Take THAT, daaahhhhhlings! Got you, didn't I? And tell your bloody friends not to trifle with me. Pebbles has won.'

Pebbles' son Bloat was a hard-drinking, snowy-haired giant of a man who blew his tough cover with a gentle voice and manner. He was engaged to Jane, who had been a nursing sister but now managed a tented bush camp. She was a tall blonde with a cheeky, freckled face and a vibrant personality. They came often to our camp to escape the tourists.

We were expecting them to visit for a *braai* on the evening of a long day we had spent observing the wanderings of Dilingane and her family. All afternoon we followed the group as they foraged, working on charting their eating pattern. Dilingane was heading straight in the direction of Farm 41, which was very convenient. The elephants moved quickly through the thick bush and we beat a path behind, making heavy weather of the terrain.

They moved over a ridge mounded by man to build the narrow-gauge railway lines that ran between Victoria Falls and

Bulawayo. Jer pushed the vehicle up the sidings, on to the tracks and into a large hole set squarely between the rails. The right front wheel was jammed deep down. Our only option was to walk to camp, which we estimated was quite close. Jer was having a long think about what to do while Kathy and I watched the retreating backs of the family. We were praising our good fortune that the elephants were moving away, when Bette Midler crashed out of the tree line coming from a different direction.

Within seconds, the three of us were back inside the vehicle. From here on, our safety would depend upon Bette's mood. She was the last cow we would have chosen to encounter without an escape route. The air in the cabin crackled with nervous tension. If Bette decided to charge, we were in trouble. For a few moments she stood ominously still, staring at us. Then she lifted herself higher and whacked her ears indignantly across her shoulders.

'Jesus wept! This isn't the time to sit quietly. We've got to stop her before she charges. Go for it, girls!' Jer shouted as he hit the horn with short staccato blasts.

Sweating hard, we screamed warnings. Unlike out first encounter with King, this time I was sitting in the middle and was more accustomed to close encounters with elephants. But memories of that meeting with the great bull flashed through my mind. Kathy banged the outside of the passenger door with a spanner. Sweet Dilingane turned around with a startled look, then gathered up her family and fled. Bette hadn't advanced, but her body was puffing up like a bolshy bullfrog's and I knew a charge was imminent.

She lifted her head even higher at the moment we heard the sound of an engine roaring. *Thank God* . . . Bloat's four-wheel-drive was on the rail tracks speeding towards us. He passed us and skewed down the embankment, heading straight for Bette. She trumpeted her rage, swung around and hurtled into the trees; back to her family, who must have been there somewhere. The horn blasts were replaced by the screams and toots of angry elephants. Once again, we had been saved at the last moment.

With Bloat and Jer taking the main strain, we rocked and lifted Bluey out of the hole. Bloat and Jane had been on their way to our camp when they heard the horn blasts, which in the African bush could only indicate a serious problem. Bloat had immediately veered off the sand track to investigate. The couple had known that someone was calling for help.

A few minutes later, the smoke-belching steam train tore along the tracks as it did every day at 5 pm. I glimpsed flashes of curious faces peering out of the windows. As usual, the train was being driven too fast through game country. Carriages had been derailed in the past in collisions with large game. Animals and people had died. This day, Bloat saved us, Bette *and* the train. During dinner around the fire we raised a toast to our red-faced knight. A few weeks later, it would be Jane who assumed the role of saviour.

It was a harsh day of cold winds, stroppy elephants, skittish game, high-flying grey clouds, chapped lips, fingers in mittens and filming problems. Skew Tusk made mad rushes at us, stopped to snort her indignation, departed, and then returned to vent her spleen on her family. We were all in her firing line. Her ire infected the family, passing down through the pecking order. Irritable cows shoved their lessers, down the chain to the lowest-ranking female, who snuck away with her tail tucked forlornly between her legs. Only the babies were left to play their usual jolly games, although even their little bodies tended to jump nervously at nothing.

Gusting winds always upset the rhythm of life on the savannah. Prey species huddled together in open spaces, their ears and nostrils flickering and quivering to catch any breath of danger. A whiff, a panicked leap in the opposite direction from the smell of the predator, and then a new gust of empty air said that all was clear – for a moment. There would be a few minutes of calm and the cycle then repeated. However, the predators didn't have it all their own way. Nervous prey may have found it difficult to track their scent, but the resulting erratic movements of the quarry could spoil the hunt at the last moment.

The wind rose with the sun. I caught sight of a leopard hidden within long tufts of grass that swished and flayed around the form of the stationary cat. Leopards know the secrets of their camouflage and melt into carefully chosen hiding places. When seen in the open, their vibrant beauty shines in technicolour which makes their ability to conceal themselves seem all the more unlikely. But windy days favoured no creature, including us. When we stopped, so did the car's heater. A teeth-aching chemical chill seeped into the cabin from the metal. It was always coldest just after dawn.

I watched the leopard remain motionless as an impala yearling grazed closer, until it was within striking distance. *Run baby run* . . . Just then, a swirling dust devil rolled across the leopard's back and on, dousing the impala with her scent. The antelope bounded clear as the leopard charged. *Hurrah! Hurrah!* I empathised with the prey, in the case of leopards. They are ruthless, sly killers with a high success rate. Their malevolent gaze is chilling.

We discussed the dreadful allure of these aloof cats while we ate apples and cheese for breakfast in the company of the elephants. By lunchtime the wind and the frayed tempers of both man and beast drove us back to camp. We were excited at the prospect of a visit from Aubrey. He would be staying the night after another game count – this time a general game tally.

Mid-afternoon, when the trees were bending deep before the wind, Aubrey's Land Rover rumbled into camp. I swung the billy on to the fire to make tea and ran to greet him. Jer was resting; still fragile after a bout of gastric trouble.

'I have a surprise for you, my girl,' Aubrey chortled. 'I've dropped a chiller box at the lodge, and dinner is on me.'

He refused to reveal the contents of the box. 'It's a secret feast,' he grinned. 'Where's the big guy?'

A pale-faced Jer appeared in the doorway and the two men shared the type of distant punching hug that is as far as such men will go with each other.

'G'day, you old bastard. How are you going?' asked my husband as he fended off another parry.

'Better than you – you silly bugger,' roared Aubrey. 'Ay-ay-ay-ay-ay! The runs, eh?' he shouted with delight. 'You need a toot, man. Keeps up the levels of alcohol in the blood. No bugs can live there.'

'Get out of it,' said Jer. 'Your blood and guts are pickled!'

'Never had malaria. Never will,' Aubrey growled. 'The bloodsuckers give piss-ants like me a wide berth. Teetotallers are suckers for the suckers!' he roared with relish.

I listened to the banter and worried for the state of Aubrey's heart. It was a great, generous heart, but he was surely living on borrowed time. As I thought this, he grimaced, pulled a tiny bottle of pills from his shirt pocket and popped one under his tongue. He noticed my concerned expression.

'Hey, the angina kicked in when I saw you, my beauty,' he smiled with all the charm of his Irish forebears. 'Make no mistake. Greg Botha keeps the ticker fit. Chr-r-i-ist! The man up top doesn't want me yet. And the guy in hell has enough trouble without adding me to the dung heap!'

From what I had heard about the notorious Dr Botha, I doubted it. It was more likely that he encouraged Aubrey's wild ways. I hoped my friend was right about the rest. We sat drinking Five Roses tea close against the windless side of the hut and discussed serious matters for a while. The clouds fled across the deep blue. Today the sky was high. The wind blew away the smoke of cooking fires and the dust that rose from the feet and hooves of a multitude of game and domestic animals. When the air was still, the hazy sky over Zimbabwe looked nothing like the intensely clear blue that shelters vast, empty Australia.

Aubrey's twinkling eyes disappeared inside wrinkles of pleasure as he stroked a hand along his mottled face and into his shock of greying ginger hair. 'The surprise awaits Cinderella. Go, put on your ball gown.'

It wasn't a ball gown, but I did drag out my one pair of elegant black slacks and a pretty pink blouse. I fossicked further and found a pair of delicate sandals studded with shells bought in a market by the Aegean Sea at Epidaurus in Greece. They smelled exotic. My feet felt elegant and light – liberated from heavy boots.

Such finery deserved some make-up. It was fortunate that the only lipstick that hadn't melted was a deep cerise colour which matched my blouse. This inspired me to outline my green eyes with plum-coloured pencil. In the past, when I was a reluctant model, make-up artists insisted that I wear plum to accentuate the colour of my eyes. Carried away by the improvement, I smudged the lids with smoky shadow and inserted a pair of large, fine gold hoops into my ears. I was dressed for a party and flounced outside to the admiring comments of the men. It felt good to be a woman.

The sun was setting when we arrived at the lodge. The wind went with it and now the air was still. A bar, fondly named The Watering Hole, sat high in a tree house on the edge of the lawn beside an artificial dam. We drank sundowners with our feet resting on the rails. Even now, deep in the dry, the grass surrounding the buildings was lush and green from the daily dowsing of bore water. Long lines of sprinklers created hazards for tourists who skipped in and out of the spray to get closer to the dam and the creatures drinking there. Dry brown leaves, stripped from deciduous trees by the winds, were already being raked into neat mounds by groundsmen wearing the ubiquitous green overalls, even outnumbering the stifling army greatcoats and head-hugging woollen caps many wore throughout every season. I assumed they must be highly valued items.

Beyond the dry moat, topped by a two-strand electric fence, the bush was dulled by dust and the ground lay rendered bare from the tread of game. A solitary crocodile rose from its basking spot to slip into the muddy waterhole. A family of kudu, three giraffes, a buffalo and several zebras watched him disappear beneath the surface. Plovers rushed about calling 'ping-ping-ping', and a family of Egyptian geese huffed and puffed towards the reeds and sleep. On the tree line, a dainty duiker ducked about as it pondered the wisdom of venturing into the open to drink.

Elephants were smiling their pleasure at a salt lick directly below us. They often broached the ramparts of the lodge, sweeping through the sizzling current at a place where the waterless moat was narrow enough to cross; it was the place where I first met Horace. Our little research bunker stood close by. I was immersed in the beauty of the moment when Jer whispered: 'Hope I don't disappoint Aubrey. Mightn't be able to eat much yet.'

I looked with concern as he rubbed his stomach with a rueful grin. 'Shame. Isn't the Imodium working?'

'Like concrete,' he grimaced. 'But there's a lot of rumbling happening. Think I'll play it safe and stick with clear soup and dry bread.'

Jane and Bloat arrived. Grins split their cheeks. They had come to share the surprise. We strolled across the grounds to the restaurant. The manager, Simon, led us to a table that groaned beneath the bounties of the sea: freshly cooked red lobsters, platters of fat oysters and shrimps, enormous fish topped with slivers of lemon and capers, and tartare sauce tucked inside coils of whitebait. And *this* on the edge of the Kalahari Desert.

Aubrey watched our reactions of delight with the beaming smile of a proud father. Jane and I fell upon his grizzled neck with gratitude. Then we all pounced on the feast: except for Jer, who played with his bread and sat quietly watching the elephants that had come on to the lawn.

When we had eaten our fill, and then some, Jane and I took our coffees to the windows to watch the elephants. Suddenly there was a crash, followed by silence.

We swung around as Aubrey shouted, 'Chr-r-i-ist almighty! Jeremy's collapsed!'

My husband was lying unconscious on the floor. I ran to him and dropped to my knees to lift his head on to my lap. His face was grey. His mouth hung slack. I wondered why I felt so calm when my heart was thudding like a piston. Jane placed her ear to his chest.

'Shit! He isn't breathing,' she muttered. 'He's closing down.'

They were the worst words I had ever heard and yet, even then, another me stepped aside and thought: *How incredible that I still feel calm.* My conscious self, meanwhile, remembered that Jane was a nursing sister. 'Thank God you're here. What can we do?' I asked her urgently.

Aubrey was panicking. 'Put one of these pills under his tongue,' he shouted. 'Fuck! It's a heart attack!'

Jane pushed his hand away and reached up to grab a bowl of sugar from the table. 'I'm the nurse here, Aubrey. This is what we need. If it doesn't work, I'll start CPR.'

Jer was very ill. His bowels had voided. Except for Aubrey's shouts, the restaurant was as silent as a tomb. I glanced at the other diners, who were all looking at us in a frozen tableau of startled faces. Some of them were wrinkling their noses. It wasn't a pleasant smell.

Within seconds, the sugar dissolved on Jer's tongue. It worked. He took a great gasp of air, and I breathed again with him. My beloved opened his eyes, sniffed the air, looked at me with shock and whispered, 'Holy shit! I've dropped my bundle.'

'Shit, yes! Holy, I *don't* think,' Aubrey chortled.

The colour was returning quickly to Jer's face. Perhaps we had given ours to him, for the rest of us were pale and clammy. Now the elephants were lined up at the windows looking inside as if they knew there was something wrong. Thankfully, this distracted the other diners, who left their chairs to rush over and watch the giants that were watching them.

Simon and Bloat carried Jer to one of the suites. I ran a bath as Jane sat with him to monitor his vital signs. When she was confident that he was recovered, the two of us lowered him into a tepid bath.

'What happened? What is it?' I asked. Now I was shaking.

'I've seen similar collapses before,' she replied. 'I suspect the vasovagal nerve in his stomach spasmed. Probably because he's been ill. It's most likely that the combination of food and drugs induced shock. He'll be fine now. But he needs to rest for a few days, eh?'

Jane led me to the well-stocked bar in the suite and poured us both a stiff Scotch. She stayed for another hour to be sure Jer had stabilised. Simon came and went, offering assistance and insisting that we stay in the suite for at least one more night. At any other time I would have jumped at the chance. Now, all I wanted was a magic carpet ride to the surgery of our dear friend Sue Newton and a positive assessment of my husband's health.

Jer cracked jokes constantly about his fall from grace until I thought I would scream. When he finally fell asleep, I crept out in search of a bin where I could throw away the awful trousers. I never wanted to see them again. In the morning I changed my mind. The trousers were his only decent pair. They were R.M. Williams moleskins given to him by a friend of the great man. In the early light I snuck to the bin to retrieve them, but when I lifted the lid I found they were gone. All the rubbish was still there, so I knew that someone had taken them. It was a sad testament to the desperate poverty of Africa.

Jer seemed to be his old self when he awoke. His stomach had settled and he was hungry.

'Are you sure you want to brave the stares?' I asked when he suggested we go to the restaurant for breakfast.

'Too right,' he replied. 'I could eat a hippo. Actually, make that an elephant!'

Even so, I decided that we should have our meal in the garden and not in the restaurant. As we passed the dining room, Simon stuck out his head and muttered gravely, 'Morning, young man. Would you like to come and lie down in my restaurant?'

I loved Simon's sense of humour, and the self-deprecating way in which my husband joked with the concerned waiters to put them at ease. He relaxed them all, but not me. For weeks afterwards, I watched him like a hawk. When we consulted a doctor later, he agreed with Jane's diagnosis. Only then did I relax.

CHAPTER 17

From desperation to elation

Jer recovered quickly. But the hard living was about to take its toll on *my* health. Early in August, at the height of the cold dry season when black frosts burned the dry grasses, the elephants moved far from Farm 41. They were on the move and we were travelling with them. Towards evening, we found a good site. I erected a folding table scrounged from friends, while Jer sorted the poles and guy ropes to pitch the tent.

The day was bleak and overcast. An unpleasant cold wind filled the air with thick dust and made the wildlife skittish. I found those bleak days of Zimbabwe's cold season the hardest to endure. The only time I ever felt completely warm was inside the heated cabin of our vehicle when it was actually moving. The temperature dropped below freezing at night and not even the hot-water bottle kept me warm in my thin sleeping bag inside the tent. We wore thermal underwear, socks and thick jumpers to bed. Woollen beanies stopped the warmth leaving our bodies through our heads. An eerie, whining wind gusted across the canvas, accentuating our feelings of isolation and discomfort and inducing nightmares.

I was quite used to being without a hair dryer, which wasn't a problem while moisture still lingered in the air, but now my dust-coated hair stood straight up from my scalp in scruffy dreadlocks. Static electricity surged through me, even lighting up the room at night when I waved my arms about. I learned to approach all metal objects with caution. When I forgot to wind cloth around my hands before grasping Bluey's handles, I sustained sharp shocks which even emitted a noise. The powdered earth choked our sinuses, causing breathlessness and constant coughing. Our tanned skin peeled and took on the consistency of cooked chicken's feet. Smiling wasn't even an option, as our lips cracked and bled with the slightest movement. Body lotion had little effect. There were always drops of nasal fluid hanging at the end of our nostrils, which we didn't dare wipe in case burgeoning fissures split open. Instead we poked lanoline cream inside our Rudolph-red beacons and accepted the ugly scene. My nose developed a wrinkle across the middle from constant swipes of my sleeve.

'Good thing it's your little button nose and not mine, Squirt!' Jer said wryly. 'My great conk doesn't need any further ruin inflicted on it, eh?'

We all suffered alike, but the toll on our bodies extended to our state of mind. We snapped at each other over nothing as we unloaded Bluey. Jer's witticisms became caustic and were met by me with a dull stare and a humourless imprecation to, 'Give it a break, why don't you?'

One day the tent was taking shape when we were interrupted

by loud trumpeting. I whirled about to see the alarming sight of a huge bull elephant bearing down on us at speed. Jer had disconnected Bluey's battery for some running repairs, so there was nowhere to go. The bull was almost upon us when Jer picked up a tent pole and charged straight at him, shouting the sounds he made when he was moving recalcitrant cattle around the yards: 'Eh-eh-getup-getup!' But this wasn't a cattle prod he was waving, and this animal was measurably less controllable than a steer.

However, the bull seemed to be impressed. He skidded to a halt just in front of us, wearing an expression of astonishment. Jer sensed his bluff was working and waved the pole harder and shouted even louder: 'Eh-eh-eh-eh-getup-getup!'

I jumped up on the little table, which was a ridiculous and cowardly thing to do – *shame and mortification* – and could barely see what was happening through the dust that burst into the air beneath the bull's legs engulfing us all in a dense cloud of claustrophobia. Then the elephant turned his attention to Bluey. He pushed his trunk inside the open tray back, knocking out a box filled with provisions. Oranges rolled on to the ground. Jer and I retreated behind a tree and watched the big fellow stuff his mouth full of fruit. He didn't miss one! Satisfied with his haul he strolled away, leaving two very startled humans in danger of nothing worse than scurvy; and, in my case, acute embarrassment.

We decided that the elephant must have picked up the scent of the fruit, as his charge hadn't been aimed at us. He was interested only in what we carried in our provisions. We realised that we hadn't carried citrus fruit with us until that day. It simply hadn't been available until then. And it was never part of our food hamper again.

That night, I cooked Jer a special meal, cracked my chapped lips without a second thought as I howled at his jokes with frenetic eagerness (even when he chortled at my table-hopping cowardice) and waited on him with the adulation due a hero.

After our run-in with the bull, we were careful to keep Bluey close to our tent, ready for immediate evacuation if the need arose. The living was hard. The animals were on the move, so we rarely stayed longer than two nights in each camp. I spent more time looking for dry tinder than watching the elephants. I swore I could smell seals on the high southerly winds blasting straight from Antarctica. When the wind dropped, a low cloud-bank obscured the sun. At night we crouched over the fire, scorching the front of our bodies while our backs froze.

The elephants looked as miserable as we felt. They roamed constantly in search of scant pickings. Dry leaves mounded in dirty yellow layers beneath skeletal mopane trees. The water in the pans shrunk into slime ponds packed with terrapins and dying fish. Everything suffered. Baboons sneezed, and vervet monkeys and I coughed with what I thought was an allergy to the swirling dust storms. But within days I was running a high temperature. I didn't give in to Jer's demands that I test the dubious nursing skills of Charity, who ran the clinic at Dete, until the cough became so uncontrollable that my hacking presence even drove the elephants away in alarm. We returned to Farm 41, where I squandered five buckets in the bush shower before the water ran clear. Then I joined the long queue outside the clinic.

Charity rose from behind her cluttered desk when I entered the room. She was awesome: a large woman with an enormous bottom and wonderful buttocks that moved independently of each other as if ferrets were fighting inside a bag. She stood well over two metres tall and wore a crisp blue uniform with a crackling white wimple perched upon a towering beehive hair-style. I shrank into a chair, exploded into a gasping fit of coughing, and awaited her ministrations.

'Aa-a-ah. So!' she bellowed. 'This is the flu!' Handing me some tablets, she growled: 'You must take this *muti*. Two of these tablets, four times in each day.'

'But you haven't taken my temperature, or listened to my chest,' I replied.

'Aa-a-a-h. No,' she responded, giving me a deep frown. 'This is the flu. I know it is. I cannot come close to you. My patients need me. You must trust me. I am the doctor.'

And so I did. But a couple of days later I was bedridden with new and unpleasant symptoms far worse than the original illness. Jer checked the packaging on the antibiotics and discovered they were months out of date. This wasn't unusual in Africa at that time. Pharmaceutical companies often donated drugs well past their use-by date to Third World countries. It was better than nothing. But we weren't confident. The time had come to seek a real doctor.

Jen radio-phoned ahead to make an appointment for me with the renowned Dr Botha in Bulawayo. 'He's a character, Sal, but he's good. Make sure you see him before lunchtime though,' she giggled.

'He's Aubrey's doctor, isn't he?' I asked doubtfully. 'The one who likes a wee dram or two in the afternoon?'

But no one was listening. In truth, I felt too sick to care. Jer drove like the clappers to get us to town before lunch. On the outskirts of Bulawayo, he swerved to avoid a woman lying in the middle of the road. I caught a glimpse of her terrified, twitching face as we passed.

Jer slowed as another driver shouted, 'Keep going! It's a set-up.'

Later we heard the sinister reason for the woman's collapse. Desperate men had been convinced by a *nyanga* (witchdoctor) that their wives must sacrifice themselves beneath the wheels of vehicles to cure their husbands of AIDS. If the women didn't do this thing, they would die anyway – and here was the most potent threat – along with their children.

When everything else failed, the *nyangas* who practised *mshungu* (black magic) wielded terrible power over their distressed clients. Their belief in the *nyangas'* dreadful threat was so strong that they often *did* die. They themselves fulfilled the *nyangas'* prophecies. It was the same in my own country. I had seen the power the *kadaitcha* man (spirit doctor) wielded over Aboriginal people. One had cursed a young couple in love, who fled when the girl was promised in marriage to an old man. He invoked the power of the *kadaitcha* man, who prophesised they would drown. They heard his curse and ran to the desert, where they assumed they would be safe. However, the healthy pair contracted pneumonia and drowned in their own fluids. It was an awesome example of the power of the mind – that what we think *is*: although I have also come to believe in a formidable power of evil that *can* afflict unbelievers.

So, for me, the reason the terrified woman waited for an innocent traveller to run her down was shocking, but not surprising. The evil, slithering *juju* the African witchdoctors wielded had already affected us. Jer was warned never to leave me alone after several white women were raped when a *nyanga* told other men this would cure them of AIDS.

I wasn't thinking of any of this when we hurtled along the wide streets that were designed by the city fathers to allow twelve-span ox wagons to turn around with ease. The space and grace of the city contradicts its dark history of tribal and inter-racial warfare that gives it the title 'Bloody Bulawayo'. Feeling pretty bloody myself, I urged Jer to hurry. I just wanted to get to Dr Botha's rooms, and was relieved to see they were on the ground floor of an elegant old colonial stone house close to the city centre. Right then, I needed solid evidence of my own culture. I settled into a chair in the waiting room. An elegant black woman wearing traditional Ghanian clothes sat beside me. Her beautiful face was framed by a vibrant turban. My efforts to control shuddering tremors failed miserably. The woman took my hand in hers and patted it with concern.

'My dear,' she said. 'You must see the doctor before me. I think you are sick with malaria.'

I assured her that it was only the flu and expected her to move away quickly. Instead, she removed a handkerchief from a copious bag and wiped my face very gently.

Just then a tall, emaciated, stooped man wearing pince-nez glasses emerged from an adjoining room. In a clipped English accent, he called my name. I had expected that someone with the name 'Botha' would be solid and bluff and speak in the guttural tones of the Afrikaaner lineage.

'My God, woman!' he exploded, when he saw the antibiotics and the dosage I was taking. 'These are dangerous drugs. One capsule three times a day is the correct dose. You're taking enough old shit to kill a horse!'

Dr Botha clipped a cigar for Jer and himself and then wrote a prescription for a different antibiotic.

'You must stay in Bulawayo until I give you clearance to

return to the country,' he insisted over the enormous cigar that belched smoke into my protesting lungs.

He bent his stork-like frame to turn the key of a magnificent mirrored mahogany cabinet. Inside was a row of crystal decanters. He lifted the stopper of one, poured two liberal tots and offered one to Jeremy. This was like no doctor's surgery I had ever seen. 'Here, man. Drink this,' he said.

I looked questioningly at Jer, who winked as he lifted the glass to his lips before wandering to the window. There were times when politics demanded that my husband keep silent about his preference for soft drinks. This was one of them.

I broke into a distracting paroxysm of coughing. Jer emptied his glass into the garden while the doctor's back was turned, and then set it down hard on the desk.

Looking both impressed and startled, the doctor lifted the decanter. 'One more time, eh?'

'Thank you, but no more. I'd better get the girl to bed. That was *lekker*,' smiled Jer, wiping his mouth with apparent satisfaction.

We arranged to return the next morning and walked back into a waiting room now overflowing with patients. *Good luck to you*, I thought. Africa's wildness wasn't confined always to its population of animals. I waved to my Ghanian friend, who stood next in line. She held her hands together before her face and bowed. I did likewise.

We had the prescription filled in a bare, poorly stocked pharmacy, before driving to the home of a friend who was a professional hunter. His lovely thatched-roof African-style house was set amidst a garden of cacti and boulders, atop a knoll with distant views of the Matopos where Cecil Rhodes's grave sits at the top of the world. Barney was away, but we had an open invitation to stay. His man welcomed us with tea and scones before leading us to separate guest quarters swathed in orange-blossomed bougainvillea and jasmine.

Jer tucked me into bed. 'How about some Chinese?' he grinned. 'Makes a change from our usual tucker.' When he returned, I didn't tell him that I could neither smell nor taste the exotic treat.

Sometime in the night I was awakened by the sound of a vehicle driving into the compound. Male voices rumbled as heavy objects thumped down in the direction of the kitchen. Jer was sleeping heavily, so I crept across the courtyard and into the kitchen to see what was happening. Barney had come home with the trophies from the latest hunt. Staring eyes of kudu, eland and sable popped despair beneath the sweeping horns of their severed heads. The smell of gore and death filled the air.

Barney lifted his cap and out tumbled a mass of golden, shoulder-length curls. They sat incongruously above the deeply dented forehead of his pugilistic face. His heart matched the colour of his hair, but he was a wild man. Years earlier, in the small hours after a heavy drinking party, Barney fell asleep in the middle of a road. A vehicle ran over his head and fractured his skull, leaving him with a steel plate set deep into his forehead where the bone had been crushed. Barney was rather proud of his battle scars, and made the most of things by telling terrible lies to wide-eyed, potential conquests about being crushed by various great beasts. But pity didn't make for enduring relationships, Barney still lived alone.

'Howzit?' he asked as he downed a beer and offered me another from his blood-encrusted hand. 'Saw your *bukkie* parked outside. Come. Tell me your news.'

'Um, not tonight, Barney. I've got the flu. Best you keep clear of me.'

I staggered back to bed quite sure that the experience was part of a nightmare. But in the morning, Barney was there and so were the grimacing heads. I asked if we could eat breakfast in the garden, away from the accusing stares of the antelope. These were female sensibilities, for I knew that Barney was a deeply committed conservationist who managed wildlife well. He donated a good portion of the hefty sums paid by his clients to shoot their victims to efforts to preserve the rest. It was the men and women who enjoyed shooting wildlife and gloated later over their dead-eyed mounted heads whom I found offensive, not the professional hunters who carefully chose aged animals and often had to finish off their clients' botched kills.

In the afternoon I felt well enough to go with Jer to the city centre, but I stayed inside the vehicle while he went to shop for food in the marketplace. In Bulawayo, a solid human presence did more than protect the goods within a vehicle; it could save the vehicle itself. Car hijacking had become a way of life in cities throughout Zimbabwe. Within minutes of a heist the thieves would have changed the numberplates and transformed the appearance of the vehicle with a quick job of spraypainting.

Jer left me on guard and walked quickly into the teeming hordes, pursued by a woman with a sleeping, pink-bonneted baby slung on her back. She shouted as she pushed large bags of oranges at him and chased away her rival hawkers. Several men, dressed in tattered clothes, ran after Jer's purposeful strides. One proffered a protesting hobbled rooster, while others pushed varying sizes of hand-carved wooden or stone giraffes and elephants into his face. He smiled over their heads without pausing, knowing that any sign of interest would be the signal for even more vendors to besiege him with their wares. And they were beautiful wares. The stone sculptures and wooden carvings were works of art that would sell for vast sums in First World countries. Instead, here, the return for hours of creativity might feed the family for one day – *if* they were lucky.

The official marketplace was located inside a large, open-sided building. Unofficial vendors spread their produce and crafts on the ground outside, each within a relatively small prescribed area. Eyes that were habituated to the perfectly attuned shades of nature blinked at the vivid colours of fruit and vegetables, hand-woven cloth, batik paintings, carts crammed with flowers, brightly dyed baskets, and fluorescent pink and green crocheted tablecloths. However, the people themselves seemed to be dressed for a funeral.

I thought of the vibrant outfit of the Ghanian woman at the doctor's surgery, but I knew why these local women wore dull skirts and faded floral blouses. Most of the clothes had come from aid packages, already old before the rock-pounding washing ritual removed the last traces of dye. The men were dressed in dark trousers and dull shirts that flapped over their skinny chests.

Some men played drums or blew into flutes, radios blared modern music, children shouted, babies cried, women laughed, men argued – or seemed to argue – when arms flew wide and heads snapped back as smiles turned into grimaces. The air was filled with dust, and smoke from tiny fires strad-dled by grids warped beneath the weight of tightly packed cobs of roasting corn. The perfume of roses massed in plastic buckets mingled with smells from pungent stews bubbling in fat cast-iron pots; from protesting caged chickens and ducks; and from the sweat of a thousand people.

When Jer disappeared into the crowds, the roving vendors made me their target. I kept the windows closed and stared at anything other than them. I felt uneasy. I wasn't indifferent to their plight, but I knew that if I bought one thing the ranks would swell, adding angry arguments to the confusion. One man climbed on to the bonnet and pressed his face to the windscreen, imploring me with his eyes as he dangled necklaces made from seed pods and ebony beads. *Get a move on, wontcha, Jer!*

Another man, dressed in an unusually bright Hawaiian shirt, came to the car door. He chased the others away and smiled at me kindly as he tapped on the window. *Don't be a sucker, Sal. This is a set-up. Oh, what the hell.* I wound the glass down an inch and asked him what he wanted. He thrust forward a sheet of paper for me to see. It was an official-looking letter, but I couldn't read the contents.

'Good morning, madam,' he said solemnly. 'Would you please sign this letter of support for my number one son to apply for a scholarship? Please help us, madam. We are very poor. My son is a good boy. He is wanting this education to help this family.' His eyes were pleading, and I felt ashamed.

I wound the window down further to take the letter. The man hammered me with his words between chasing away the returning hordes. Now his eyes were hard. His voice grew louder, but I heard a click to my right and turned to see that another man had already sprung the driver's door and reached across the seat to grab the straps of my handbag. I lunged to grasp the base. A tug-of-war began in earnest. I was boiling! Thinking, thinking . . . *Roll up the window with the left hand; try to push the bag into the horn.*

Glowering straight into the eyes of the thief and clenching my teeth into what I hoped was a look of intense judgement, I said: 'God is watching you. This is a very bad thing you are doing.'

His eyes were muddy and glazed, I supposed from *gunja* (marijuana).

'There will be no place in Heaven for one who steals. God is telling me this now!' I stressed, assuming a steely expression of certainty while my heart hammered the walls of my chest. *Don't let my mouth quiver . . .*

The aspiring thief was leaning well into the vehicle, still pulling on my bag. I've been told that my Scorpio eyes can look into the souls of others. This was a time to use them. I felt my gaze burn into his eyes, and soon his face softened into a rueful smile. He dropped the straps, turned and ran. The man with the letter, who had served as a distraction, was long since gone.

People were running towards me, their faces creased with concern. A woman began to cry as she lifted her hands in imprecation. 'We are too sorry. These are bad men. Please believe me, madam. They will be punished.'

At that moment, Jer appeared laden with foodstuffs. When he saw the people swarming about and the look on my face, he accelerated into a run. 'What the fuck is happening here?' he roared. 'Get away from my wife!'

'No, please don't be angry with these people. It's not them,' I said. Jer is hard to rile and harder to calm down. I blurted out my story quickly.

The woman who had apologised was pushing a lovely necklace towards me. 'Please? Take this gift,' she offered. 'Those bad men bring my people shame.' She was dressed in tattered but clean clothes. Genuine tears dripped down her cheeks. Jer's shoulders dropped from his ears as he took a deep breath, but his eyes were glacier cold.

'Thank you, good woman,' I whispered. 'I know the truth.'

I accepted her necklace and then bought three more at the asking price, which isn't the way of things in the marketplaces of Africa. Bartering is expected, and enjoyed, by the people. They laugh at foreigners who don't join in the game. The woman knew from my attitude and refusal to bargain for her goods that I didn't judge her people by the actions of the thieves.

It wasn't over, though.

Jer said he wanted to take me back to Barney's and then return alone to visit some government offices on elephant business. 'I'm fine now,' I said. 'Someone has to look after Bluey. You won't be long and it's away from the market.'

No one bothered me during his brief absence, and he returned quickly with a friend in tow. The three of us were leaning on the driver's side of the vehicle catching up with the news. The passenger door was locked. A man approached.

'Sir, you have a problem with your tyre. I will fix it for you.' A concerned expression wrapped across his face like a veil.

It puzzles me still that we went to look at what was indeed a very flat tyre. I suppose we thought we wouldn't be hit on twice in one day. This time it was our friend who heard the click. He ran around the vehicle and rugby tackled another man who had forced the lock of the passenger door and was about to flee with the most enticing handbag in Bulawayo that day. The thief squirmed like a snake, and like a snake he was slippery. He got away and disappeared into a side street. His accomplice, who had obviously punctured the tyre while I sat unsuspectingly inside, was nowhere to be seen.

Jer shook his head. 'Strike me pink,' he marvelled. 'You wouldn't credit this could happen again so soon.'

By now I was trembling from exhaustion, an emotional and physical wreck. I looked around and for the first time, I longed for my home among the gum trees in a safe world.

Back at Barney's, I bowed to the strain of the illness, the isolation from my loved ones, and the pressure of living in a harsh environment in primitive conditions. I wept for hours – missing my children, my mother and my friends. Women need their friends. We celebrate joyful happenings, and console each other when we are sad.

Jer tried to fill their role by patting me and making endless pots of strong tea. He disappeared into town for an hour and I fretted that he was being robbed and bashed, until I finally decided he had been murdered. The tears began again when he walked in with twinkling eyes.

'Hush now,' he comforted. 'When you're feeling better we're going to Botswana. I've made a plan with Hugo Langdon to return to Savuti. We'll visit his camp for a few days.'

'But we can't afford it,' I snuffled into his shoulder.

'Yes, we can. And that's not all! Remember how Skiv has been asking us to come see his camp in the Okavango? Well, I radioed through. We'll go there from Savuti.'

Jer held me away from him and looked into my face. 'You'd like that, wouldn't you? Maybe we'll find those Bushmen you've been looking for. Now, how well out of a hundred do you feel?' he jollied, as he would have to his children when they were small.

I felt a tiny ripple of excitement and a renewed sense of

wellbeing. 'Oh, I guess about seventy-five, which is an improvement on zilch.'

Three days later, we were in the wild frontier town of Maun, in Botswana, standing in a safari office holding a phone. Hugo shouted into his radio: 'Stand beside the pile of groceries at the end of the strip. I'll find you there.' He was flying his light aircraft from the camp in Savuti to collect supplies – and us.

At the arrivals hall we wandered about looking for a way to get on to the Tarmac without being questioned. There was a window of opportunity when a South African Airways turbo prop aircraft arrived from Johannesburg. Airport officials were occupied with the throng and didn't notice us heading outside as passengers poured through the gate into the building. Gasping at my temerity and from the swamping heat, I sidled close to the surrounding fence, with Jer following closely. We began an illegal saunter towards a distant mound of crates.

Steam fogged my sunglasses and rose in quivering motes of electricity from deep craters of muddy water beside the runway. Rain had fallen in the night and the air was thick with clammy moisture. It was more like swimming through the atmosphere than walking. Our backpacks weighed heavily long before we got to the isolated group of cartons bulging with tomatoes, cabbages and tinned goods.

We waited and waited, tense with the fear that someone would see us and call the infantry. Light planes came and went. Pilots swung their headphoned heads our way out of curiosity at the strange sight of us and the produce while they prepared for take-off.

'Come on, Hugo,' I willed him.

Finally we watched a small Cessna taxi closer. I knew it was Hugo whose trademark cap was just visible above the cockpit windscreen. He screeched to a halt, wheeled the aircraft around in a ridiculously tight turn and jumped on to the shuddering wing. The engine was still roaring.

'How're you doing?' he whispered in a lazy tone which decried the speed of his advance. Hugo was fast. Everything about him was fast. If he could run he would, and when he was forced to walk, it took the form of short steps on the edge of a canter.

'Ah, it's Sally, Sally . . . girl of our alley! Very good to see you, m'dear.'

He grabbed me close to his short, hard body with immense strength before Jer engulfed him in a cap-popping embrace. I was always startled at the way Jer could do this in Africa with his men friends, when he wouldn't have done so at home.

Hugo adjusted his cap back into position, peered at the towering mound of boxes and asked, 'Who's got the longest arms?' I regretted that it was me when I began pushing the crates deep into the body of the plane. When there was no room left for more, we balanced another atop the pile.

'Right, let's get out of this hole,' Hugo said, rubbing his hands together and looking determined.

Then I realised there was no room left behind the two forward seats. Before I could ask where I was to sit, he said: 'There's a space for you beside the door, girl. You'll be on the floor. Had to take the seats out for the groceries.'

Jer looked concerned but there was never time to argue with Hugo, and before I knew it, we were on board. I was pressed hard against the door amid canting cartons with my knees pulled high into my chest. I couldn't see the men in front. It was insane, but what the heck. This was Africa, and a short flight to Savuti sure beat ten hours of dune bogging and bush bashing in the Toyota.

Within minutes the tiny plane was tearing along the strip, weaving dangerously from side to side. It seemed to be an endless take-off. Just when I thought we would plough into the trees, the Cessna lifted, but the stall buttons were wailing – and kept wailing. The plane was hovering only a few metres above the ground, which I could just see through a tiny unobscured section of window. I thanked God the scrub was low. The men were shouting to each other above the noise of the siren, but I couldn't make out what was being said. Later, Jer told me Hugo had been trying to reassure him. My stomach knotted as I remembered that Hugo had walked away from several crashes.

At last, the plane ascended to a safe height. The crates shifted, crushing me harder against the fragile shell. I braced my legs against some of the boxes and held others away with my arms. Now my face was pressed against the glass. My nose was actually flattened there. My anxious breathing escalated until I was on the verge of having a panic attack. *Settle, girl – NOW!*

When we reached the prescribed altitude, the load settled. I didn't dare drop my limbs, but I could ease the intensity of pushing. *It's just a short trip. I can do it.*

Until I heard Hugo yell, 'Elephant below! We're going in for a closer look.'

'No!' I shouted. But he didn't hear me.

The wing on my side dropped as he turned the plane and began to descend. Boxes began to fall on top of me. I didn't see one of those elephants as I sank beneath the weight. We lifted again and for another hour I lay inert, not fighting the weight or trying to shift it. I discovered that if I remained still, I could endure the ordeal.

I almost wept with relief when the wheels touched down. Within seconds, a dark-faced Jer opened the door and I fell out, along with several freed cabbages and tomatoes. He just managed to pull me away as some boxes followed.

'Are you all right?' he asked me over and over. 'I couldn't do anything to help you. Shit, I knew you must be in trouble.'

Meanwhile, Hugo had run to one of two Land Rovers waiting beside the rough bush strip and was fossicking for something. Two of his staff, Custard and Kaiser, began to load the produce into the vehicles. Obviously unsuccessful in his search, Hugo turned to the men and frowned deeply. 'Where's my Scotch?'

With calm grace, Custard pulled a silver and leather flask from his pocket and threw it to him. Hugo caught it, opened the top and downed a great gulp as he jumped into the driver's seat and fired the engine. 'We're away,' he said quietly.

Patting the seat beside him, he indicated where I was to sit and handed me the flask. This time there was no room for Jer behind. He climbed into the other vehicle with the men. We set off along a dusty trail towards the horizon and a red Kalahari sunset. A distant purple *kopje* made the only projection above the desert. The rusty sand stretched on forever, studded inter- mittently with stunted scrub and thorny salt bushes. Occasional wheels of dry sedge rolled with the wind. The air was dry at Savuti. There had been no rain in a long time. The country was crying in pain, but it was more beautiful than ever to my eyes. I remembered a mummified crocodile I had seen there years before, released from the cave where it had retreated when the Savuti Channel dried for the final time. It was impossible to believe that not so long ago here, crocodilians had ruled vast pools of water.

'She's left me,' Hugo said. He was driving hard, looking straight ahead.

Startled, I turned to look at him. I had heard the words, but I didn't understand them. Tears were streaking down his tanned, bunching cheeks.

'Say again?' I replied.

'Olivia! She's bloody left me for Dries. *Today!* The mongrel animal!' He started to cry. Great wrenching gobbles of sound.

'There, there,' I said stupidly as my own tears began. In that instant I forgot my anger at the dangerous flight. It was too awful to see this man so defenceless. I passed him the flask. He gulped down the entire contents in one hit.

'They've gone to her favourite lion hide-out,' he wept. 'I want to die'.

With that, he pushed the accelerator to the floor. I was astounded that he was sharing this awful sadness with me – I was almost a stranger. I supposed there was no one he could talk to at Savuti. Perhaps he could unburden more easily with an outsider, a woman. We flew over jaw-jarring holes in the track, leaving the vehicle following us far behind. Once again I feared for my life, in a vehicle that was out of control and in the hands of a desperate man.

'Slow down, Hugo,' I pleaded. 'It's no use wrecking the Landy as well!'

My words seemed to calm him. He eased back on the accelerator. His wife had fallen in love with the camp manager and was leaving him, he repeated. 'She wanted to spend one last time with her fucking lions – *with him!*' he growled.

I listened and crooned words of support all the way to the

camp. When we arrived, I ran straight to the ablution block where I shook so hard I couldn't pee. Jer found me there. He was furious. 'The bastard doesn't want to live. He almost took you out with him!' he raged.

'And you, too,' I said between hiccups. 'He's almost demented with pain.'

I looked up at the stars that shone down on Savuti and remembered my epiphany there so long before. 'This is the place of my freedom,' I whispered, 'I was reborn here. It's a strange, beautiful, gut-wrenching place. Maybe this had to happen for Hugo, too.'

That night I sat with Hugo's guests beside the campfire watching his leprechaun figure act out his larger-than-life stories. But they were all true. His wasn't a usual life. For a short time he forgot his problems as he amused his audience; becoming an elephant, a zebra and a pearl-spotted owl. The English couple next to me had saved for years to come on this safari. Hugo was a professional. He wasn't going to let his personal pain affect their holiday. He paused once, placed his fingers to his lips and directed our attention to the shadows. Two dirty yellow lion forms slunk past. Hugo's captive audience trusted him. They sat higher in their chairs, but they didn't wince. I did. This was just a hundred metres from the place of my long night of the lions. Yet, though my breathing grew shallow, this time I knew I was safe.

A grinding headache was beginning to pound my brain, demanding I go to bed, when the others left the fire. Instead, Hugo insisted we join him in a hide overlooking a tiny seep below the camp. He didn't want to be alone, and he talked and talked as we listened. Elephants came to drink and left without a sound. Hyaenas and lions spoke in the distance. I felt small and insignificant when I looked at the squashed egg-shaped moon that would rise and fall over the eternal desert when I was no longer a memory. I spoke of this to the men. Hugo took my hand and kissed it. Maybe my thoughts offered him solace. All of us were fleeting things in the universe and our torments and joys transient.

At 2 am I was woken by a nightmare. I was shivering with cold despite the heat. The pain in my head was explosive. Every part of me ached as I staggered from the bed with griping pains. I had to use the chamber pot within the tent, and was evacuating from every orifice. Jer took my temperature. It was 40°C. For a short time I felt better and then my body began to burn. I have never felt so ill. I thought I was going to die. I wanted to die.

Jer offered me three pills. 'It's malaria, darling. Take these now and in a few hours I'll get you the next dose.'

Somehow I kept them down and began the fight of my life. We couldn't call the doctor to confirm our fears. If it *was* malaria, we couldn't wait for a diagnosis to start treatment. I remember the next few hours as being a misery of strange dreams, delusions, humiliating symptoms and fear.

Two long days later, Hugo ran into the tent, his elfin face lit up with excitement. 'Come on, guys! Wild dogs have a leopard cornered in a tree on the marsh. You can't miss this!'

I suppose the pills were working as, despite Jer's objections and my exhausted state, I was determined I wouldn't miss such a spectacle. As it turned out, I would regret my decision within minutes of leaving, but I managed to get through the trip and saw the leopard make its escape straight over the heads of the dogs.

I expect I succumbed to malaria because I was run down after the bout of flu. Incredibly, I recovered within days, which Hugo said was a bloody miracle and probably thanks to Jer's immediate drug therapy. However, I believe that Savuti wove its magic again. Just being in the place where my second life had begun was itself a potent healing force. Instead of languishing for weeks, I was pumped and eager to push on deeper into the Okavango for our visit with Skiv.

A week later, I was standing beside Jer's sick bed at Skiv's camp in the Moremi.

'For heavens' sake, go, girl,' he growled miserably.

'I can't just potter off and leave you here feeling dreadful,' I said. 'You might have malaria as well.' I swiped the wet wash-cloth across his forehead.

'Rot!' he burst out. 'It's just the flu. I caught it from you.'

Skiv was calling me from outside the tent. 'Hurry, Sal, the aristocracy's not amused!' He was referring to a Scottish lord and his family who were ready to leave on a game drive. I was keeping them waiting.

I thought Jer was right about his diagnosis. Malaria doesn't present with a streaming nose and bronchial cough. Even so, I felt like a traitor leaving him behind while I enjoyed myself.

'Go! I just need to rest,' he groaned.

Skiv's partner, Maree, arrived with a concoction of freshly squeezed lemon juice and honey. 'It's definitely not malaria. I'll keep an eye on him. He's best left to sleep.'

Reassured, I made my way along the wooden walkway that wound high above the ground. The ecologically friendly struc-ture allowed animals to wander freely about the camp while the guests walked in safety. The Scottish laird and his wife were sitting in the first row of the tiered seats of the open-sided Land Rover. Their teenage son and daughter were seated above and behind them. 'Sorry if I kept you waiting,' I apologised. They didn't respond and refused to make eye contact. Daunted by the frosty atmosphere I hurried into the front passenger seat. A canvas hood protected us from the sun.

We rolled out on to the plain on a perfect autumn afternoon. The floods of the Angolan rainy season months earlier had finally arrived and were beginning to seep into the waterways of the delta. The area throbbed with game. Skiv stopped regularly to point out the different species and explain their habits to the haughty family, who made no comments and asked no questions. Their silence suited me well. For once I could just relax and enjoy the wildlife.

When we came upon elephants, there was no need to scurry to record data. It was heaven! That is, until we bogged in a rapidly swelling floodplain between islands of trees. Skiv and I decided that we needed to collect branches from the island up ahead and place them in front of the wheels to gain leverage out of the sludge. The Scottish family remained firmly ensconced in the Land Rover. Arching an expressive bushy eyebrow, Skiv muttered: 'Do you think they'll descend to our level when we're ready to roll?'

I giggled and shrugged. 'They're probably scared witless.'

Skiv stood up and said pointedly, 'Perhaps you should get out and stretch your legs?'

There was no response. Either they didn't get the hint or they were absolute morons. I thought the strapping son might respond, but no one made a move. So Skiv and I sloshed through the ankle-deep water to the island on a wood-gathering mission.

I wasn't yet back to full strength. My heart did cartwheels inside my chest, and my head felt set to explode as I struggled to drag my pile of branches back to the vehicle. This had no effect on the group, who sat stolidly, raking the terrain with sweeps of their binoculars.

Several trips later we had enough branches in place to make an attempt to pull clear of the mire. Puffing and panting, I stayed beside the vehicle to lighten the load while Skiv fired the engine. The wheels screeched as the Landy burned rubber trying to get a grip. Skiv's quiet cursing soon got louder. The lord lifted his snooty nose higher in disdain. The situation was worrying. Skiv tried to call base on the radio but without success. It seemed we must be in a black area for communications. The sun had set. Rising waves of sound rolled from the drumming wings of a thousand cicadas to welcome the night. I could feel hot anger vibrating from the pores of my friend. He was steaming! *Uh, oh! Skiv's about to blow.*

At the same time as the thought crossed my mind, Skiv twisted around abruptly to face his passengers. His wide, strong features were set in granite. His black hair stuck up in spikes like a porcupine's quills. 'OK. Get out! Now!' he commanded.

'I say. What if there are lions?' neighed the woman. She was speaking for all of them.

I spoke up: 'Goodness, no. We're quite safe and Skiv really needs our help to get this vehicle free.'

Meanwhile, Skiv was muttering over and over, 'Ay-ay-ay-ay-ay!' He jumped over the driver's seat and we set off towards the island again, where we had to plunge deeper into the bush to find more sticks. When we returned, the family were huddled close to the Land Rover. Without their considerable weight she leapt across the mound of wood and Skiv roared out of the bog.

He kept going at speed to reach the firm surface of the track on harder ground. Lords and ladies danced quickly behind without any trace of dignity to clamber inside before the vehicle had rolled to a stop. I brought up the rear trying to suppress my howls of mirth.

I stopped laughing within a minute. Around the first corner we came upon a pride of twenty-nine lions, lolling on the highest knoll of the island. They would have had us in their sights the entire time. When Skiv and I were gathering wood we had been only fifty metres from them. Suddenly the Scottish family found their tongues all at the same time. Skiv was embarrassed and tried to fend off their angry remarks with light banter.

We now had radio reception, and within an hour Maree joined us. Beside her sat a bundle of grey blankets. It was Jer, looking like Scott of the Antarctic. A beanie was pulled low over his forehead and he shivered within the heavy folds. It seemed that nothing was going to stop him seeing such a phenomenal gathering of lions. The Scottish family forgot their anger and became as enchanted as the rest of us with the antics of the cubs and their patient mothers. Eventually, the bitter cold drove the pride into dense scrub and us back to hot showers. Jer returned to bed with a hot-water bottle.

Over a silver service dinner, as with everyone who has been to the edge, the Scots told and retold the story of their adventure. Skiv winked at me. Our usually abstemious (at least while he was on duty) host tossed back shots of Scotch with the lord until they were both staggering about clutching each other in wild Scottish reels. I remembered my own heritage and joined them. Much later, I returned to the tent to find Jer sleeping peacefully amidst wet bedding. His fever had broken. I woke him to change the sheets.

He chuckled sleepily, 'Your African spirit saved you again, eh? Just as well. I never seem to be there when you get into strife with wild animals.'

I wondered if he were right. It seemed wise to express my gratitude to my unseen friend just in case.

I had even more to be grateful for the next morning, when a tiny Bushman walked into camp. His wrinkled ochre cheeks were held wide by a calm smile. My longed-for meeting had arrived. At last, a child of Mantis! Mantis (as in praying mantis) is a deity. The deities' names really express the peoples' reverence for nature.

'Look who I found waiting at the well,' smiled Skiv. 'I believe this young man has come looking for work.'

Lively, slanting eyes watched us above his permanent smile. His tiny peppercorn-studded head turned from face to face as each person spoke. He understood nothing of the language and everything of our intentions. His expression of innocent happiness never altered. When his bright eyes met mine, they sought my soul. I was enchanted. By the expressions on the faces of my companions, I sensed they were equally affected.

There was a pause in the discussion about the possibility of finding a job for the Bushman. He responded with a torrent of earnest clicking sounds. His body leaned forward eagerly. He pointed a gnarled finger at the grass, at shrubs and up to the trees. He laughed, and threw up his arms in a gesture that said, 'This is useless. These people do not understand me.'

Then he took Skiv's hand and led him to a wheelbarrow. Gesturing for the rest of us to follow, he grabbed the handles and pushed it about. He chattered non-stop, while looking at

307

us to see if we understood his meaning. Our puzzlement was evident, so he reached down to pull a weed that he placed carefully in the barrow; then another, and another.

'I see,' said Skiv. 'I think he's telling us he wants to work in the garden.' He nodded at the Bushman, then shouted towards the kitchen: 'Hoy, does anyone speak San?'

A coloured man poked his head through the doorway. His eyes grew large when he saw our companion. He called to the little fellow, 'Click-tut-clickety-tuck.'

'I think *he* does,' grinned Skiv, nodding towards the cook, who was aptly named Benevolent. 'Is it? What does the little guy want?'

An energetic discussion was taking place between the cook and the Bushman, who continued to mime frenetic gardening activity.

'This Bushman is asking for work here. He is telling me he can do many things. He is known as Twee.'

An hour later, Skiv returned with his new handyman, who was proudly inspecting the smallest uniform the housekeeper could find. Even so, the khaki shirt swamped him, and his wiry calves poked out below shorts that were held up by a length of string. But he appeared to be ecstatic. Twee took our hands one by one, gazed deeply into our eyes and expressed gratitude, humility, knowledge, joy, humour and love without saying a word. He was all, and more, than I had ever imagined. I saw the same wonder shining on my companions' faces.

'This is the sweetest little guy, eh?' whispered Maree. Her grey eyes moistened. Jer blew his nose and Skiv cleared his throat. No one was immune to the Bushman's charm and innocence.

Twee set to his work with bouncing enthusiasm; his naked feet leaped and danced behind the wheelbarrow. He sang all day and I followed him about, fascinated by his perpetual joy. It was difficult to estimate his age. Bushmen wear wrinkles from their youth. He seemed ageless.

He paused often to watch the maintenance truck rumble about the camp; to smell the air; to push his wide nostrils into exotic flowers and to giggle at their perfume. The bougainvillea gave him a fright for a moment; he jumped away from the thorns and then pranced about, shook his head and laughed out loud at his foolishness. He stood for some time beneath a mighty baobab with his head bowed as if in prayer; then placed his small bow and a quiver of arrows against the smooth pink trunk.

That night we were wakened by a tremendous crashing sound. We grabbed flashlights and ran out to see what animal might be creating havoc. It was the Bushman. The truck was canted up the trunk of a tree with the little man perched behind the wheel. His head sat so low in the cabin that I wondered if he had been able to see through the windscreen. It was a scene straight from the film *The Gods Must be Crazy*! But I thought that no one who had seen the movie would believe me when I told them of this night.

Skiv was already there. 'Chr-r-r-i-st almighty!' he yelled.

'Click-twitter-click-tuck,' said the culprit with earnest nods of his head as he climbed out the window and walked towards us. He took Skiv's hand gravely, 'Shhh-shhh-shhh-shhh,' he reassured, over and over again, addressing each of us in turn.

'Get Benevolent,' Skiv ordered one of the kitchen staff who was watching the events with a mischievous expression. Someone else was in trouble for a change.

When Benevolent arrived, the Bushman nodded at us as if to say, 'Now we can sort this out.'

An earnest conversation ensued between the cook and the

309

unperturbed Bushman. Every little while he would turn to us, reach out his hands and pat the air. 'Shhh-shhh-shhh-shhh.'

The tiny man, smiling broadly, encouraged Benevolent to tell us his story. He said he loved the big thing (the truck) and wanted to learn its secrets. That was all.

Skiv examined the truck. The damage was more cosmetic than structural, he said, but it would be out of action for a few days. Benevolent interpreted, as Skiv told Twee that he would have to pay for the damage to be repaired.

'I don't want to sack the little guy,' he told us. 'But he needs to be taught to ask before he goes looking for secrets, eh?' Speaking through Benevolent to the now sorry-looking Bushman, he frowned and growled: 'I must take some money from your pay each week until the bill is paid to heal this truck.'

A wide smile again lit the Bushman's face and he nodded vigorously in agreement. 'Shhh-shhh-shhh-shhh,' he comforted, taking Skiv's hand in his. And all was well.

The next afternoon I spied Skiv as he sat behind the wheel of the truck with the tiny man perched on his lap. He was giving him a driving lesson. The bumper bar was crumpled, but the engine roared and growled, to the delight of the Bushman. His face was split by a joyful smile.

Twee brought healing to the camp: Jer recovered quickly. No one could resist the Bushman's transparent honesty and infectious pleasure in life. He appeared to live each moment with total relish. There was much to learn from his free and loving spirit.

CHAPTER 18

Would they
remember us?

Armed with the extra blankets we bought in Francistown on our way home, we returned to Zimbabwe restored and ready for action. The blankets weren't just for us. A special visitor was due soon. Before she arrived, we spent every waking hour checking elephant movement across the transects to assess their browse patterns. Until then, our work had revolved around identifying individual herd members. Now we had concrete evidence of an important aspect of their behaviour. The elephants were selective in their feeding habits. No one species of tree or bush was decimated from an area. It was certain they left food in the larder for another time – at least, in this time of relative plenty. However, we knew that the next drought would test this theory. At last we had some results to take to Mandebele.

For the first time since we began the research, Skew Tusk came close beside Bluey and dozed comfortably, as if to say: 'Welcome home, guys.' I was overwhelmed with gratitude at the great privilege she granted us. All was well in our world, and it was about to get better.

A beautiful girl stepped out of the plane, holding a wide-brimmed hat over her long blonde curls. It flew away when she ran towards us with arms outstretched. My vivacious daughter, Mary-Louise (known to us as Lou), had come to visit. She chattered constantly all the way to camp, stopping only to clap her hands with excitement at the creatures we met along the way.

Steve Mpofu had erected a tiny rough shelter for her beside ours, but her doubtful expression made it clear that at least for the first few nights she should sleep with me in our sturdy hut. Before she had even rolled out her sleeping bag, the first admirer arrived for a closer look. Brian had seen her at the airport. By tea-time there were four preening young men vying for her attention. She was too busy telling me about her flying lessons, and of her intention to become a commercial pilot, to pay them any attention. I couldn't know then that years later she would be flying Hercules aircraft on aid missions into the Sudan for the United Nations. This was the beginning of her love affair with Africa. But it would be a trial by fire.

Stevie had spent the day setting up an electric heater to warm the water in the shower head. Quite illegally, he managed to tap into a power line that serviced a game farm. Stevie 'Wonder', indeed! We were chuffed with this luxury and proudly allotted Lou the first shower. Still bubbling with excitement, she took her towel into the reed structure. A minute later, we heard a shriek. My first thought was of snakes. I ran to find her lying naked and shivering on the floor. Jer was close behind me but retreated quickly when he saw her state. Water was still running from the shower. I leaned forward to turn it off.

'Don't touch the water!' she screamed. 'That bloody shower head electrocuted me!'

With great care I stretched across the pooled water to reach around the flow and turn off the taps. Lou staggered to her feet and snatched the towel I was holding. Her intense hazel eyes were blazing with the 'Louie look'. 'Are you trying to kill me? That bloody thing threw me against the wall!' she shouted.

I calmed her down while Jer disconnected the heater. So much for dreaming about hot showers! Stevie was fallible, after all. Looking dismayed and disappointed, he came to cut the wires the next day.

Lou's ruffled feathers settled. She helped me prepare a meal while Jer turned away a stream of curious young men who were arriving with all sorts of excuses and in numbers way beyond any previous visits to our humble camp. The jungle drums were beating up a storm. However, this was a night to share our news and enjoy family time alone. We sent them all packing. At midnight, we wished Jer a happy sleep and settled into our sleeping bags. Lou expressed some doubts about using a shovel to seal the door, and I assured her it worked very well.

'Oh, yeah? Just like the shower?' she replied.

I was on the verge of sleep when the sound of clattering saucepans broke the silence. 'What's that?' a tiny voice quavered.

'Probably hyaenas,' I muttered.

Surely not tonight . . . We struggled out of our sleeping bags and tip-toed to the glassless window to see what was causing the disturbance. The moon was hidden by cloud. All I could glimpse were movements in the shadows. Another crash. A series of tiny 'aoo-ous'. Lou was hanging on to me tightly.

'What is it, Mama?'

'I think we have lions,' I whispered, just as a roar split the air.

Lou almost crushed the breath out of me.

'It's all right, Chicken. They can't get in. They're playing with the utensils.'

It was a rule that we cleaned up after meals to deter wandering hyaenas and jackals from scavenging incursions. Distracted by our reunion, we had stacked the pans to wash in the morning. The smells of leftover food must have attracted the lions into camp. I coaxed Lou back to bed. For a long time, the lions beat up our goods.

For a longer time, Lou repeated the same question: 'Are you sure we're safe? What about Jersey?', the name she called Jeremy.

I knew that Jer would be chuckling at the possible scenario in our hut. He certainly couldn't come to see how we were managing. In the morning, we awoke to chaos. Pots were scattered everywhere. Our precious deckchairs were gone, which was a disaster. They were hard to find and very expensive. But, more importantly, they provided us with real comfort. From here on we would have to make do with logs and no back support. Lou placed her hand into the huge spoor of a male lion. It was as big as a dinner plate. In the light of day she chattered incessantly about the thrilling adventure provided by the visitors of the night. *So much for my squashed ribs* . . .

One by one, the rangers appeared. Lou made it clear she had a boyfriend in Australia, which dampened their ardour. After much consideration, she finally accepted an invitation from Rob to go on a night drive. She'd taken to the courteous jolly giant and deemed him safe. I suspected Rob had no intention of being a saint.

Already Lou's day had been filled with excitement. She had met the elephants and watched them wallow. My ears felt battered from her ceaseless questioning. She absorbed information quickly, which was just as well, because Rob was taking a group of Americans on a night drive and she had to pretend to be a guide in training. Rob arrived in camp in the early evening to collect her. We waved them off.

At midnight they still weren't back. I steamed with anger. 'Rob is usually so reliable. He promised to have her home by ten,' I fretted, in full mother mode.

Jer had just decided that we should head out on a search mission, when the Land Rover rolled in. Lou's second night had turned out to be even more electrifying than her first. She kept us awake for another hour telling her story.

The first few hours of trolling about with the clients had been perfect. They stopped for sundowners overlooking a favourite watering hole of the elephants. Many of the herd came in to drink. Lou was enjoying her role of 'trainee ranger' and the enthusiasm of the American tourists. A large crocodile basked on the bank in front of the Landy. Lou could speak knowledgeably about these reptiles: Australian saltwater crocs were part of the scenery back home and this creature wasn't so different from them.

When night fell, Rob packed away the hamper and cooler box to go looking for leopards, genets and other nocturnal creatures on the way back to the lodge. Lou was looking forward to having dinner there. Rob turned the key and was met with the sound of silence. The battery was dead.

'It's cool,' he reassured his charges. 'I'll call another vehicle for assistance.'

Unfortunately, the flat battery meant the radio was also out of action. Rob pretended to make contact with base, so as not to further alarm the clients. Lou also thought help was coming until he whispered that the radio wasn't working and no one knew where they were. 'Don't let on that anything's wrong,' he stressed.

Lou felt scared, she later told us, but she managed to smile confidently. 'Let's see what the croc is doing,' she chirped, as she reached for Rob's spotlight.

He stopped her hand and said softly, 'Remember? It runs off the car battery, too . . .'

That was the final straw, Lou said. Or, at least, she thought it was; for at that moment a lion roared close to them. They could see nothing. The Land Rover used on night drives doesn't have a canopy, so they were completely unprotected in the open vehicle. They couldn't see the lion *or* the crocodile.

'Mum, for all I knew there could have been an enormous pride of lions stalking us. What an idiot!' she snorted.

From that distance, knowing they had all survived, I could feel for shy Rob, who had been the unlikely choice of the new girl on the block. As it turned out, his failure to impress her as a potential suitor made him safe for reasons other than actual physical security. He became her friend, which I thought must have caused him further frustration.

However, that first night they were in real trouble. Fortunately, the Americans had no idea of the possible perils. They had complete faith in their safari guide, who admitted later to having no idea what to do about their predicament.

After an hour, they heard the welcome sound of a vehicle: another night drive had followed the roars of the lion in search of a sighting. The lights of the vehicle illuminated Rob and his hapless crew parked right beside an interested lioness. The second vehicle chased her away. There was just enough room for the Americans to crowd aboard, but Rob and Lou had to wait until another vehicle could arrive from the safari camp to tow them back. The second guide left them with a powerful spot-light. It was a long wait, and Lou said there were many times she wanted to crawl underneath the Land Rover for safety.

At noon the next day, my daughter bounded out of her sleeping bag and asked for breakfast. She looked at me eagerly with my father's large hooded eyes, and I hatched a plan. My father had fallen in love with orang-utans in the jungles of Borneo during the Second World War. He had never returned to the island, but his passion for wild creatures was as much a part of my childhood as were the numerous Australian crea-tures that passed through our home. My father's unfulfilled dreams of living in wild places fuelled my interest in conser-vation. He taught me to care for orphaned kangaroo joeys, wallabies, reptiles and birds.

His legacy continued through me to his grand-daughter. I bought her books about the work of Jane Goodall and Stella Brewer with primates – particularly with chimpanzees. She saved her pocket money to send to Gerald Durrell's refuge for endangered species in Jersey. I also longed to see chimpanzees living in the wild. This was our chance to accomplish a shared dream: observe the elephant situation in Uganda and realise my singular ambition to sight a rare shoe-bill stork. By evening, Jer had agreed to stay behind with the elephants while Lou and I went on a quest to Uganda.

* * *

A week later, we flew to Kampala and into a quietly simmering Uganda. A fragile peace had been established following the reigns of terror of Idi Amin and Milton Obote. The aircraft swooped low over Lake Victoria and into Entebbe. Customs officials were welcoming and full of questions about life in Australia. We were corralled in the arrivals hall by locals who were eager to tell us their stories and ask for ours. They were hungry for knowledge. Their hearts were sore, but they said they held hope for a return to calm if the proposed general elections were held. All of this took place before we had even left the airport.

The road to the city skirted the lake, where fishermen lounged in boats as fish virtually jumped into their hands. Or so it seemed, for during the journey I counted five lines flashing silver cargo being tossed back into the craft. Our driver drove wildly (with little regard for the clapped-out taxi that was probably owned by someone else) over pot-holes so deep he must have thought speed would carry the wheels right over the holes without making contact. I was terrified we would run down some of the people among the hordes who walked, or cycled antique bicycles, in an unending stream of humanity.

Huge, flamboyant trees in run-down parks, and derelict houses of grand size and architecture, indicated that Kampala had been a stunningly elegant city in its heyday. Now coffins lined the road, and prospective buyers bartered with the vendors to purchase the final resting places of their dead.

We passed the bloated corpses of dogs and a donkey. The grotesque throat bags of marabou storks swayed as the grim reapers fought over the remains. People picked their way around a human body that lay on a roundabout where the taxi was forced to stop in a traffic jam. Wide-eyed and pale, Lou leaned into my side. My stomach heaved at the indifference of the passers-by. The driver shrugged when I asked him what could be done. Death was a constant companion here. *How could I sit in judgement? I know nothing of such things, of unspeakable atrocities. Breathe deeply. Take it all in, but don't say anything.*

We fled from Kampala the next day. For nine hours we drove across a great green land towards Murchison Falls National Park. Away from the dross of the city, Uganda was stunningly beautiful. Fertile red soil fed the roots of growing things which produced harvests of fat fruit and vegetables, and immense corn cobs that lost nothing in sweetness due to their size. We stopped for lunch and I thought I had never tasted produce as good. Rich juices dripped down my chin with every bite of food. The land hadn't lost its energy. People would come and go, but the earth could never be destroyed. I knew the wildlife was less fortunate. Without help, many species here would be lost forever.

In the evening, we arrived at a run-down lodge that was struggling for existence in a country without tourists. The manager, Krishna, was of Indian extraction. He was a second-generation Ugandan, but the ethnic cleansing in the years before had forced many like him to flee to a motherland they didn't know. Krishna had just returned from India to the land of his birth and was eager to begin life anew. He was a communications technologist. He told me that his business and the family home in Kampala had been requisitioned by an infamous army general during the turmoil. Now he was forced to work for others in a field outside his expertise, but he was keen, clever and enthusiastic. I hoped his energy would be rewarded.

There were only six guests staying at the quaint lodge that

lay within hearing distance of the Murchison Falls. None of us were regular holidaymakers and I wondered how a safari operation could survive without tourists to fill at least half of the twenty *rondavels* scattered through its grounds.

The vast dining area rang with hollow echoes when Lou and I joined our fellow guests to eat at one table. Two of our companions were on a mission for the United Nations. The others were medical staff working for Médecins Sans Frontières. A herd of kob, a roan antelope and five buffaloes were drinking at the small waterhole in front.

After dinner, I took a chipped mug of aromatic coffee (locally grown and ground fresh) on to the flag-stoned terrace. Krishna joined me. I asked him why there was a wreath of flowers around the huge horned boss of a buffalo that was mounted on a post nearby.

'That is Arjuna,' he replied. 'He passed a month ago. I will tell you his story, but first I must give *prasad* to my sacred bull.'

Krishna rose from his recliner, poured some milk from the jug into his saucer and approached the boss of the buffalo. Reverently, he placed the offering on the small table beneath, which I now understood to be an altar. He held his hands in prayer before his chest for a moment, then returned to begin his tale. By this time I was bursting with curiosity.

'So . . . It began eight months ago when I had just started this job.' He paused, and then turned his sad, deep brown eyes to mine. 'You know, I was very grateful to be given the work here, because we Indians are not so welcome in Uganda – not since the trouble started.'

I nodded. There was nothing to say. We both knew he was right. Efficient and hard-working, Indian merchants and traders tended to corner the economic market in their adopted countries. Consequently, they were often resented by many local people.

Krishna leaned forward with his fingers steepled beneath his chin in the pose of all good storytellers. Just then, Lou appeared. 'Wait for me,' she said. She pulled a chair close and clapped her hands at the possibility of a story. We settled in to listen. Krishna began his tale.

'I was concentrating deeply during the cleaning out of the cupboards behind the reception desk. Things were in a mess after the long years of war. I was kneeling down when I heard a strange noise on the other side. I knew it could not be the labourers, who were the only other guys at the lodge. You see, I'd sent them to the village to collect materials. You have seen that the main building has few walls. The thought came to me that there might be a rebel looking for big trouble.' He shook his head sadly. 'I am telling you, it is too sad that this is how we think now in Uganda.'

I nodded in understanding, while Krishna dipped his ears towards each shoulder in the Indian manner of agreement.

'I could not be seen by whoever was there. I took the loaded revolver that was in place for such an emergency. I jumped up with the gun, pointing it straight ahead.' Once again, he paused to look at the remains of the buffalo.

'It was this guy here,' he pointed. 'He was a very large buffalo and he was just standing there chewing cud. I ran into the storeroom to hide. He stayed for a long time on the first visit. I kept looking through the doorway, but he just stood there resting. When he left, I thought he would never return. I had never heard of such a strange thing,' he said.

He was right. Buffaloes are wild creatures who would normally avoid humans.

'Well,' he continued. 'He came back the next day. I was standing in the pool cleaning the sides with a wire brush when three buffaloes ran to the water to drink. Those guys were very belligerent – very! I was frightened and went to the centre of the pool to get away from them. They were tossing their heads and grunting. I thought they would come in and kill me. Just when I thought I would die, another buffalo charged towards the pool and chased the bad guys away.'

Krishna leaned forward intently. 'It was the same buffalo. You know, the old man who came into the lodge. Over the next few days, he visited the reception area each day. That buffalo would just stand there ruminating.'

I chuckled. 'Perhaps he wanted to book a room for the night?'

Krishna nodded from shoulder to shoulder and smiled gently. 'Maybe, but I think he knew me in a previous life and wanted to remake our friendship. He was very quiet. I learned to trust him, you know. He followed me about the grounds like a dog. In the end, I could stroke him. I even sat on his back. Look, here is the photograph.'

And there was the proof of an astounding friendship. Krishna was perched atop the back of the most feared of Africa's 'Big Five', who was christened Arjuna by his human friend. The story didn't have a happy ending. Krishna heard lions roaring one night. The next day the buffalo didn't come to the lodge. On the third day, Krishna went looking for his friend. He found the remains of his carcass nearby. Lions had ended the life of a remarkable animal.

Krishna walked to Arjuna's boss and stroked the great sweeping horns. 'I will meet him again in another life,' he said. 'We are bound together for all time.'

It was a sacred moment. I felt deeply moved by Krishna's devotion to the creature, and humbled by his willingness to entrust to me something of his eastern tradition.

The next morning we rose early to be at the mighty Murchison Falls before dawn. While Lou climbed to a viewing point, I sat alone and happy as the ozone showered over me from the spume that was tossed from the brown waters of the Nile as they thundered down into the gorge. Monkeys skittered in the branches of trees overhead; a hippo lumbered back into the pool above the cataclysm; flocks of vibrant carmine bee eaters plunged in and out of the mist; and far below, on the banks beside the boiling river, an elephant stood. We saw only one small herd of elephants during two days of long drives in Murchison Falls National Park where once they had roamed in herds a thousand strong.

The strange palm trees that grew there, that were propagated through the digestive processes of elephants, had no young. There were few great bellies left to break down the hard nuts for future germination from their dung. Murchison was a glorious vast savannah almost emptied of game. During the time of civil unrest, Ugandan soldiers and local villagers had decimated the creatures to feed their hunger. Everyone and everything had suffered. I feared that I wouldn't find chimpanzees when we visited the forests the next day.

However, that day I *did* find the fantastic bird I had sought and failed to sight in Zambia's swamps, and in the papyrus fields of the Shire River in Malawi. When one least expects to see something, it is suddenly there.

We were picnicking with our guide beside the Nile, sitting in the shade of a sausage tree, when I heard a guttural call. Before I saw it, I sensed that the source of the sound was a shoe-bill stork. And there it was – strutting out of the reeds nearby. I knew that shoe-bills were very large birds. However, I wasn't prepared for the metre-high, sturdy, prehistoric-looking creature that was passing by.

The stork had an enormous head and beak, but the eye that slowly blinked a white eyelid was almost as large as those of nocturnal birds; large and lazy. A much smaller, yet equally prehistoric-looking, Hammerkop was following in its trail. The birds were framed by the papyrus and I thought that at any moment a dinosaur might join the parade. It was an incredible scene and I wanted to share it with Jer, who would understand my wonder.

Lou and the guide were sleeping, so I said to the shoe-bill: 'Thank you for your kind visit. Would you like some tea? Or perhaps a biscuit? No? Then how about posing for a photograph?'

The great bird stopped mid-stride and turned its strange head towards me. The Hammerkop did likewise. But before I could take a photo, the beautifully ugly bird cloaked its eyes one last, slow time and stalked into the papyrus. It didn't matter. I would always have the memory, which I could revisit whenever I wished.

We left Murchison in the evening to re-cross the Nile on an ancient, rickety barge. The indolent boatman lit a cigarette next to the engine that leaked diesel. Lou looked at me in amazement, but we said nothing. An AK-47 was slung across his shoulder. The sun was sinking in the west as the full moon rose in the east, and both were reflected in that most mysterious of all rivers. Hippos left the Nile as crocodiles returned to the mercury water from the sandbanks.

Over an early dinner I told Krishna of my experiences and

he shared my wonder at seeing the shoe-bill, which made me happy. I fell into bed as excited as a child on Christmas Eve who knows the sooner she sleeps, the sooner she will unwrap her presents. Tomorrow we would search for chimps.

Once again we were on the road in the predawn light. This time it was Krishna who drove us to the small encampment at the edge of the vast rainforest where the primates lived. He introduced us to a young woman with a monkey sitting on her shoulder. Zahra was one of the carers of the wild. Krishna said he would return to pick us up in the evening. We watched him leave and I wondered if the day would be long and fruitless. At that moment I heard the sounds of chimp-speak close by!

'You are very, very lucky,' said Zahra. 'They have come in the night. The chimps sometimes seek our closeness when a leopard is hunting.'

I knew these chimpanzees were habituated to the presence of humans, but I couldn't believe our good fortune.

Zahra smiled. 'Many times they are very deep in the forest and people are here for a week without a sighting.'

I nodded eagerly. 'Let's go. Before they change their minds.'

The monkey was now perched on Lou's head and lifting the long blonde strands of her hair, as if fascinated. Lou was totally relaxed and grinning with delight. I admired her nerve. I had become wary of monkeys following several recent clashes with cheeky robbers who were after food. Zahra retrieved the little monkey and handed it, now screeching in indignation, to a young boy. After filling our water bottles from a fast-running stream, we hefted our packs on to our backs and set off into the dimness beneath the dense canopy.

We followed a game trail that wound between great roots and thick undergrowth. Branches whipped my face as we hurried towards the noisy chimpanzees. I didn't notice the scratches until later. Zahra was wearing a red beret and I regretted not having a cap to protect my head. The jungle was steaming. Within minutes I was wet with a combination of sweat and the water that seeped from the leaves. There had been a torrential downpour in the night, Zahra said.

Chimpanzee-speak rolled through the canopy. They were all around us, but I couldn't glimpse them among the denseness of the leaves, although I could smell the strong odour of their bodies, which resembled the stench of an exceptionally dirty human. It was a fat, full, pungent call to be still.

Zahra indicated that we should sit down on the forest floor. The noise of the chimpanzees' screeching vocalisations built up to a crescendo that I found disturbing. I sensed they were angry. I hoped it wasn't our presence that was causing the problem. Zahra looked worried.

She whispered, 'Don't move. There is something not right today.'

At that moment, a black body rushed backward down the trunk of a tree beside us. It was a male, puffed out even more by stiff black hair that stood on end. He came to earth, turned around and stood erect, glaring straight at us. I shrank in shock as his angry eyes locked on us. His lips curled into a grimace of rage, revealing red gums and a daunting set of discoloured teeth.

At once, he launched an attack on Zahra, who fell backwards holding her hands across her face. Terrified, I threw my arms around Lou. Another chimp was on its way. I was startled at the size of the primates. Then the large male ran from Zahra, holding her red beret in one hand and using the other to knuckle run on the ground.

Chimps were streaming down the trees all around us, screaming as they ran to the male who was now bashing the beret against the ground. The others surrounded him in a frenzied attack on the thing that had created such disharmony. Two males kept breaking away to grab and shake low branches. All the while, they screamed and hooted.

Lou and I had been frozen in alarm. Now we went to Zahra, who was unharmed. Shock had replaced fear and she was shaking. We huddled close together as the attack continued. 'My God!' she said, clasping her hands to her mouth. 'Nothing like this has ever happened before. What is wrong with these chimps today?'

Within minutes, the primates had returned to the trees. Except for occasional contact hoots, they were once again at peace. We discussed the episode, looking for clues to the mysterious attack. They had long accepted Zahra's presence among them. In the end, we thought it might be the red colour of the beret which had thrown them into panic. Zahra had never worn it in the forest. It was the colour of blood, which must have signalled danger to animals that see blood only in the context of death. Or perhaps it was a colour they associated with the rebel army, who preyed on their species for bush meat.

I soon forgot my fears, and our presence was accepted again. For the rest of the morning we wandered with the chimps. We followed them when they came down from the trees to walk along the game trail. We lay on our backs beneath the branches where they foraged. One even peed on me, and I could swear she laughed at my disgust. Babies peeped at us from behind leaves, no less interested in our doings than we were in theirs.

They looked like little people with ears too big for their comical faces. And Lou laughed with me.

We ate our packed lunch beside a trickling stream of water. One female chimpanzee brought her tiny infant down from the trees to drink about four metres away. This was testament to her trust in Zahra and it restored the young woman's faith in herself. It wasn't her they had attacked. It was the beret.

I have never since experienced the kind of otherworldly serenity I felt that day. Nothing else existed. I was at one with the forest; with the chimps. Every breath I took was long and deep. I thought like a chimp. My thoughts were slow and only of the forest, the itch from the leeches I must leave to take their fill lest I bleed (and it didn't matter), the trail of ants through the mouldering leaves, tiny vivid birds that darted, the tinkle of streams, the breeze when it came, the swelter when it didn't, the sound of trees growing and the presence of Lou, who was shining with elation. I think that Jane Goodall will live to be a very old woman, given the quality of her life during the time she lived in her beloved Gombe Forest. I felt utterly blessed to have experienced even one such day.

We told Krishna of our fantastic day when we returned to the lodge. He smiled knowingly as we ate dinner that night. The next day we left Uganda, covered in tick bites and deep scratches on the outside. Inside, I glowed.

When we returned to Zimbabwe, I spoke little of my experiences. I felt that speaking of them would diminish my joy, which was indescribable. The wet was approaching, which would bring an end to the research season. It was time to leave the herd in peace. Soon they would depart for the deep forest and be out of reach. *Would they remember us?*

Jer and I dismantled our camp with heavy hearts. The drum that had fired our cooking and warmed our bodies was tucked away in the tiny shelter, along with the furniture Stevie had built. Our tenure had been brief; the wild would continue its rhythm. I thought of Effie the horn-bill. Perhaps she might have missed us. But things were as they should be, I knew this, yet I mourned the leaving.

We couldn't leave the project and Africa immediately. It would be too harsh. So we planned a journey into Namibia to search for desert elephant and rhinoceros. Lou would be coming with us. The civil war was over. Or so we had been told.

Lou was aware of our reluctance to leave. She hurried us along with silly jokes and bossy orders, for we were sad and slow. Then we drove across the *vlei* and away. We arrived at the national park's bungalows at Victoria Falls in time for lunch. Each of us went our separate ways until evening. Lou walked by the Falls. Jer took Bluey to a garage for a service; and I sat by the Zambezi alone with my thoughts. Later we played Scrabble; my letters formed words that spoke of my tears. Jer piled wood into the *braai* for an early meal. Tomorrow would be long; longer and more dangerous than we could ever have imagined.

The border post at Kasangula was empty when we arrived the next day at 5 am. I watched the darkness lift over Botswana from the Zimbabwean side, then turned my face into the rising sun at the place where four countries converge around the silky waters of the mighty Chobe River. As it had been when we came through at the beginning, a herd of elephants reflected shimmering orange from their wet backs as they lumbered from the water on to the Zambian banks. Further away, a block of black buffalo bodies grazed on an island that lay within Namibian territory.

Our travel documents were processed quickly when the customs officers arrived to begin business. What a pleasure. It's a requirement that shoes, boots and tyres are disinfected when passing between many African countries. I regretted my choice of footwear that day. My exposed toes curled back into my leather sandals when I stepped gingerly into a wide metal bowl of muddy liquid. Jer drove the vehicle through a depression filled with the same substance and we then set course for the next border post seventy kilometres away. There was just enough room in the back of the Toyota for one of us to stretch out between driving shifts.

We travelled fast along the gravel road spanning the length of the floodplains. Chobe throbbed with game that had been forced to gather near the eternal waters during the height of the dry season. This put tremendous pressure on the sur-rounding vegetation. Vast herds of elephant had decimated the scrublands; hungry mouths and myriad hooves had stripped the soil bare of grass. Stunted mopane trees crouched bare of leaves, almost hostile in their stolidness as if they dared the pachyderms to try to kill them with another assault on their stubby branches. The arid land resembled the site of a catastrophic bomb blast, and I understood why some conservationists were calling for a cull on Botswana's elephant population, but this was the country that seven months earlier had rejoiced in a flush of verdant growth. It was certain this would come again when the rains returned, when nature created anew, when the wild beasts departed for fresh fields deeper in the Kalahari.

A hot wind howled about the vehicle, blowing dust through the vents and into our nostrils. I was coated with the stuff. I was driving when we crested a hill that overlooked the northern border post into Namibia. A stationary herd of hundreds of buffaloes blocked the road ahead. I slammed on the brakes; irritable with the delay, for we had far to go that day. After a long time the buffaloes finally moved into the bush and I saw that a government vehicle had been waiting on the other side.

Two policemen emerged. They sauntered slowly towards us, side-stepping piles of dung without looking down. Their hard gaze never shifted from us. *Sinking heart.*

One officer slowly drew a revolver from the holster that sat on his hip. The other was hitting a baton into his free hand. From the driver's seat, I turned and opened the window that divided the cabin from the back, where Lou was taking her turn to rest amid the luggage and equipment.

I whispered, 'Don't speak or move.'

Her expression was anxious as she nodded and shrank down deeper. She knew that the brother of a friend of ours had been shot in front of his wife and small children when he disagreed with a policeman at a roadblock.

Jer stepped out of the passenger's side to greet the men with the offer of a handshake. Like honey badgers on a mission, they ignored him and moved to my side of Bluey. I looked into faces set hard with hatred.

The man with the revolver ordered, 'Get out. Now!'

I reached down to undo my seatbelt and discovered I had forgotten to wear it. We had become accustomed to driving without seatbelts in Zimbabwe where it wasn't required by law.

'Woman! You are not wearing the seatbelt,' the policeman shouted; his dust-shot eyes boring into me.

The other officer had walked on and was now bending down to peer in at my daughter. He tapped his truncheon against the metal. My heart thudded with fear for the girl with the golden hair whose long legs, like mine, were exposed beneath cut-off shorts. They quivered in naked embarrassment.

With cast-down eyes, a forced smile and a shamefaced shrug, I apologised. 'I am very, very sorry, sir. We have come from Zimbabwe today. It is not compulsory to wear seatbelts there. I did not know it was a law in Botswana.'

Jer spoke up quickly. 'Excuse me, officer. My wife did not mean to break the law. What can we do to make it right?'

The officer spun around and lifted his revolver to Jer's chest. 'I am talking to the woman!' he roared.

The sights of the revolver turned back into my face. 'I am the law. I am dealing with this now. You have committed an offence. Get on to the road!'

I heard a sob from Lou as I opened the door. The other officer had returned and was eyeing off a carton of cigarettes on the dashboard. He spoke to his comrade in Tswana. The discussion was heated. Jer walked quietly to me and pushed me back gently. With a deferential expression he addressed the officer who had taken the sights of the revolver off me for the moment. 'What is the fine, sir? Can we pay it now? We wish to make amends for our mistake.'

Holding one hand over the forearm of the other in the customary gesture of obsequiousness I offered the men cigarettes from a loose packet. The mood had changed; their expressions altered from darkness to calculation. They took the cigarettes. I gave my inquisitor the packet. My husband rushed to fire his lighter and lit the cigarettes. 'We are just passing through Botswana today and need to pay the fine now.'

Everyone understood the language of corruption. With eyes still cast down and my teeth exposed like a submissive chimpanzee, I blurted: 'We are sad to be rushing through this beautiful country so fast. Soon we will be coming for a long visit.'

The men knew I was ridiculous. Why shoot a ridiculous thing? They shared amused looks and the revolver was returned to its sheath. My interrogator, who appeared to be the senior policeman, produced a book and began to write while his companion looked me up and down in a manner that made me feel dirty. Without speaking, the first officer showed Jeremy the paper. He looked to the horizon as Jer took out his wallet and produced a wad of notes.

It was an exorbitant sum that we handed over, and the carton of cigarettes went with it. I felt sure that the money wouldn't reach government coffers. The policemen insisted on escorting us to the border post, where they insulted Lou and me with their eyes as they ran their hands over our bottoms. I was grateful that Jer was inside with customs officials and didn't see what happened.

At last we crossed over the border into Namibia and immediately bought several cartons of duty-free cigarettes and a supply of vegetables from roadside stalls; just in case. Jer drove, while Lou and I huddled close together for the silent trip along a paved road to Katima Mulo.

On this day we would cross two borders, visit three African countries, and look upon two others. We had been told of the resolution of the Namibian civil war, but were not aware the peace treaty had been signed only that week. The intention had been to spend the night in the pretty town that marks the eastern perimeter of the Caprivi Strip: a narrow corridor of Namibian territory that stretches more than 500 kilometres west between Botswana, Zambia and Angola.

Instead, we made an instant decision to change our travel plans. Although the day had already been long, the hour was young. When we discovered that a wildlife conference was under way in town, and accommodation was full in lodges and rest houses, we decided to push on across the Caprivi to the town of Rundu. Jer calculated that the journey would take us about seven hours, which would bring us into Rundu before nightfall. There is no doubt that this was a foolish decision.

Fear had been replaced with a surge of energy and happiness. As we set off on the tarred road we sang our exit song, 'We're on the road again', and shouted a nonsensical phrase which had become the family mantra for joy: 'Shu-u-u-ut yo-u-r-r GOBBBBBBBB!'

'We'll do the trip in no time on this fine surface,' I assured my loved ones with supreme optimism. 'On the road again – and again.'

And then the tar ran out. The road was wide, and full of corrugations. We had been driving for an hour without meeting any traffic when Jer decided to move on to the wrong side of the road where the surface was marginally smoother. He drove like the clappers, which is the only way to deal with such a surface. I was alert for antelopes that might bound across our path. We caught glimpses of elephants as we sped along. The country had changed into riverine forest where tall Jackal-berry, mighty Leadwoods and Marula trees towered green beneath layers of dust thrown up from the road.

Then, two hours into the journey, we hit a roadblock. Once

again, Lou was in the back. I asked her to dig out a couple of sarongs so we could cover our legs. An impassable row of evil spikes spanned the road in front. A cordon of soldiers carrying AK-47s and wearing camouflage clothing was closing in. This wasn't how the trip was supposed to develop. My skin became cold and clammy as I realised we once again had relinquished control over our destiny. But then I thought, *Who ever really has control? Here and now, these guys rule. They can use us any way they like.*

Jer muttered, 'Shit! Place some cigarette cartons and cabbages in sight,' as he pulled over slowly.

Once again, we saw hatred in the faces of men. This time the leader spoke to us in Afrikaans. We put our hands up to indicate that we didn't understand what they were asking, but it was also a sign of surrender. Visions filled my mind of a home among the gum trees, of Lachy, and of my faithful terrier waiting at the gate.

Then I remembered that Australian soldiers had joined the UN forces during the battle for Namibian independence. I scrabbled through a bag looking for our Australian passports and visas and offered them, along with a face-splitting smile, to the soldier who seemed to be in charge. This time I made eye contact. I wasn't without compassion for these men, for what the war had done to them. I didn't know it personally, but I understood the rage created by wars and the agony that goes with the injustice of innocent's deaths incurred by bullets, bombs and land mines. War corrupts, as it alters the human perception of future progressive movement. It is always there. My eyes expressed these thoughts to the men who held sway over our lives.

The long body of the leader relaxed as he strung his AK-47

over his shoulder to examine the documents. He moved the weapon again. It became a stick to lean upon. 'Ah, Australian,' he said.

We nodded like sideshow clowns waiting to be fed ping pong balls. Everyone relaxed, until a soldier suddenly shouted in alarm behind us. He had been circling the vehicle looking at our goods – and at my daughter.

My earlier altruism dissipated. *Go-to-hell-bastard*, I thought. But my chimpanzee face said to the leader, *You have the strength of Shaka. A lion is as a lamb beside you – oh, great one.*

Once again the weapons were all pointed at us: a row of evil things with dead black eyes. The officer in charge pulled Jer out of the front seat and hauled him roughly to the back of the vehicle. He indicated that he wanted the back opened. He reached in and pulled out the binoculars in their camouflage-coloured case. Once again the bloody things made us suspects. *Should have chucked them long ago . . .*

Another soldier emerged from the guard hut. He adjusted an important-looking cap and strutted to indicate his importance. Speaking perfect English he demanded, 'Explain this, Mister white man. I think you are a foreign spy.'

He ordered us to unpack the vehicle. Grubby, elegant long fingers tore our clothes and equipment out of cases and threw them carelessly on to the road. Every item was picked up with the barrels of the weapons they used with careless familiarity.

Black people all have wonderful fine hands, I thought, as I watched my delicate frothy underwear being mauled by those magnificent fingers. A soldier with hard eyes, not at all like his delicate hands, challenged mine. Slowly, with a pink tongue flicking, he wiped his face with a pair of my lacy pink panties!

'Keep them for your wife,' I offered the pig. I would have burned them anyway. They disappeared into a pocket.

Jer bowed his head to each man as he proffered and lit cigarettes. In a quiet voice, he continued to explain the source of the binoculars. He told of our work with the elephants in Zimbabwe. It wasn't the first time his easy charm had relaxed the atmosphere with angry Africans. I remembered another man I had known. He would be dead already if he were here. He would have become brutal with his arrogance. The man who bowed his head to these men made me feel safer.

Lou and I got down in the dirt to repack our possessions. It was the best place for us. When we were finished, we clutched our sarongs close and crept back into the cabin where we sat still with our eyes downcast. Jer went with the soldiers into the hut. I could tell from the sounds of laughter that he was succeeding in putting them at ease.

An hour later, the leader casually waved us on. We were down fifty rand (about thirty Australian dollars), two cartons of cigarettes, three cabbages, a bag of tomatoes and a tattered water bottle. It was a small price to pay. Our spirits had descended into our filthy sandals. But we thanked God for our good fortune in having escaped with our lives.

By now it was mid-afternoon and we were hungry. We pulled off the road for a forlorn picnic under a mighty sausage tree. It felt as though a week had passed since I made the sandwiches in our Victoria Falls lodge at 3.30 am. They tasted a week old in my dry mouth. Jer had his head under the bonnet. He called me over and whispered, 'The engine's running hard. We've got problems.'

He continued to do the things that men do with engines, while I wandered back to Lou, who was looking as exhausted as I felt. She gathered a pendant of carmine-red flowers from the sausage tree. I knew the bell-shaped flowers held a secret beneath their beauty and grinned when I saw her bury her nose into a bloom. She snapped her head back and dropped the pretty things. 'Whew, these flowers smell really awful,' she gasped. 'Like mice.'

I laughed. 'It's awful, isn't it? *Kigelia africana* has to protect itself so that it can fruit. Bats are about the only creatures that like the flowers. They pollinate them, you know.'

'Wow! I wonder if the sausages taste like mice?' she asked, trying to lift one from the ground. It was about forty centimetres long.

Unfortunately, the distraction hadn't worked. She frowned. 'Mama, the engine has been coughing. Are we in trouble again?'

I tried to reassure her that nothing more would go wrong. But the Toyota started up reluctantly, and then cut out again within fifteen minutes. The old girl stopped and started every few minutes for the next two hours. Since leaving Katima Mulo we hadn't seen another vehicle. It was evident we were travelling in a virtual war zone. The conflict might be over, but the soldiers were still in battle mode. We had made an incredibly stupid decision.

Ah, to hell with it. I began to sing and chant the silly mantra until my family joined in. Then another roadblock loomed ahead. This time several of the soldiers spoke English. They also seemed to be impressed by an official document I found in a folder during our lunch break when I was looking for anything that might be of help. It was a letter of verification that was given to me by Golden (the official who told me the spirit of Africa saved me) to validate my status to the villagers he had asked me to visit.

The soldiers' breath stank of alcohol, and eyes peered myopically from a delta of red veins. Joints hung from their lips. They were intoxicated enough to be happy and amenable; not yet stoned and careless. 'Where is our gift, father?' one grunted.

Such was the way of Africa: another cabbage; three cans of baked beans and four packets of cigarettes. They waved us on quickly. This time the engine turned over immediately and we covered a good distance before it died. The sun was about to set, and by our assessment, Rundu was still 200 kilometres away.

'It's an adventure,' I sang.

Four eyes looked at me in disgust. Jer decided we should let the engine cool completely each time it stopped. The longer pauses gave us even longer periods of mobility. Our route now ran beside war-torn Angola. Just before darkness fell, we almost hit a man who ran out of the bushes waving a rifle and mouthing shouts, soundless to my ears above the drone of the engine. His dusty feet were bare and his tattered clothes flapped on a skeletal frame from coathanger shoulders. His wild face was framed by long dreadlocks.

Jer maintained our speed as he swerved around the man and hurried on. We decided he was probably an Angolan guerrilla fighter on the wrong side of the border, daring to risk the lesser of two evils. If he managed to merge into a community, and remain undiscovered on the Caprivi, he would eat. If he didn't, he would die. But if he stayed in Angola, conflict, starvation and death would be his constant companions. We were all hunched closely together in the cabin. No one spoke.

Barely suppressed fear turned into rabid panic when the engine cut out near the first settlement we had sighted. Light twinkled from the windows of a large concrete building. Drunken shouts and laughter replaced the sound of the motor.

Jer groaned. 'Bad timing. But I don't think they know we're here. I can't wait for the engine to cool. We have to get the old bitch out of sight.'

He took my hand. 'Salda, I want you to control the steering from outside the door.' Then, 'Lou? We'll push.'

'Mama, I'm frightened,' she sobbed quietly. 'I didn't come to Africa to die.'

I was overwhelmed with guilt. Her body was as rigid as mine. I whispered, 'Nor did I, Louie. We are going to get out of this. But we need to stay focused.'

Both of us were only too aware of the possibilities if the soldiers found us. There would be no escape from hardened soldiers, celebrating liberation from white oppression. We all had white faces and were therefore the 'enemy', even though we had nothing to do with their war. By now, we knew, they must have been fuelled with alcohol and *ganja*.

Steering the wheel with one hand, I leaned my trembling body hard into the door as Jer and Lou found superhuman strength at the rear. Inch by inch, the lights of the building receded. We crawled back inside to wait for the engine to cool. Holding each other's hands, without any prompting, we began as one to croon 'Waltzing Matilda'. It was the song of our homeland. When it was done, Jer leaned across to plant quick kisses on two sets of moist cheeks.

'I'm going to start the engine,' he said. 'If it doesn't kick in and the soldiers hear us and come looking, we'll run into the bush and hide. We need to stay together. Do you understand me?' and his eyes asked me to understand the worst of possibilities.

At that moment all the tension drained from my body. I sensed a calm presence with us. It banished any doubts I had. *We were going to survive*. I looked back at my husband, at peace for the moment. He turned the ignition and the engine purred into life. Bluey flew over the corrugations, soaring above the pot-holes with disdain. Lou and I slumped into an exhausted, restless sleep. I kept waking and wondering how I could doze off when anxiety had been pumping adrenalin all day. And it wasn't over yet.

I woke with a start as the car slowed. The headlights framed the form of yet another soldier, who was reeling towards us waving an AK-47. He aimed the weapon at Jer, whose face was riven with exhaustion. For a second we looked into his mad, bloodshot eyes. I knew he was going to fire.

'Don't stop!' I screamed. 'Gun the engine. He's going to kill us.'

Jer slammed his foot down; the vehicle roared ahead, just missing the man. We heard the rattle of automatic gunfire as we fled.

Lou then shocked me with a shout of triumph. 'We beat the bastard!' Fired by victory, she took the wheel for the final leg. It was midnight when we rolled into Rundu to begin the search for lodgings. A bullet-pocked sign directed us down a narrow track and into a tiny camp perched on the banks of the Okavango River. We stumbled into the lights of a thatched-roofed bar and into the company of a band of Irish soldiers; a very startled-looking unit of the Green Berets. When we told them we had crossed the Caprivi Strip they lifted their caps in salute and ordered us huge jars of beer.

'You must be *mad*. No civilians travel there. And certainly not at night,' roared the bull of a man who manned the bar –

above the sound of Roy Orbison who was shrilling at the crest of 'Crying'. It is a song I detest, but at that moment it was a glorious reminder of Western civilisation.

A soldier asked, 'Are you Irish? If it isn't the luck of the Irish, then the angels would be liking ya.'

I smiled at Jer as I croaked, 'I think it was an angel'.

Flushed with relief and the beer she had downed in one hit, Lou cried: 'But we *did* make it. Who's buying me the next one?'

In Namibia we visited the town of Swakopmund, a moon landscape, where the houses are modelled on those in Bavaria, hornless rhinos, the Skeleton Coast, where beautiful naked orange women smoked pipes, and another place where a painted white lady waits patiently to be understood. We watched an elephant dancing, snakes walking sideways, trees that shot arrows, animals that never drink and birds that cannot fly. We frizzled in mindless heat and froze in sub-zero temperatures – on the same day. It was a world cloaked with mist and mystery that would call me back.

We put Lou on a plane in Swakopmund and returned to the elephants in Zimbabwe for our final farewell. The season was changing. Heat came one day with the clouds. It would be some time before they dropped their blessing, and when they did the elephants would once again retreat to impenetrable forest. The project was now a strong entity with a solid set of parameters. Others would join the team next year when the rains were over and the elephants returned to the *vlei*.

Kathy and Neil would marry soon, Des and Jen were moving on, and Aubrey and Siti were leaving for a holiday in England. I began the process of detaching myself from our human friends – but not from my elephant friends. I would never detach from them. I knew I could manifest their presence in my mind at will.

On the last day we searched for the herd without success. By evening, my heart was aching with despair. Determined to have one last moment with them, we drove towards their least-loved waterhole, hoping and praying they would be there. Ignoring the possibility of connecting with a blister beetle, I hung out of the window to search the sandy track for spoor. There was no sign of elephant.

A male kudu with fantastic tri-twisted horns burst out of the thick bush in front, forcing us to stop. He stood for a moment looking at us, and then veered off along a narrow game trail. He paused again, turned to look at us and came back a few paces. I felt a strong urge to follow. 'Jer, he's leading us in there. Please follow him.'

'What? Down that game trail?' He looked at me as if I were crazy, but what he saw on my face was enough. 'Let's do it then, Squirt.'

The kudu moved off down the trail and we followed. The cool night air was transforming the heatwaves lifting off the earth into a gentle fog. The antelope disappeared into the bush. The light dimmed. Branches whipped along the sides of the vehicle.

I knew she was there before I saw her. Skew Tusk walked on to the track and turned to face us. She lifted her head high to look down her trunk in a posture of regal pride. Small streams of emotion were dripping from her temporal glands. Tears wet my cheeks. Jer reached out to hold my hand.

Skew Tusk had been the first of the herd's elephants I met and she would be the last to farewell. The matriarch stood quite still as swirling tendrils of mist licked across her back and eddied about her feet. She was unaccountably alone.

We remained together for a time, until she lifted her trunk, smacked her ears with a deep nod from her marvellous head and moved into the bush. The magic went with her. Our time with the elephants was over – for now.

The kettle is smiling
– July 2006

'Tenzi. What is in the black bag in the freezer? It smells awful.'

'That bad thing is a giraffe. He is dead. *Ye bo.*'

'Ah,' I say, as if dead giraffes in freezers are everyday findings. 'We must move that dead giraffe now and dispose of it.'

Shouting earnestly (he always shouts), Tenzi replies, 'I will run with him to the staff village. This giraffe will make good biltong.'

My nose twitches with alarm. 'But that giraffe is bad. It will make you sick.'

Tenzi becomes even more earnest. 'No, Saa-lly, that giraffe is long on the foot. His body has grown old. He will be good food. Yeee-bo.'

His patience with the village idiot is considerable. I have much to learn as a safari slave living with the Damara, Herero and Himba people in the Namibian wilderness.

It is seven o'clock on a freezing morning in July 2006 when Tenzi and Redney take flight, swinging the head and remains of the giraffe between them. Mist bursts from their mouths with their laughter. Lean and wiry, with shining white teeth, they skip like children across the kilometre of gibber plain to their camp. It is hidden behind the range of craggy basalt hills, away from the eyes and ears of guests. I hope the staff shout and sing into the night there, because they have to quell their naturally effusive natures in order to be quiet around visitors. I watch the young men disappear into dust thrown from the hooves of a small herd of springbok that scatter in alarm.

'Come back quickly. There is much work to do here,' I call after them, hoping they can understand my Australian English; that they won't decide to begin the long salting process before their work is done in the kitchen. I don't want to have to chase after them. This morning we sighted fresh lion spoor crossing the path between the encampments. The lions of the desert are cunning, rarely roaring in the night. You don't know when they are around.

These men speak many languages. English is new to them, yet they are endlessly tolerant of my efforts to speak slowly and their fluency grows daily. I know I will never be able to learn Damara. The words roll from their tongues with a mixture of clicks and liquid vowel sounds. But if difficult communications sometimes cause a feeling of alienation from humans, my other senses are comfortable with the environment. Forbidding hills of a thousand faces and forms encircle the sand and gravel valley, studded sparsely with umbrella thorn acacias. I recognise friends and animals amidst the leers of monsters. Their grimaces don't bother me. Rather, they have become solid, protective presences.

Each morning I greet my rocky companions, who are always there in a place where nothing else is certain, especially the availability of water. There are springs in the Hoanib, but they must be left to the wildlife. Most days, an antique Nissan rattles off before dawn to fetch water from a borehole ninety kilometres away. The exhausted driver returns after his second round trip at night. He drives a total of three hundred and sixty kilometres each day. Guests are always astounded and impressed by this information and, for the most part, acquiesce with requests to shower sparingly. I joke that we should bathe in beer, as it is cheaper than water. But I am not really joking. Water is more valuable than diamonds in this fragile desert environment.

Six safari tents are placed far apart between the hills, connected by a meandering stone-lined path. Each night, a campfire burns in front of a large dining tent that faces the bank of the mysterious Hoanib River, where rare desert elephants roam and shy brown hyaenas and sly leopards slip through the darkness. The presence of these creatures is why I have volunteered to work as a safari slave for Wilderness Safaris. As well, it is a wild place where I can write the final chapter of this memoir of other elephants. Coming to the Hoanib to chronicle my recent reunion with the Presidential Herd of Zimbabwe seemed perfect. Now I'm not so sure. Being a safari slave is challenging. I had not anticipated the long hours of work running an isolated camp, being first to greet the dawn and last to bed at night. As well, the lengthy days are not just about making people happy. There are temperamental chefs to placate, local staff with their own personal problems, logistical nightmares of monumental proportions, and constant breakdowns of vehicles and satellite communications with the outside world.

I had begun to despair that I would find time to write a word until this first break between guests has come. *Ah*, I think. Now I can unwrap my little word processor and use some of the precious 700 hours of battery power. I flop onto a chair with my back to the sun, nod to the monsters and promptly fall asleep. A while later, I jerk awake to the thunder of hooves. Seven scimitar-horned gemsbok (oryx) are galloping past my tent, lifting clouds of sand that envelop the precious machine and me. A bucket shower and two coffees later, I type one sentence before the wet fog from the Skeleton Coast sweeps over the crags to cloak the valley in a heavy curtain of cold and the word processor in dust-clotting moisture.

Such is the way of life in this harsh, beautiful land of changing circumstances. The freezing Benguela Current flows close against the bleak Atlantic coastline, just forty-five kilometres away (as the vulture flies), although you could not imagine it. Often, when the cold air meets the heat of the dunes, life-giving fog forms, bringing moisture to the parched land. Hard-shelled black tok-tokkie beetles stop, lift their bottoms high and wait for drops of water to run down to their mouths; antelope and oryx take moisture from the leaves of vegetation that lives because of the moisture-laden fog, and predators take theirs from the blood of prey. The heavy mist brings life.

I remind myself of this and try not to dread the bitter cold that comes with it. When the fog lifts, curling back spectacularly from the glistening hills, I begin to peel off layers of clothes until the sun re-ignites blessed warmth. At least for a while. It is winter, but the heat of mid-afternoon is intense if the fog and wind are absent. Of all these contrasts, it is the wind that irks me most. Suddenly it arrives. When it howls hot from the east, dust storms blow and these are hard to bear. Sand and grit creep into every orifice. Solar panels, canvas and all the crockery and food in the kitchen are hidden beneath coatings of grime. Flapping tents complain with eerie shrieks. Birds stop singing. Game disperses into the deep protective shadows of trees and cliffs. If the wind blows for longer than a day it creeps into the psyche of humans until stretched tempers explode.

Somehow, the camp cook, Janaman, creates miracles from whatever questionably fresh vegetables and fruit we can find at the local store – just 300 kilometres away. Before each group arrives, we have to make the two-day round trip. Two days, because the first seventy-five kilometres is through the deep sand of the mostly dry river bed that stretches wide between towering canyons. Whenever elephants are ahead, we stop until they move onto the Ana tree and mustard bush-lined banks. This can take time. Disturbing them – or the giraffes, oryx, springbok, steenbok and ostriches – is not an option. Human invasion is kept to a minimum. If only it could be so for the equally precious Presidential Herd in Zimbabwe.

Two months before, I left Australia on the journey back to Zimbabwe for a reunion with the elephants. A long day later, the aircraft flew into the dawn over Africa. The usual brown smog of pollution bruised the salmon sky above Johannesburg as the wheels touched down for the extended braking taxi of high altitude. I was grateful we were simply passing through the airport of the dark city where Lou had been shot in the leg during a car-hijack two years earlier.

Hours later, we flew on to Victoria Falls. Unlike our arrival in Johannesburg, we were greeted by smiling customs officials who responded with brilliant beams to my Ndebele greeting, '*Lichonanjani* [Gooday]'.

'Ah, madam, *Siyabonga*! [Thank you]' and one man stamped the passports with a flourish as he waved us through the barrier.

A driver was waiting to transport us to our old stamping ground on the Dete *vlei*. Amidst the spray from the Falls, I glimpsed rainbow shafts thrusting high into the sky as we turned west onto the main highway toward Bulawayo. It seemed the wet season had been kind. Thick green mopane scrub lined the sealed road; two- and three-span donkey wagons hauled piles of wood; happy children dressed in beige uniforms leaped and danced their way home from school along the sides of the road. Women wearing bright sarongs strolled along carrying on their backs babies with nodding bonneted heads. The road was well maintained. We crossed Matetsi Bridge, passed by the Hwange colliery, Lukosi Government School, and thatched-roofed villages teeming with fat cattle and goats. The driver told us the harvest had been good. The familiar great baobab looked just the same and the Inyantu River held water. Yellow-billed hornbills (fondly known as flying bananas) cackled and swooped in the air, and I remembered Effie. My head was woolly, but my shoulders began to unlock.

Several years had passed since our last disturbing visit. So far so good for this re-entry. I was delighted to be on the road to our second home. Even so, I felt some fear because now

Zimbabwe was a nation in even deeper crisis. Jer was unusually edgy as well. The Australian government and the world media painted a grim picture of political strife and the resulting tragedy of the human condition in Zimbabwe. Some of our expatriate contacts had been equally explicit in their description of the chaos. They had less to lose than our Zimbabwean friends, who sent carefully coded messages by email. My replies were just as circumspect.

I knew that Marius and Wilmarie had been thrown off their land with only the clothes they could pack into two suitcases. Not yet born during the guerrilla campaign which became a civil war from 1972 to 1979, the so-called 'war veterans' had come one day to take the farm. They were opportunistic young thugs. As others had done to white farmers elsewhere, they intimidated, invaded, ransacked and claimed everything – not only the land they were encouraged to see as their birthright by those in power. Less than ten white people had been slaughtered in Zimbabwe. This was appalling, but it was thousands less than the rarely reported murders of South African farmers – mostly elderly people carefully chosen by thieves as easy targets. However, there was a subtle difference between the crimes: a government by turning a blind eye sanctioned one; the other was the result of random crime. Tentacles of fear coil into the minds of democratic nations when a dictator condones and even incites acts of terrorism. Therefore, though the death rate was higher in South Africa, tourists still visited.

However, they had deserted Zimbabwe. A tyrannical, rabid minority who were destroying the economy and the livelihoods of their compatriots was crucifying the lives of the peaceful majority of Zimbabweans. Tourism had been the second-highest source of revenue in Zimbabwe, but now only a trickle of intrepid travellers dared to visit, even though the trouble spots were scattered across areas tourists rarely visited.

I dozed in the warm car and thought of my life since 1990 and our farewell to Skew Tusk in the evening mist.

When we had returned to Australia I fell to earth – in more ways than one. I kissed the Tarmac of the Lucky Country and was grateful to be home. But I carried with me an unwelcome part of Africa. Doctors were unable to identify the parasites that flattened me and I was ill for a long time. This meant an early return to the research project was not a realistic option.

Instead, I turned what energy I had to Elefriends Australia. Jer and I visited schools and service organisations to spread the message of endangered species in Africa, and to communicate the commonalities and differences between races as we shared our vulnerabilities, hopes and fears.

To sustain a living, we bought another derelict avocado orchard, restored its quaint old cottage and planted an organic garden. I again fell in love with the birds of Australia; with the evening flyby of spectacular parrots whose call is harsh, while the song of the plain butcherbird was the sound of angels. These rapacious little buggers wrought havoc on the worms we overturned with our spades. I thought it was their calling to be the munchers of the chicks of other birds – the lions of the air. And when the wind blew twigs into broken piles on the ground, I would joke, 'Elephants have passed through recently.' However, even I was annoyed with my propensity to compare creatures and nature in Australia with those of Africa. But what could I do? The herd continued to thunder through my dreams and Jer also longed to return to Zimbabwe. Sometimes when the lush habitat became claustrophobic, we drove west into the vast space of the arid country to breathe its freedom. I caught myself looking for movement amongst the eucalyptus trees that in Africa might have been antelope, but here was cattle or a mob of kangaroos.

I think many people thought we were quite mad to want to leave our safe motherland and return to somewhere that lacked freedom and peace, and had brought me physical grief. Rightly, they perceived Zimbabwe as driven by conflict, steered with savagery, and ravaged by HIV/AIDS, malaria and extreme poverty. I understood their concern and tried to explain why I was drawn to a world where the strength of the spirit almost manages to overwhelm the baseness of the human condition, whereas it seemed to Jer and me that in our society money had become more than a means to live.

By then, Lou was a commercial pilot flying in the Northern Territory and Lachy was taking a sabbatical from his law degree to roam the world searching for the perfect wave and inspiration for his music. To pay his way, he worked the salmon run in Alaska and crewed on tuna boats in southern Australia. Jer's daughters, Jenny and Jackie, brought their babies to visit and the youngest, Kate, came to stay during school holidays.

We became nomads, Jeremy and I. We sold the orchard and returned to Africa for a few months in 1993. Even before leaving Harare, we were troubled. Stress creased the faces of young men who took us aside to speak openly of their rage against the government. They were angry and said they spoke for the new intellectuals. One of them told me he was HIV positive. I ached for him and the AIDS-induced genocide that was killing the cream of Zimbabwe's youth, taking hope for a better land with them.

Des and Jen were managing a game farm surrounded by high electric fences. The homestead was a fortress that had been made even more secure after a terrifying incident when 'war veterans' (armed with axes and machetes) threatened Jenny during an attempt to invade the farm when Des was away. The police ignored her call for help. Terrified for their baby boy, and aware they were defenceless against a lawless terrorist force sanctioned unofficially by the government, the young couple secretly planned to emigrate to Australia.

Harold was just holding on at the Gwaai, but he saw the writing on the wall. Soon he would be forced to leave his beloved sanctuary for South Africa. Life was grim for them and for many of our black friends, some of whom had been subjected to violence and intimidation and were struggling to feed their families.

Trouble had come to Dete as well. We were unable to drive through the concession where the herd roamed. From the tarred road we looked longingly into the bush, hoping to sight the herd and Skew Tusk. It was Tunny we saw. The triangular hole in her left ear identified the great cow that emerged from the bush to rush her family across the road. They were flighty. She sent them ahead, then swung towards us flapping her ears in anger. I placed my hands around my mouth and rumbled to her at the moment I thought she might mock charge. Tunny lifted her trunk to test the scent and froze for a precious moment. There was no doubt she recognised us. The sighting was frustratingly brief – over within a minute.

* * *

Back in Australia we bought and renovated houses, which were never homes, and along the way turned a derelict cattle property into a viable operation. The purpose of submitting ourselves to endless moves, hard work and constant change was to create the means to return to other parts of Africa; which we did, between each project. If moving house every year or so is one of the great stresses in life, then we are suckers for punishment. But I believe these things are relative. I had a passion that was shared by my husband, so creating the means to fulfil our need became a mechanical issue rather than a difficult life change. Oh, every now and then I longed for stability of place and wondered if I would ever have the security of a permanent home. I tried to mirror the décor of each house so there was a sense of familiarity for us all.

Jer and I knew there was no chance of getting off the nomad trail while Africa remained such a magnet. Whenever letters came from friends in Zimbabwe, tidal waves of longing swept through us. I think Aubrey knew this when he wrote:

Our beloved elephants have departed temporarily after a freak and I mean freak accident. A few mornings back one of the guides from Sikumi Tree Lodge was returning after his early morning drive. He was coming back from Kanondo along the road that runs parallel to the power line that feeds Hwange Safari Lodge. He heard a crashing and saw a flashing. On approaching he found the 33000-volt high-tension line down and resting on the body of a large elephant bull. He rushed back to Sikumi and the two us shot back to the scene. The line was still live and the elephant of course dead. After the electricity authority shut down the power I was able to reconstruct what had happened.

Checking the spoor very carefully it appeared that two large bulls had been fighting. The dead bull had three large tusk wounds around the face and the second bull, that obviously departed the scene in a hurry, also left a minor blood spoor. What had happened was the one bull pushed the other who then reversed into the power pylon breaking it into three pieces. The cables then came crashing down and initially fell on his head burning three distinct lines across his forehead. At that stage the animal fell on its left side and the cables came to rest across his stomach. I know cardiac arrest would have caused instant death. Ay ay ay ay ay! In all my life I have never heard of such a thing although they do sometimes push each other into our land rovers as you know!!!

You know too that elephants react when one gets shot. On the morning in question, the whole herd, with the exception of the wounded bull was standing around. I am sure the matriarch decided the bull had been shot and told the whole lot to bugger off!! As if someone had come along with a giant vacuum cleaner they all pushed off although five scouts were seen near Kanondo yesterday evening. I hope they tell the others to please come back. We all miss them very very much. Pity we can't explain exactly what happened to them. It would be a tragedy to break trust with our gentle giants.

President Robert Mugabe has finally given special protection 'In Perpetuity' to the herd. I am honoured to have been appointed to the Board of Trustees. We have already had our inaugural meeting in Harare and our first proper meeting when the President makes the project public is scheduled for the 18th February 1992.

We had great excitement today during lunch. 'Banda' the waiter, rushed in to tell me three cheetah were hunting impala right in front of the lodge. I alerted the guests who rushed out just in time to see the mother cat nail an impala! Imagine the thrill – in full view of the lodge. The three cheetah and ourselves then all sat down to lunch!!

To you both I send my warmest greetings and a snog for you Sal.
Aubrey Packenham.

And, of course, my world tilted again. I wanted to be there to celebrate the bittersweet victory with our friends. Mandebele had achieved his purpose of protecting the herd by ingratiating himself with the president. I could almost hear him and Aubrey apologising to the elephants. But it was worth pandering to the president's vanity to place a mantle of safety over the elephants. Sadly, this would not be a permanent victory.

Every two or three years, after selling our latest property, we hefted our swags and returned to Africa. Until the late nineties, Zimbabwe was always included in our travels, but we also came to know Kenya, Botswana and Namibia. Each trip we would have to endure Johannesburg while we searched for a vehicle. Bluey was replaced variously by 'Snow', 'The Beast' and others that didn't earn a nickname. There were tents on top, bedrolls in the back and the occasional luxury of staying in national parks' lodges or with friends, and eventually with Lou in Kenya, where she worked for the United Nations flying Hercules aircraft on aid missions into the Sudan.

In 1998 I made a pilgrimage back to the place where it all began – to Savuti in Botswana. On my first day there heat ironed the shirt against my back as I walked out from the shade beneath the awning of the tent. I perspired for a moment until the ravenous sun slurped up the moisture. The sweat dried as soon as it broke onto my skin. God knows what extremes the temperature reached – the thermometer cracked, set forever at 44°C. It was October and rain hadn't fallen that year.

Twenty-seven emaciated elephant bulls stood still on the sand of the dry channel below the camp. A host of antelope and a family of wart-hogs were there, also waiting to drink. Flocks of namaqua doves landed, crooned and left without relief. Reptiles and raptors were the winners now. Hunting kites and eagles swooped in effortless vertical dives to feed off the hapless or those who had died from heat exhaustion. A pair of exquisite pythons and a family of boomslangs coiled motionless in two Leadwood trees waiting, ready to make lightning strikes on red-billed queleas when they descended in swarms. Aside from tail flicks and occasional slow flaps of cabbage-shaped ears, nothing moved except the birds and the air. You only ever sight air in intense heat or cold. In the heat, air shimmers in waves; in the cold, it steams as it leaves warm mouths. Both are illusions. In the drought, life was being sucked from all living things, even changing the form of inanimate objects.

While I sketched, a prehistoric painting of a praying mantis warped when a rock cracked in the sacred *kopje*. The dreaming of an ancient human, the very heart of his creation myth, was split. But I knew the rains would come again and change the desert so that once again life would regenerate, one moment at a time. Humans would regain the strength to care about each other and for the creatures of the wild. I hoped this would happen soon. For now, there was no fuel to run the pump that watered the pan. Animals were dying of thirst. Hugo was being bloody-minded about not pouring more hard-won money into the rescue, and why not? It had been months since government sources dispatched fuel.

I watched more bulls lumber into the only water source they knew. They dropped their trunks to search listlessly where the liquid should have been. Then they leaned their great bodies to one side, either leaving the tips of heavy trunks fully extended onto the ground or lifting them to rest across their tusks. One peed a short gush of thick yellow fluid. Another reached out to suck up the acrid urine before it hit the sand. I felt sick. The elephants were too weak now to make it across fifty kilometres to the next water source, the Linyanti River. They didn't try because there had almost always been the certainty of water at Savuti, since humans decided to create an artificial pan when the Savuti Channel dried for good. I feared for Skew Tusk and the herd. Were they safe? They also depended upon bores pumped by man.

On the fifth day, Hugo gave in – to the pleadings of humans, to his own pain and to the animals he adored. He fuelled and started the pump. Shrivelled grey bodies expanded, as did my spirit. I remembered the elephant that snored his song into my consciousness just before dawn in 1984. He saved my life and stole my soul. Savuti would always sing me back to the arid, mysterious, singularly beautiful Chobe, where some day the Savuti Channel might flow again.

Jer called me back to the present – Zimbabwe in 2006. 'We're at the turn-off, Sal. Almost home.'

The driver turned the vehicle off the main road onto the secret track that wound through the forest towards the Dete *vlei*. I cringed as we passed by Marius's house. It was falling down and the formerly beautiful garden sprouted rusting vehicles and rubbish. The 'war vets' were there, but they were either unable to run the operation, or had no intention of doing so. A stately bull kudu bounded before us and then we had arrived. A man was waiting at the gate of Sikumi Tree Lodge, where we would stay.

'Welcome,' he said as he stepped forward to shake my hand. 'I am Bheki.'

My heart tipped over as recognition flashed across his strong face. Then he grabbed me close, held me away from him and then hugged me again and again.

'Mama Ndlovu! Is it you?' he said, and to Jer, 'Madala, you have come home.'

'Oh, Bheki, I never thought to find you.'

I watched the two men embrace. This was an unusual gesture for a Matabele man to make to an outsider. Bheki's eyes were as wet as ours. Unashamedly, he took a large handkerchief from his pocket and blew his nose. He continued to ask disbelievingly if it was really us as he lifted his legs high to slap his hands hard against his thighs. I looked at the boy who had become a man. Bheki turned excitedly to the other men who had appeared. His arms flew about as he spoke urgently in Ndebele. Sixteen years had passed since we had met. I was delighted to see Bheki had retained employment when so many had been retrenched since tourists deserted the country.

'Come. Let me find you a cool drink. Or is it tea? I am now the barman.' His deep voice rang with pride.

Later he spoke of getting his professional guide's licence, but he was unable to progress further until he saved enough money to apply for a driver's licence. Over the next few days, we shared life stories but he stood with us rather than sitting unless we were alone. I understood. It would have been ill-mannered for an employee to sit with guests.

I was enchanted when light suffused his grave face with each wide smile he gave, but his eyes were sad.

'Ah, Mama, I am an old man now and those were the days of joy. Those days when we were all together and Zimbabwe was happy.'

'Bheki! You're only 33 years old. That is still young.' Yet, I knew that, for a Zimbabwean, he *was* an old man, for people's life expectancy has dropped to the mid-thirties. I thought how very old we must seem to him.

'Ah, I am a married man now. My wife has a name like yours. She is called Saliwe, Sali, and I am the father of two beautiful children. They are Perfect, who is five years, and Ability, who is two years.' He pointed to the waterhole. 'There are the naughty baboons, Sally, and three sable have come to welcome you.' His face lit up with a mighty smile. 'I will call for the elephants to be here soon.'

'Then you must ask especially for Skew Tusk, Tunny, Dilingane, Bette Midler and Inkosikasi to come,' I joked.

'Ah . . . it is right that you have elephants on your mind. I am told that old cow Skew Tusk is still here somewhere,' he intoned with his old gravity. 'But I am always here looking after the guests, so I cannot know with my own eyes.'

On that first day over tea and biscuits, I asked where Dingindawo, Lovemore, Jabulani, Shadrick and Stock were. Bheki dropped his head and clasped his hands across his chest in a reverent posture. 'Ah, Sally. I am sorry to tell you this sad thing. They have all passed away.'

I gasped and sat down quickly. We both looked out towards

the waterhole and Bheki rested his hand softly on my shoulder. I did not ask him why the youngest of these men was gone.

'However,' he continued in an encouraging tone, 'Dumisani, Elton and Pious are all now living in South Africa. Our good friend Dickson is a professional guide and Raphael is fat and strong. He is now a professional hunter. He is a very success-ful man. Only rich men become fat.'

'Is it, Bheki? That is good news indeed.' But my heart was heavy for those who had gone so young. We already knew George Ndlovu had died without welcoming the new century, as he had planned with the son he named Millennium.

Later, Bheki joined me by the fire to speak of his life now. He said that at the beginning of the year he had saved Z$10 million for his driver's licence. The money might have covered the cost but his brother died and Bheki gave the money to his brother's wife, and agreed to educate her three children as his own.

'What can I do?' he shrugged. 'I must share what I have.'

Bheki said that that week he went to the supermarket with 10 million Zimbabwe dollars (his monthly pay packet) and couldn't afford a small basket of groceries. He dropped his head with shame when he said he had to take most things back to the shelves – even a packet of flour. 'My family cannot eat bread.'

Two kilos of sugar cost Z$6.5 million. The economy was in a tailspin, with inflation running rampant and rising daily. In 1990 two Zimbabwean dollars were worth one US dollar. Now one US dollar bought a staggering Z$100,000. One week later, Z$150,000 would buy one US dollar, and the value of the Zim-babwean dollar was plummeting daily. And that was the official bank rate. On the black market, one US dollar bought Z$300,000.

Bheki told me in his measured way of financial worries. It took a long time, and I neither interrupted nor offered any comment. Anything I might have said would have been irrelevant. He simply needed to be heard. I listened until my front was scorched and smoke began to waft from the tips of boots thrust too close to the flames. My back was frozen. I stood to move out of the smoke trail that was hell-bent on pursuing me around the pit.

'Look, Sally. The kettle is smiling,' Bheki laughed, reminding me of his sixteen-year-old self's charming confusion of language as he struggled to learn English. A kettle was steaming on adjacent coals to fill hot water bottles covered in furry covers. I wrapped my hot water bottle inside my coat, said goodnight and climbed the ladder to a cubby-house tucked away within the branches of a large tree. The gurgling bottle (actually a rubber container) was a small ray of comfort when I snuggled into the blanket-laden bed.

I couldn't sleep. I was overwhelmed by human misery, jet lag and the bitterly cold air that flowed over the rail high walls through my woolly cap and onto my head. Resigned to a disturbed night, I entered the realm of mad monkey thoughts where no sensible monkey surely goes. To banish them, I imagined the first glimpse of the breeding herd. Would they know me? As the air seemed to crystallise until I felt the hairs in my nostrils had become icicles, I prayed for the street children; for all the homeless, undernourished Zimbabweans who might die of exposure that night.

The temperature was hovering at freezing point just before dawn. Dressed like an Eskimo, I clambered down the ladder in a rush to stoke the coals. Bheki had pre-empted me. A huge log of Leadwood blazed even brighter than his welcoming smile. We sat cross-legged in the pit, toasting bread and drinking bush tea while we discussed elephants. Mist curled over the silver back of a honey badger making its single-minded way to the water's edge to drink. A line of kudu broke and stepped aside as the bossy badger hurried in. Wisely so. His typically arrogant body language broadcast an ominous warning to keep clear. He drank quickly, lifted his heavy head for a bone-headed glare at the hovering animals, and then trotted off on a well-worn game trail into the long grass.

Baboons vocalised morning greetings before emerging onto the *vlei* from the heights of tall trees. Tiny black babies rode high on their mothers' backs like miniature jockeys. They rolled off to play beside fresh elephant droppings while their elders scattered the hardly digested stuff, fossicking for juicy titbits and dung beetles. Elephants had been to the pan in the night. Somewhere close, in the surrounding forest, I heard an indignant blast. My pulse rose. Maybe I didn't have to go searching if they returned to drink during the morning. I decided to stay put. But the elephants had other plans. My strained ears and searching eyes were sore by lunchtime.

Mid-afternoon we set out in a clanking old Land Rover driven by Pembas, a gentle-eyed professional guide and trusted friend of Bheki. We drove through the burnished copper grasses of the *vlei*. I feared our noisy progress would clear the *veldt* of wildlife. The familiar excited wings were fluttering in my stomach. Everything looked the same, which was somehow shocking because I knew things were different. The mopane scrublands were dense after good rain and not yet losing their butterfly-shaped leaves, though the winter cold had already been of long duration. A herd of 200 buffalo were drinking and wallowing at a fresh hole one hundred metres from camp. Mean-looking bulls corralled their charges in a wildly spinning wheel that drifted slowly toward the forest. The buffalo looked fat and healthy. I thanked God for the blessing of a good wet season this year. How many humans would have died otherwise? How many animals would have perished without water? There is now no money to pay for fuel to pump the majority of the artificially watered pans.

Impatient to find our elephants, I hardly noticed the giraffe, sable, impala and wart-hogs we passed on our way to the much-loved acacia grove. I knew this was the place to start. There would be enough late pods to attract bulls to the beautiful park-like area where the Gang of Eleven once thrust their great bodies against the trunks to shake down the delectable *Acacia erioloba* pods.

Blood surged into my head as I sighted my first elephants. Two large bulls melted their grey camouflage into the shade beneath a massive tree. Unless there were obvious identifying features, I knew the possibility of recognising any of the herd would be difficult, particularly bulls without the presence of known cows. We stayed near them for a long time. I was home, relishing the familiar sweet game smell, the woofs of dust when great ears flapped, the sight of baggy bottoms jiggling as one great leg scratched another – and the relaxed trunks with tips extended onto the ground. The oldest bull squinted at us before he wandered away, followed by his head-shaking, protective young askari. Their ease in our presence indicated they were definitely Presidential Herd bulls, but I didn't recognise them.

As usual, the baboons and impala were there, busily gathering pods left on the ground by the bulls, and a pair of jackals were their false friends – waiting for the time the ewes would drop their lambs. I was completely in the moment, the fog of jet lag having lifted from my brain. There was nothing except the wildlife. This was my personal heaven and Jer had what looked like a permanent grin parting his heavy beard. We waited in silence, hoping a family from the breeding herd might come. I was willing it.

And then they broke from the thick bush, walking fast towards the vehicle just as they always had done. My heart sang as I scanned the faces of the cows to see who was there. Then one female strode purposefully towards us demanding full attention. I noted her wide forehead and large eyes, and she turned her head. A triangular piece of skin in her left ear was missing. It was Tunny. I couldn't believe the synchronicity. She came right beside my door and looked at me beneath the long lashes of a warm amber eye. My breath caught in my throat; tears ran down my face. I whispered, 'Hello, Tunny.' She reached out her trunk and blew hot air on my arm. I sat very still, but wanted to reach back and stroke her.

The tiny baby of another cow gambolled close. Her young mother came behind with an anxious expression on her pretty face. Tunny stood firm, still looking straight into my eyes. The younger cow relaxed. We had been introduced. Tunny stayed close for half an hour, occasionally reaching out to test my scent and blow her own. I blew back gently. Her family relaxed enough to gather pods, and one large cow laid her trunk hard and high onto a tree, and leant her massive weight to shiver and shake bunched muscles until pods dropped. It was rare to see a female try this. Jer thought she could be the graceful cow known as Grace, but I wasn't so sure. Before she led her family away, Tunny flopped her head amiably and flapped her ears gently as if to say, 'Bye for now.'

We drove on to Kanondo, where many of our favourite times were spent with the herd. Even knowing the state of affairs, I was shocked to find the once verdant string of lagoons almost silted up. The luxurious reed beds were gone and dust devils raked across the arid space. Kanondo was deserted – gone to the dogs, as had Zimbabwe. Not even the usual suspects were there. Always, always, there would have been waterbuck, impala, baboons, wart-hogs and spectacular bird life. But today there was another reason for their absence. A lean lioness and her scruffy sub-adult cub were draped across a termite mound, waiting for unsuspecting game that might come in to the little water remaining in Kanondo's once-wide waterholes.

I closed my eyes to spend a moment in the past with Aubrey as he teased Cathy and me, and rabble-roused Skew Tusk to chase the Hwange bulls. I lifted a sundowner of Zambezi beer to his memory. 'I know you're here somewhere, you old ginger fox.'

The full moon lifted above the eastern horizon. In the west, the sun set fast: the air turned cold in an instant. I pulled on my woolly cap, leather gloves and a warm jacket before we returned along the Dete *vlei*. I'd almost forgotten the bitter winter cold of the open plain, made even more so by a sharp wind that sheered across my face and teared my eyes. A white rhino bull meandered along the track, reflecting the moonlight off his wet back. Evidently, he didn't mind the icy conditions.

Flames were licking high from the coals of a campfire when

we drove into camp. We ate dinner beneath the ball of silver light, as hyaenas whooped and jackals wailed. By nine pm, I was in bed in the tiny tree-house. Jer went out like a light. But for me, sleep was once again elusive because of the biting cold, my disturbed body clock and my excited re-enactments of the meeting with Tunny.

I woke to another frozen dawn. Grotesque marabou storks reflected unusually elegant shapes in the waterhole: glossy starlings, long-tailed shrikes and doves flocked to drink. Five ground hornbills boomed amidst fossicking, fighting baboons with hair puffed out from the cold – or was it to indicate rage? The soft pastel colours of the early light washed into my heart. I would enjoy this Sunday without thought of the sadness of Zimbabwe – just one day.

We didn't find elephant. 'They must be going to the church,' laughed Pembas. It didn't matter. How could I be greedy after the previous day's reunion with Tunny and her family? I had observed many times that there are bird days, giraffe days and all-game days. This was a day for trees and birds. Pied babblers and white-helmeted shrikes shouted from their perches in an 'ordeal tree', so called because once (maybe even now) those suspected of crimes were forced to drink a brew made from the poisoned bark. If they were guilty, they died; if they were innocent, they recovered. A brutal judgement, but maybe the prospect of such horror was enough to give some with dishonourable intentions pause.

When we returned to camp, Bheki was waiting. 'Are you winning?' he asked.

When I replied that the elephants were missing, he said,

'Ah, instead I have called the "boooofallo" for you. And there is a lonely elephant hiding there in the trees.'

His finger was aimed at a point behind me. I turned to see a large herd of buff galloping towards the waterhole. Further back, the form of an elephant stood still in the shadow of dusk. I could see by the pointed outline of her head that it was a female. And then she was gone.

The following evening, an unseasonable storm chased us down the *vlei* after another day without elephant. Lightning split the evening sky.

'Damn the storm,' I thought. It would spook the game, that would now not return for a few more days. Yet, I knew it was selfish to curse rain in a place where water is the supreme treasure. It pelted down as we ate dinner with two white Zimbabweans who were re-visiting from South Africa. They were angry men, who spoke with passion of their love for their homeland. One had been evicted from his farm. When he returned a year later, the war vets gloated, 'Go look, white man. Pigs now live in your house.'

'Good,' barked the man. 'Do they like it?'

The other was a seventh-generation Zimbabwean living in exile in South Africa.

'I fear for my life every minute there. I never did here,' he whispered. 'You know, I don't fit the tough criteria to emigrate to your safe country. I have money to buy a house there and support my wife and myself. Ay-ay-ay . . . it seems I am too old and useless.'

There was a long, deep silence. What could I say to this? I blushed with embarrassment at the rigid immigration policy of

Australia that refused entry to elderly refugees, unable to contribute to the workforce: unfortunate beings who had been evicted by force from their homeland. This man was descended from white settlers who came at the same time as the Shona and the Zulu people (from then on known as the Matabele tribe). The three groups of immigrants had displaced the indigenous San Bushmen. I wondered who really had ownership of this great land. If man can lay claim to territory through long habitation, then surely the San people were the real victims.

These men and others spoke of the reign of terror. The economy is crashing without the input of the white farming and business community, which was the axle upon which Zimbabwe's prosperity wheels rolled. A few thousand farmers had employed around quarter of a million workers. Now, voodoo economics, hyperinflation, cronyism and corruption are the tools of trade amongst the ruling elite. I knew that criticism of the president was a criminal offence, punishable by imprisonment. However, not once did I hear the name Robert Mugabe ever spoken by black Zimbabweans – for good, or for evil. He has granted free rein to thugs loyal to Zanu-PF, as he distances himself from his people. Even the mandatory photos of him on walls in every entrance hall have faded to ghost-like images. It seems to me this man of many honestly won academic degrees (excluding the utterly unspeakable self-acclaimed 'degree in violence') has become corrupted by ultimate power to the point where he is totally disaffected from the groundswell of human misery.

Robert Mugabe began his presidency with a reconciliatory stance: 'If yesterday I fought you as an enemy, today you have become a friend and ally with the same national interest, loyalty, and rights and duties as myself. If yesterday you hated me, you cannot avoid the love that binds you to me and me to you.' These words promised a splendid future for Zimbabwe, and Mugabe was revered as a great man. He was even given an affectionate nickname – 'Good Old Bob' – by white Zimbabweans, many of whom had gained their wealth by owning the majority of fertile land, businesses and by utilising cheap black labour. Undoubtedly, a black government wanted to see justice done and the imbalance redressed; rightly so, but this could have happened without banishing their peoples' oppressors with their essential knowledge and skills.

Sadly, either the president's vision was limited or his heroic attitude when elected had been a sham. There's no doubt the man was a brilliant thinker, with the potential to become a great statesman and lead a united nation forward to stability and peace by offering justice to all. Unfortunately, he betrayed himself – and Zimbabwe – as hatred overwhelmed good sense. Ten years later, 'Good Old Bob' had descended into paranoia and tyranny, inciting terrorism, murder, repression and oppression against not only the white minority, but also the millions of Matabele people who supported the MDC (Movement for Democratic Change). No one knows how many black Zimbabweans lie in mass graves but it is thought to be scores of thousands. Many more have been tortured, raped, beaten and broken. They have been denied aid relief of food, clothing and medicine and been forced to watch as their homesteads, crops and livestock have been destroyed.

The white Zimbabweans told of 'The Brigade of Green Bombers'. Children between the ages of twelve and sixteen are compelled to do three months' terrorism training – basically, they are brainwashed about the evil wrought by white colonialism and taught to harass whites. This can take strange forms. In one instance, Green Bombers swarmed into the small shop of a white trader, arrested him and interrogated him about why he was selling white, not black, jumpers, vanilla, rather than chocolate, milkshakes, and sugar and flour in white packets. Fortunately, he was well liked by the local community, which came to his rescue, as did the police, so he was closed down only briefly. It seems that Mr Mugabe has learned well from 'White Imperialism'. The bitter years of aparthied have left a terrible legacy.

But not all in power are corrupt, or ignore common sense. A female minister in the Zimbabwean Cabinet appeared on national television to interview a war veteran who had been given a white farmer's dairy farm. She said the farmer had been producing 5000 gallons of milk daily and asked his usurper how much he was sending to the factory. When the man replied, 'Five hundred gallons,' she exploded. 'We have given you this farm. Why are you not producing as much milk?' She tore him to shreds and threatened to return the farm to the white farmer.

Many say that the president is terrified to let go of power due to the Matabele massacres, as he knows he would be taken before the Tribunal at The Hague for crimes against humanity. But perhaps his greatest fear results from the traditional belief that when he dies he will meet the spirits of the murdered and be held accountable. It seems he will hold hard to life, and others will shield him as they rule behind his paranoia.

Intellectuals, doctors, highly efficient farmers, teachers and tradespeople are continuing to evacuate – overseas and to neighbouring countries which are recovering, or have recovered, from political turmoil. This gives hope that the cyclical nature of African development will see Zimbabwe also rise from her knees before Mugabe, starvation and disease destroy her.

Meanwhile, a morgue near Dete has had its power cut off. The locals' sufferings are beyond description. They smell the family members they have already been unable to honour in death. So many people die of AIDS-related diseases that there is no time to perform the traditional funeral ceremonies of respect.

I never spoke of these matters with Bheki. The closest he came to commenting on political issues was when he said quietly, 'My heart is heavy for this Zimbabwe. I am struggling to make sense of the problem.'

His words were not inflammatory. Even so, he looked over his shoulder while he anxiously clasped and unclasped his hands. I also checked behind, as I would continue to do until we left the country. In that same moment of backward scanning, we both jumped at the sight of a figure standing in the shadows. I feared it could be someone in camp whose appearance always caused the others to slip away, whose emotionless eyes made me shrink. Thank God it wasn't him. It was Pembas, 'the kind'. He must have been listening, which was unsettling, because he picked up the threads of the conversation where we'd left off.

As if he were describing the *sadza* he'd eaten for breakfast, he said in a quiet, matter-of-fact way: 'Poverty is terrible here. Death is with us always. It is my thought that malnutrition is the sad factor why people die quickly from AIDS, malaria and simple diseases – even from having the cold.'

I could smell Bheki's fear. He was uncomfortable with a discourse on the unmentionable.

Spooked, I changed the subject. 'But it isn't malaria season, is it?' I asked while my eyes searched the air; this time for another feared enemy, the mosquito.

'No. This is the dry season. You see, these people get the malaria, which is living always in their blood because they are starving and worn down with worry. They cannot afford to buy medicine. Instead they take the bark of the acacia tree and boil it. When it is cold, they drink it. Ah . . . it is very bitter.' Pembas whispered gently through steepled fingers: 'Very bitter. Like the living in Zimbabwe. But we are tired. And we are a peaceful people. We do not want war.'

That night, the fire flared high, sending trails of embers dangerously close to the thatch above. A hapless gecko fell and frizzled. Bheki shrugged, lifted his hands in a gesture of surrender and I nodded.

Some days later, Bheki asked for just two things: exercise books and pencils for the school where he sends his brother's children; 'Where Perfect begins her education next year.' He showed me a photo of a group of teachers and children in worn uniforms mostly without shoes (education is not free) standing in front of a school with no roof and holes in the walls. 'There is no hope here, Sally.'

I replied, 'I know, Bheki.' But I couldn't really know and was ashamed.

After this statement (which was as candid as he could be without actually saying 'the forbidden name' or the words 'government' and 'politics') Bheki did not speak of the sadness. Whenever my thoughts headed in that direction, he returned to my old title, saying, 'Mama Ndlovu, let us be with the days of joy. We must think of happy times and make this day good. We will call those elephants.'

The world view of Bheki and many other African friends, and their ability to be happy in the moment is magnificent and calming. Their philosophy requires them to speak few words.

A week after our arrival, Bheki left on long overdue leave. It was two months since he had seen his family. I thought of the joyful reunion in which Bheki would be the Lobengula of his *kraal* for a brief time, as I warmed my feet in the sun and gave gratitude for my blessed existence. Without the opportunity to live in Third-World countries, I might not have recognised the good fortune of my Australian birthright or how precious is freedom.

I started when a deep voice growled over my head: 'I am Godfrey. The one who has malaria? Bheki is my friend.'

I looked into sunken and milky eyes that came with the cursed disease. 'Godfrey, it is good to meet you. But you are still ill. Please stay in bed.'

'Ah no. All in all, I am feeling healthy today. The roof is no longer falling into me. My passion has returned.'

And so, Godfrey joined the ranks of Pembas, and another friend, Cleophis, who cared for me and made it their mission to help us find our beloved elephants. These men were professional guides who knew and loved the herd.

A few days later, Cleophis and Godfrey found elephants again near Mpofu, where the boomslang once swayed around my ankles in the tree hide. The boomslang is no longer there; nor the great Leadwood tree, nor the deep pool. There is no money to pay for the water to fill the pans that are the lifeblood of the wild.

The family group of nine cows and calves stood listlessly beside the dry curls of ancient mud; seeming to look longingly at the place where once they could sink their entire bodies into the cool lightness, where they would wallow and rid their skin of irritating parasites. They accepted our presence calmly, which is typical of members of the Presidential Herd. However, their despondency depressed me. One cow was heavily pregnant, her breasts swollen and leaking milk. Perhaps the birth of her baby would bring joy to the three youngsters who stood together in a solemn huddle.

Once more I closed my eyes to remember the happy times when the entire herd swam, wallowed and played in this place. I recalled exuberant calves clambering over each other, chasing birds with wild, bleating charges, and testing their mothers' patience in attention-seeking screams of distress when they were really quite able to escape from the mud. But when I opened my eyes, I saw mud long hardened.

Cleophis drove on to Mataka, where there was a small amount of green-slimed sludge seething with terrapins. This had been the place where giraffe appeared on cue at sunset, stretching legs wide and necks low to drink, reflecting on the still water immaculate mirror images in front of the luminous clouds. So far we had only sighted one known cow. Time was limited and frustration was building – not only in me, it seemed.

'This is VERY bad,' bellowed Godfrey, startling the silence and me. 'We will call your old friends from their hiding places. Cleophis, let us try Kanondo again.'

We hadn't seen elephants visiting Kanondo: the beloved pan where Rembrandt hogged the fresh flow of water from the bore pipe; where Skew Tusk, Dilingane and their friends lost their dignity in a wild game while the children huddled in shock; where a government minister sanctioned hunting for four terrible months from 2003 to 2004. Elephants have long memories. I wondered if they continued to avoid the pan that was once their favourite place because their trust had been abused.

I was standing when we rounded the great teak tree on the bend just before Kanondo. No elephants. But we saw a white rhino bull (re-introduced from the Matopas) and that was good. He grazed peacefully. I sighted three more rhinos lumbering along the *vlei* as we returned home. It is encouraging that the numbers of the Presidential Herd have also risen despite the changes.

The next day, we set out with a clench-jawed Cleophis at the wheel. 'I am telling you, Sally. We will not return before we find these elephant.'

Mid-morning, a large number of elephants ambled out of the forest onto the *vlei* and into the acacia grove. Sitting before the vanguard of a long line of elephants is thrilling – especially when you are looking for old friends. They loom larger and larger as they approach; striding with immense decorum – that is, unless they are running excitedly to water, or bouncing with their floppy greeting walk into a reunion with others.

This time they were coming with the steady regal progress I most loved. We didn't even consider moving from their path. Their attitude was calm and accepting. I didn't know where to look first. As each cow passed the Land Rover, I peered at their ears, faces and tusks. I lost it when the third cow arrived.

It was Inkosikasi and behind her was her best friend, maybe

her mother, the equally tuskless old Granny (Gogo). They stopped beside the vehicle. I beamed into the face of Inkosikasi and I swear she beamed back. She and Granny each had a calf at heel. They were venerable old ladies now, and to my eyes still utterly beautiful. Cleophis patted my leg as I sniffled. Inkosikasi made a strange low, droning sound I had never heard, before she continued on to the small artificial waterhole. I twisted back to look for Skew Tusk. In the old days, she had always been with them, guiding and protecting in her haughty manner. I searched every set of tusks for her, but she was absent. Godfrey told me her deformed tusk had been broken halfway and that she was rarely sighted. I was puzzled that the supreme matriarch wasn't with her charges and could only hope luck would continue to be with us. Finding the other cows was a gift as it was.

Later that day, we touched base with a woman who has been guarding the herd for five years. She has many times been pro-active in saving elephant's lives. Most often this has been by alerting veterinarians from anti-poaching patrols who immobilise and rescue snared elephant calves and crippled game that struggle for breath as snares cut slowly into their windpipes and hobble in agony on legs gripped in the vice of thick wire. Several elephants have lost portions of their trunks to snares; that most delicate, important and miraculous tool cruelly sliced off. Unfortunately, many die in agony because the resources of the anti-poaching patrol are stretched in these harsh days of economic ruin. The necessary drugs are expensive and those who can dispense them are thin on the ground. Elephant infants die slowly as evil snares cut deep into growing flesh — until gangrene sets in, or their throats are slashed.

I don't know how I would react if I came across such horrors without the means to help. And yet, I understand the plight of desperate humans who are in survival mode. They can only think of basic needs – the search for food to save their families from starvation. The gangs who brutally prey on the game for meat, which is then sold at inflated prices to hungry humans, are another matter. They are an ugly reflection of the corrupt 'elite' and deserve to be punished harshly.

That night we talked with the three guides about the conundrum. This was a discussion they could have safely and they were eager to express their views. I asked the men if they thought it callous to fight for the preservation of the remaining wilderness and its creatures in a place where humans are starving; where misery is the means by which power-hungry potentates drive their ambitions. Their shock that I should even ask the question was heartening.

'Ah no. We must not become like Mozambique. All wild things have been killed in their terrible war. That Africa is now barren,' Godfrey scowled.

Pembas nodded and said quietly: 'Those hungry people ate for a while. Until the game was gone. And still they are hungry.' He sighed. 'Now they want the animals of Zimbabwe. If we let them and our own people destroy this wildlife, then soon there will be nothing. And one day, when human rightness has returned here, our hearts will call out for the creatures of the wild.'

Lions roared in the distance. Four wild dogs, one wearing a collar, dappled the firelight as they slipped by. Another stopped for a moment to look through me with his wild gaze. I wanted to run hard with them, free and unaware of the danger man creates.

* * *

It was a relief to immerse myself in elephants the next day; a joyful relief, because it was beautiful, serene Dilingane that strode purposely onto the *veldt*. If possible, her charm had grown. When she sighted the vehicle, she stopped, then lifted her trunk to test our scent. She must have been satisfied. Her lovely head began to nod; she smiled and proceeded towards us with the joyful floppy walk of greeting. I wished I could run towards her shouting my pleasure as Skew Tusk had done so many times. Dilingane brought her family close to inspect us. Sixteen years later, her tusks were a little worn and her matronly back swayed lower. However, her playful, loving spirit shone in her sparkling eyes. Being with Dilingane had always made me feel especially happy. The cows and youngsters with her emulated their matriarch's affable nature.

The reunion was sweet, if brief. The family was on a mission to a further place, perhaps to meet up with Skew Tusk. We couldn't follow them into the thick forest. They left, as another family appeared.

This group, though, kept their distance. And then I knew why. Bette Midler stumped by. The old girl was still acting true to her nature. She flapped her ears belligerently against her head for a moment and shouted an insult or three before continuing to the water trough. She seemed shrunken in both form and spirit. For a moment, I longed to see her attempt with a mighty charge to reduce me to a trembling wreck.

It was our last day. Soon we would leave for Namibia to spend three months living within the rugged ravines and harsh desert where the mysterious Hoanib River shelters the unique desert elephants.

Sunset came without Skew Tusk. We may not meet again, for she is quite an old lady now. I hope she has in her wisdom taken her family deep inside Hwange National Park, where they might swim and wallow in the deep water of pans far away from the eyes of hungry humans. Perhaps her descendants will be amongst the first elephants to migrate freely through the proposed Transfrontier Peace Park corridors that will cross the breadth of Southern Africa from Hwange to the Atlantic Ocean. It's a fantastic thought that humans are working to make this happen by re-creating at least one ancient migratory route roamed by the vast herds of elephants that once were.

Being accepted by Skew Tusk and the herd has been the greatest privilege of my life. They have been my teachers and through them I've learned about myself. Living in Africa observing nature with them and with other friends has taught me about living in the present. It hasn't always been easy to keep to my quest of retaining my highest values. But I endeavour never to take life for granted or linger for long on a negative thought, or in an unproductive space. Such things are wasteful, best displaced quickly by optimism and hope.

And I know there is hope when I sink into the savage peace of the African wilderness. The elephant striding purposely towards the waterhole knows nothing of me, or of the human condition. It is too busy being an elephant. The lioness dragging down the wildebeest knows nothing other than the need to kill in order to eat. She doesn't agonise over whether the kill will be successful. She has nothing to prove, she is simply hungry. There is no malice toward her prey, which dies without thought for a life hereafter. It has lived fully within the moment and dies within another. It never knew of the havens for other wildebeest in predator-free zones. The world it sees is all there is.

ACKNOWLEDGEMENTS

I am extremely grateful to all humans and to creatures great and small that appear in my memoir – even to those who threatened me, for their challenges offered valuable lessons in common sense and compassion. Every story is true and every character – both human and animal – is real.

Particularly, I would like to thank:
Skew Tusk and the herd. Without them there would be no memoir. They brought me joy and gave my life purpose.
The spirit of Africa for watching over me.
Kathy Rogers and Hans Knupp for their guidance and treasured friendship.
Alan and Scotty Elliott for their generous support.
Harold and Sylvia Broomberg, Des and Jenny Delange, Buck deVries, John and Delle Foster, Steve Mpofu, Karen Ogilvie, Paul Perez, Steve and Nookie Perry, Geoff and Nookie Randall, the Williamson family and Lloyd Wilmott. I would never have managed without them.

My special friends Tammie Matson, Celia Mundy and Sue Newton. When I trembled at revealing intimate moments of my life, they offered encouragement, support and love.

Bhekizizwe, Barmi, Butzi, Douw, Edda, George, Hopi, Marthin, Tenzi and Steve for their kindness.

The Brightman family, Cleophis, Dries, Godfrey, Golden, Hendrik, Ian Russell, Johan, Josh, Mark, Mick, Neil, Pembas, Rob, Ron, Salim and Skiv, for sharing Africa with me.

My big brother, Peter Bain, and all of my family – especially Jenny Kefford, Kate Martin, Catherine Mancham, Ginger Hollis and Adrian Fitzgerald.

My agent, Lyn Tranter, for believing in my manuscript.

My very patient publisher, Alexandra Craig, who endured communication nightmares between Sydney and Africa with equanimity and humour.

Senior editor Sarina Rowell, for her gentle guidance, and all the crew at Pan Macmillan.

Saba Douglas-Hamilton for the secret tryst with our heroine Blythe Loutit.

Iain Douglas-Hamilton, Cynthia Moss and Daphne Sheldrick for their inspiration.

Elefriends Australia, the Elefriends family (especially John and Naida Watkins and Sue Delaney) and the wonderful community at Montville who generously supported endangered species and sustained us with aid parcels. Sisi Macfarlane for her care.

Dave van Smeerdijk and Rob Moffett of Wilderness Safaris, Namibia for placing a roof over our heads where I could write the Epilogue. Touch the Wild in Zimbabwe.

ACKNOWLEDGEMENTS

I would like to pay tribute to the memories of:

Aubrey Packenham. He would have chuckled at the stories of 'the Ginger Fox'.

Jenny Russell for her dignity and courage and for her faith in my ability to write.

Blythe Loutit, who devoted her life to SAVE and the rhinos.

Finally, and most important of all, I am utterly indebted to:

My fantastic husband, Jer. His love sustained me through every step of the journey.

My beloved Louie and Lachy for understanding and encouraging their mother.

My parents, Colin and Sylvia Bain. They would have loved to read *Silent Footsteps* and see how their child fulfilled the dreams they sowed.

S.S.B. for teaching me about loving and serving, and for persevering with a wayward student.